# AMERICA'S GREATEST COACHES

Michael D. Koehler, PhD
Deerfield High School
Deerfield, Illinois

**Leisure Press**
Champaign, Illinois

**Library of Congress Cataloging-in-Publication Data**

Koehler, Mike, 1938-
   America's greatest coaches / by Michael D. Koehler.
     p.   cm.
   Includes bibliographical references.
   ISBN 0-88011-330-8
   1. Coaches (Athletics)--United States--Biography. 2. Coaches (Athletics)--United States--Rating of. I. Title.
GV697.A1K63   1990
796' .07'70922--dc20
[B]                                                                                                                 90-34980
                                                                                                                                            CIP

ISBN: 0-88011-330-8

Copyright © 1990 by Michael D. Koehler

All rights reserved. Except for use in a review, the reproduction or utilization of this work in any form or by any electronic, mechanical, or other means, now known or hereafter invented, including xerography, photocopying, and recording, and in any information storage and retrieval system, is forbidden without the written permission of the publisher.

Acquisitions Editor: Brian Holding
Developmental Editor: June I. Decker, PhD
Assistant Editors: Julia Anderson and Timothy Ryan
Copyeditor: Wendy Nelson
Proofreader: Maggie Kanonse
Production Director: Ernie Noa
Typesetter: Kathy Boudreau-Fuoss
Text Design: Keith Blomberg
Text Layout: Tara Welsch
Cover Design: Jack Davis
Printer: United Graphics

Leisure Press books are available at special discounts for bulk purchase for sales promotions, premiums, fund-raising, or educational use. Special editions or book excerpts can also be created to specification. For details, contact the Special Sales Manager at Leisure Press.

Printed in the United States of America

10 9 8 7 6 5 4 3 2 1

**Leisure Press**
A Division of Human Kinetics Publishers, Inc.
Box 5076, Champaign, IL 61825-5076
1-800-747-4457

*UK Office*:
Human Kinetics Publishers (UK) Ltd.
PO Box 18
Rawdon, Leeds LS19 6TG
England
(0532) 504211

To Pat—who makes loving so easy
and so complete.

# PHOTO CREDITS

Photos in *America's Greatest Coaches* were used by permission of the following sources.

Photos on pages 9, 39, and 185 courtesy of National Federation of State High School Associations.

Photos on pages 12, 155, and 169 courtesy of University of Southern California Sports Information Office.

Photo on page 19 courtesy of National Baseball Library, Cooperstown, New York.

Photos on pages 44, 179, and 240 courtesy of UCLA Athletics.

Photos on pages 50, 205, and 210 courtesy of Hickock Library at the Naismith Memorial Basketball Hall of Fame.

Photo on page 61 courtesy of Gordon Wood, Brownwood, Texas.

Photo on page 67 courtesy of University of Notre Dame.

Photo on page 75 courtesy of Grambling State University.

Photo on page 78 courtesy of Green Bay Packers.

Photos on pages 95 and 127 courtesy of Penn State University Athletics.

Photo on page 105 courtesy of U.S. Hockey Hall of Fame, Inc.

Photo on page 109 courtesy of University of Michigan.

Photo on page 114 courtesy of Scott Bowman, East Amherst, New York.

Photo on page 121 courtesy of Gene C. Baker, Granite City, Illinois.

Photo on page 135 courtesy of David A. Robertson, 7723 Pointview Circle, Orlando, Florida, 32819.

Photo on page 140 courtesy of Yale University Sports Information Office.

Photo on page 151 courtesy of Jay Kramer, Hinsdale, Illinois.

Photo on page 163 courtesy of Alan Rowan, Honolulu, Hawaii.

Photo on page 190 courtesy of Sports Information Office, University of Iowa.

## Photo Credits

Photo on page 219 courtesy of Nancy J. Cole, Centereach, New York.

Photo on page 222 courtesy of Athletic Department, Ursinus College.

Photo on page 228 courtesy of Sports Information Office, University of North Carolina.

Photo on page 235 courtesy of Richard G. Rasmussen, Ankeny, Iowa.

Photos on pages 245 and 251 courtesy of Stanford Sports Information, Stanford University.

Photo on page 262 courtesy of Sports Information Department, Tennessee State University.

Photo on page 270 courtesy of Norma J. Bellamy, Safford, Arizona.

Photo on page 275 courtesy of University of Hawaii.

# CONTENTS

Foreword  ix
Preface  xi
Acknowledgments  xv

## Part I  Men's Sports  1

### Chapter 1  Baseball  3
High School Baseball  9
College Baseball  12
Professional Baseball  19

### Chapter 2  Basketball  33
High School Basketball  39
College Basketball  44
Professional Basketball  50

### Chapter 3  Football  55
High School Football  61
College Football  67
Small College Football  75
Professional Football  78

### Chapter 4  Gymnastics  93
College Gymnastics  95

### Chapter 5  Ice Hockey  103
High School Ice Hockey  105
College Ice Hockey  109
Professional Ice Hockey  114

### Chapter 6  Soccer  119
High School Soccer  121
College Soccer  127

### Chapter 7  Swimming  133
High School Swimming  135
College Swimming  140
Club Swimming  146

### Chapter 8  Tennis  149
High School Tennis  151
College Tennis  155

### Chapter 9  Track and Field  161
High School Track and Field  163
College Track and Field  169

### Chapter 10  Volleyball  177
College Volleyball  179

### Chapter 11  Wrestling  183
High School Wrestling  185
College Wrestling  190

## Part II  Women's Sports  197

### Chapter 12  Basketball  203
High School Basketball  205
College Basketball  210

### Chapter 13  Field Hockey  217
High School Field Hockey  219
College Field Hockey  222

### Chapter 14  Soccer  227
College Soccer  228

### Chapter 15  Softball  233
High School Softball  235
College Softball  240

### Chapter 16  Swimming  243
College Swimming  245

### Chapter 17  Tennis  249
College Tennis  251

### Chapter 18  Track and Field  255
High School Track and Field  257
College Track and Field  262

### Chapter 19  Volleyball  269
High School Volleyball  270
College Volleyball  275

References  281
Index  285
About the Author  295

# FOREWORD

**M**uch of what has been written lately about coaches involves sensationalized peeks at college abuses. The attention received by the unprincipled few in certain major college sports seems to have obscured the accomplishments of *all* coaches. One result has been the media's scrutiny of recruiting practices, graduation rates, and such specifics as the NCAA's Proposition 48. Unfortunately, the newly discovered facts have been used by many writers to bury coaches, not to praise them.

This book was written to praise them. The vast majority of coaches in this country receive little recognition. People don't realize *how* little until they read books such as this one. Mike had to dig deep into obscure records simply to find their *names*. When finally he uncovered information about them, he discovered a commitment to the youth of our nation that distinguishes coaches from people in almost every other walk of life.

Most coaches, for example, are not "flesh merchants," exploiting their athletes like expensive but expendable gladiators on the Coliseum floor. Instead, they are heads of "families," concerned about their players and seeking always to create the sense of unity that results from mutual respect and common purpose. The players on a team may be its arms and legs, but the coach is its head—and often its heart.

Through this book you and I discover that most coaches are the living standards in the team's search for personal excellence, the instruments by which athletes transform a selfish desire for individual recognition into a selfless commitment to team goals. They are the source of the accumulated experiences that shape a team's character, that make commitment *visible*.

Finally, we discover that many coaches are able to develop personal excellence in their players without ever having reached athletic greatness themselves. We find that some of history's most demanding coaches were forced to accept mediocrity at least once during their careers—in their own performances as athletes. They found in their own limitations as players an adversity that influenced their growth as human beings and that led ultimately to their success as coaches. They join the thousands of others who seek out adversity for themselves and for their athletes in order to find the sense of accomplishment and personal growth that accompany an obstacle overcome.

I have *sensed* much of this throughout my career; this book proves it.

Lou Holtz<br>
Head Football Coach<br>
The University of Notre Dame

## SELECTION COMMITTEE

**Elmer Blasco**
Publisher, *Athletic Journal*

**Tricia Bork**
Director, Women's Championships-NCAA

**Lou Boudreau**
Hall of Fame Baseball Player

**Jack Brickhouse**
Hall of Fame Sportscaster

**Mickey Cochrane**
Sports Historian

**Brice Durbin**
Director, National Federation of State High School Associations

**Bob Devaney**
Athletic Director/Former Coach, University of Nebraska

**Pat Harmon**
Sportswriter

**L. Oval Jaynes**
Athletic Director, Colorado State University

**Donna Lopiano**
Athletic Director, University of Texas

**Ray Meyer**
Former Coach, DePaul University

# PREFACE

When Theagenes returned triumphantly to his village after the Olympics of 776 B.C., the townspeople of Thasos carried him to his new home, where they gave him money and the promise of free meals for a lifetime. Two centuries later, Spirodan Louis, a shepherd from the hills of Greece, won the marathon to conclude the first modern Olympiad in Athens in 1896. He, too, was carried through the front door of his home, where townspeople feasted his victory. In both instances, their coaches—if indeed they *had* coaches—probably had to find their own way in through the back door.

In the history of sport, the popularity of coaches is relatively recent. Before the Civil War, sport in America was secondary to the tasks of developing a nation and managing an ever-expanding frontier. The first recorded amateur competition in the U.S., for example, involved a cricket match in 1838 between two clubs from New York and Philadelphia. No coaches were involved. Shortly, cricket gave way to baseball, which gained popularity after its first recorded contest in 1846. Still no coaches were involved. Track and field, basketball, and football didn't appear until after the Civil War.

Coaching didn't appear until much later still. During the early development of football, for example, leadership and strategy were the responsibility of elected captains. Many of these later become coaches because of their knowledge of the game and their ability to communicate its fundamental skills. However, team captains in all sports, not just in football, were limited by their inexperience and by the absence of recorded knowledge about their sports. So they sought the counsel of former players who volunteered to help.

By the start of the 20th century, all the major sports in the United States had salaried coaches or managers who were responsible for the organization and success of their teams. The advent of coaching paralleled the

xi

transition of sport from diversionary to serious competition, but the relationship between coaching and an emerging emphasis on winning was not necessarily causal. Even today, coaches inspire and motivate more than they cause players to seek victories in every contest. More likely, they complement each athlete's learned desire to win—if not to be a national champion, then at least to be a first-stringer. The coach's job is to help players realize such success, to inspire when necessary, and to teach when possible. Like great teachers, great coaches don't fill buckets; they light fires.

And let's be honest. By complementing each athlete's preoccupation with winning, coaches bring to their responsibilities the potential for abuse. The win-at-all-costs philosophy in some schools has resulted in under-the-table payments, doctored high school transcripts, "Mickey Mouse" curricula, and general exploitation of young athletes. It would be unrealistic to deny that some coaches have tried to ensure their own survival by neglecting the educational and human needs of their athletes. Fortunately, such coaches are in the minority. Their failure to uphold decent standards of athletic competition simply underscores the self-restraint and high principles of those many fine coaches who *do* play within the rules and succeed in shaping their athletes as well as their programs.

This is a book about such coaches. The process of identifying them was gratifying—and at times frustrating. Even our expert panel of sport personalities and nationally recognized coaches had difficulty selecting from among the many truly accomplished people who have influenced the world of sport. Those of us who owe much of what we are to a coach or coaches realize that the term *great* is not restricted to the few people in this book.

A significant number of young people in our society are influenced each year by a caring and usually insistent coach. Whether the sport is football or field hockey, coaches and players enjoy a unique relationship, strengthened by common interests, mutual respect, and the shared desire to realize individual perfection. The coach is the catalyst in this relationship, the force that imposes obstacles and then provides ways to overcome them.

Coaches are unique in our culture. In a nation where our love of "things" is reflected on TV and brightens the eyes of every child who wanders rapturously through shopping malls, coaches emphasize denial and self-sacrifice. In a society sometimes characterized by its excesses, coaches demand self-control. In a culture emphasizing "Me first," coaches emphasize team commitment. And in a world grown increasingly tolerant of mediocrity, coaches represent a personal commitment to excellence.

Coaches and noncoaches alike will find enjoyment and inspiration in these pages. There is an inherent drama to be found in any person's search for excellence, especially in the face of adversity. It is the stuff of which great stories are made. Such stories can be found everywhere. They are in the home, the school, the workplace—anywhere people reach beyond their immediate grasp. Nowhere, however, are they more dramatic than in athletics, where men and women *seek* adversity and pain in order to realize individual perfection.

*Finding* their stories, however, was no easy task. Writing a book takes only a fraction of the time required for researching it. The selection committee and myself were in frequent contact with several regulatory and coaching organizations, including all the halls of fame. Baseball, basketball, and football were exceptionally cooperative. Most of the halls of fame and coaching organizations of the other sports provided some information but simply didn't have the kind we needed. Some of them didn't even have the win/loss records of their coaches.

Most of what we eventually found resulted from personal research and had to be supplemented by university sports information directors. We organized the information into lists of names for each sport at each level of competition (high school, college, and professional) and mailed the lists to the respective halls of fame, coaching organizations, and members of the selection panel, asking them to rank the names and to supplement the lists with suggestions of their own.

Fortunately, we received responses from people such as Bob Paul from the United States Olympic Committee (USOC), Bob Devaney and Tom Osborne from the University of Nebraska, Barry Switzer from Oklahoma, Joe Paterno from Penn State, Lou Holtz from Notre Dame, Bo Schembechler from Michigan, Elmer Blasco from the *Atlantic Journal*, Mickey Cochrane, Bill Deane from the Baseball Hall of Fame, Joe Horrigan from the Pro Football Hall of Fame, former pro football great George Allen, Wayne Patterson from the Basketball Hall of Fame, athletic directors Donna Lopiano from Texas and L. Oval Jaynes from Colorado State, Jack Brickhouse and Lou Boudreau from WGN Sports in Chicago, Nelson Campbell, Mike Chapman from the Wrestling Hall of Fame, Dan McGill from the Tennis Hall of Fame, Bob Rose from the Track and Field Hall of Fame, Tricia Borke (the NCAA's director of women's championships), Brice Durbin from the National Federation of State High School Associations, Skip Morris from the National High School Athletic Coaches Association, Pat Harmon from the College Football Hall of Fame, and Ray Meyer from DePaul. Their assistance gave the process excellent credibility.

The lists were combined, and in each category the coach with the highest ranking was selected as the nation's best. In almost every instance, first choices were unanimous or near-unanimous. Only a few names involved controversy. In such instances, the votes of the selection panel were determinative. Each evaluator was reminded of the criteria to be used in making his or her selections. Win/loss records were our first criterion but only to determine each coach's eligibility for selection.

Once we narrowed the field to the consensus best coaches in each sport, win/loss records became less important. Final selections were based on championships won, especially consecutive championships, testimonials from other coaches and players, demonstrated influence on athletes and other coaches, innovations, and contributions to the sport.

Readers will notice, therefore, that some coaches with outstanding win/loss records may not be ranked as high as others. The information provided for each coach will explain the reasons. Everyone involved in the selection process agreed that winning is an essential and, perhaps, the most obvious criterion to determine a coach's success. They also agreed, however, that the values of coaches and players should reflect much more than winning. Contrary to the win-at-all-costs philosophies that prevail in some schools, the coaches in this book reflect a commitment to excellence and a devotion to the advancement of their sports. Their greatness inheres in a dedication to their players and their sports that transcends win/loss records.

In spite of hundreds of letters and phone calls, we acknowledge that we may have missed some names. Even the major regulatory and coaching organizations in the country admit to an inability to compile information on *all* their coaches, even some of their great ones. We are dependent, therefore, on our readers' sharing information about coaches whom they feel should be included in a book of this kind.

Also, because the book contains so many pieces of information, we may have made some inadvertent errors. We also welcome your calling these to our attention.

Please forward such information to:

> Dr. Michael Koehler
> c/o Leisure Press
> Box 5076
> Champaign, IL 61825-5076

We are anxious to acknowledge this very special class of people who have devoted their lives to the search for excellence. Their greatness was thrust upon them not from without but from *within*, a result of their uncompromising commitment to seek within themselves and to demand from others the absolute best each of us has to give. Recognition of their accomplishments is our ultimate tribute to them.

# ACKNOWLEDGMENTS

The author wishes to express his gratitude to a number of persons for providing special assistance in the development of this book. In addition to the obvious help provided by members of the selection panel, he wishes to thank Ron Good, the editor of the *Amateur Wrestling News*; Bill Dean at the Baseball Hall of Fame; Joe Horrigan at the Football Hall of Fame; Sandy Vivas at the American Volleyball Institute; Marian Washburn at the International Swimming Hall of Fame; Carol Barr at the USA Field Hockey Association; Mickey Cochrane, soccer historian; and Betty Jaynes at the Women's Basketball Coaches Association.

Additional gratitude is extended to Berny Wagner at the Athletic Congress; Cathy Peterson and Gene Rauzi at the Hockey Hall of Fame; Jack Rose at the National Track and Field Hall of Fame; Carey McDonald and Skip Morris at the National High School Athletic Coaches Association; Micki Christians at United States Swimming; David Benjamin at the Intercollegiate Tennis Coaches Association; Bruce Howard at the National Federation of State High School Associations; Dan McGill at the College Tennis Hall of Fame; Lee Eilbracht, the former executive director of the American Baseball Coaches Association; and Gene Szypula, the former head gymnastics coach at Michigan State University.

Special appreciation is extended to my wife, Pat, for mailing literally hundreds of letters; Nelson Campbell, author of *Grass Roots and Schoolyards*, for his special input on high school basketball coaches; Todd Petr, assistant director of research at the NCAA, for going out of his way to provide additional information; Wayne Patterson at the Basketball Hall of Fame in Springfield for diving in with such enthusiasm; Mike Chapman at the College Wrestling Hall of Fame for providing information well in excess of my requests; George Kelly at the University of Notre Dame for his friendship; and the hundreds of sports information directors and high school athletic directors for providing information that made this book possible.

The task of identifying and recognizing the hundreds of coaches out there who deserve this honor would have been impossible without their help.

# PART I

# MEN'S SPORTS

Sports in "settled" America are as old as the Declaration of Independence and as enduring as our love of individual freedom and self-affirmation. Ever since the Colonial times, when Calvinist proscriptions against "frivolity" annually gave way to Thanksgiving games of strength and speed, athletic competition in America has provided fun for the participants and entertainment for every segment of society. It may have risked an unnecessary emphasis on winning and, at times, a preoccupation with violence, but the athletic arena has displayed this nation's commitment to excellence as consistently as any other social institution.

The greatest growth of men's sports in America came a few years after the Civil War, when games like golf, tennis, baseball, and football emerged as popular pastimes. Born in universities, many of them were nursed through their infancy in halls of ivy by undergraduates who managed the total sport programs. By the turn of the century, however, intercollegiate athletics had become so popular and profitable that coaches were hired to organize and control them.

Faculty indifference forfeited control of intercollegiate athletics to coaches and alumni. The potential for abuse, therefore, was as predictable as the spectacle that was sure to follow. The situation remains much the same today, although the NCAA is seeking to eliminate abuses by encouraging greater control by university officials.

"Abuse" is often the companion of achievement. The athlete's search for personal and team excellence may at times be obscured by a disregard for fair play. But the commitment and dedication of millions of coaches and players will forever mark such abuses as regrettable but momentary interruptions in the relentless human search for excellence in the opportunities provided by American sport.

# Chapter 1

# BASEBALL

Abner Doubleday was not the father of American baseball. Although credited by early National League president Abraham G. Mills as founding the game in Cooperstown in 1839, Doubleday is only one in a succession of people who claim to have played the game, or a version of it, in the early 1800s. Oliver Wendell Holmes, of Supreme Court and sometime "base ball" fame, wrote of playing the game at Harvard, when Doubleday was just 10 years old. Sometimes called "rounders," a game transplanted from England by immigrants in the 17th century, and sometimes "base ball," the game didn't become uniquely American until 1845 when New Yorker Alexander Cartwright assembled a committee of friends to standardize the rules.

From this union of common interest was born the game as we know it. It seems fair to assume, therefore, that the distinction of being the Father of American Baseball belongs to Alexander Cartwright, who in 1845 proposed a set of rules that, in large part, is unchanged to the present day. Cartwright's "code" provided for foul balls, three strikes, three outs, and a "base ball square" that consists of bases 90 feet apart. The dimensions of his "diamond" are unchanged in almost a century and a half of play, in spite of the Baltimore Orioles' John Lowenstein, who recommended a couple of years ago that first base be moved back a foot "to eliminate all close plays."

Close plays were not the order of the day on June 19, 1846, when the distinctly American game of baseball was first played in Hoboken, New Jersey. The New York Knickerbockers were humbled by the New York Nine 23-1 in four innings. In the earliest days of baseball, the team to first reach 21 "aces" won the game, regardless of number of innings played. The "nine-inning" rule didn't appear until 1857. The Knicks paid off by buying dinner for the Nine; and one of the Nine—a man named Davis—earned the distinction of paying baseball's first fine. He swore at umpire Alexander Cartwright and paid 6 cents for putting in his 2 cents worth.

It didn't take long for the new National Association of Base Ball Players to realize the financial rewards of a rivalry between New York and Brooklyn. On July 20, 1858, the outstanding players from the several teams in the area staged an All-Star game. The Association charged admission for the first time and waged a close but high-scoring contest for the 1,500 fans who paid the 50¢ to watch New York beat Brooklyn 22-18. Still an amateur sport, baseball was showing signs of being a money-maker. Unlike popular games that started in college, baseball originated among the people. "Bleacher bums" cheered then as they cheer now when players "hit the dirt." Baseball quickly became the blue-collar worker of the sports world.

Although the first college game was played between Amherst and Williams colleges in 1859, baseball's growth was nourished only incidentally by colleges and universities. Players worked hard all day, and they *played* hard on weekends. They would rather "take their licks" than give it the "old college try." The game belonged to any male, regardless of station, who could get his hands on a bat and ball. Even today, baseball's greatest growth is visible in pickup games on vacant lots in Chicago and stickball games on the streets of New York.

While football in 1869 was being nursed through the halls of ivy in Princeton, New Jersey, baseball was earning its own way in Ohio. The game's first professional team, the Cincinnati Red Stockings, under baseball's first manager, Harry Wright, embarked on a 66-game schedule, playing all comers and winning every game but one—a draw with the Troy Haymakers. Manager Wright drew a yearly salary of $1,200 and paid his brother George, an outstanding shortstop and hitter, $1,400. Other players received lesser amounts.

The gate receipts for the Red Stockings that year came out to just under $30,000—so did the team's expenditures. As a matter of fact, the team's net profit for the year was $1.39—not the kind of margin that stimulated investment. It may have been the first and best example of baseball's tenuous relationship between player salaries and management profits. Be assured, however, that the Red Stockings of 1869 *earned* their salaries; baseball mitts weren't introduced for another six years.

In just two years, several more teams became professional and enjoyed the money that baseball fans were willing to spend on behalf of the "home" team. The Chicago White Stockings, for example, under one-year manager Tom Foley, traveled to New York to play the Mutuals before a crowd of 6,000. The Mutuals' manager, Brooklyn-born Bob Ferguson, also caught and played second and third base to lead his team to an 8-5 victory over Chicago and keep happy his team's owner—political bigwig "Boss" Tweed.

In that same year, 1871, Harry Wright moved to Boston, taking the Red Stockings' name with him. He settled for a second-place finish his first year but won the National Association championship, followed by the

National League (NL) championship six of the next seven years. More importantly, his Boston Red Stockings played with a "professionalism" that all but eliminated the swearing and fighting characteristic of so many other teams of the era. Manager Harry Wright was one of early sport's best examples of the fact that a team's play often is a reflection of the coach's personality.

"The coach's personality" was just what the Chicago White Stockings were looking for when team president Bill Hulbert lured pitcher and future sports-equipment tycoon Al Spalding away from Boston to manage and pitch for his team. Perhaps the best pitcher of the day, Spalding took the job and then proceeded to pirate three of his teammates away from Boston, followed by two more from Philadelphia. The very next year, in 1876, Spalding's White Stockings won the National League championship, proving that a manager's first duty during baseball's formative years was not to devise solid strategy but to surround himself with solid players—no matter how he got them.

The "reserve rule" went into effect three years later. Fed up with players "revolving" from one team to another for more money, the league established a rule that "reserved" the right of each team to negotiate exclusively with five of its players. Within a few years, the reserve rule governed all of baseball. The resultant player restrictions are still sore spots for many professional athletes, in spite of the change in 1976 that allowed players to become free agents in five years. The predictability of player personnel for managers and owners, however, shifted management's efforts from getting and keeping players to building teams and coordinating their play.

In 1884, Henry Lucas, a realtor from St. Louis, sought to break the bondage of the reserve rule by creating a third major league, the Union Association. "Liberated" players with fatter wallets escaped the National League and the American Association (AA) so fast that some teams were left short-handed in midseason. Charles Radbourn, a pitcher for the Providence Grays, for example, suddenly found himself the only thrower on the staff who could do the job when teammate Charles Sweeney jumped to the Union Association. Manager Frank Bancroft used the only strategy available and pitched Radbourn for the remaining 38 consecutive games of the season. Radbourn concluded the season with a record of 60-12, including three straight in the World Series, and earned a place in the Hall of Fame with the nickname "Old Hoss."

The Union Association faded after one season; Lucas, the millionaire rebel who had conducted so many forays into NL and AA camps in the name of "player freedom," bought the National League's Cleveland franchise, transferred it to St. Louis, and subjected his players to the same reserve clause he had so openly opposed a year earlier. Another significant change that year was the lifting of most restrictions on pitchers. No longer required to release the ball below the waist, pitchers were now free to vary their deliveries, except that they were permitted only one step during the pitch.

The new rule provoked sudden changes in coaching technique and strategy but didn't have much effect on *batting* averages. In spite of the fact that pitchers were only 50 feet from home plate (they wouldn't be moved to today's 60 feet 6 inches until 1893), James "Tip" O'Neill of St. Louis batted .492 in 1888, the highest batting average recorded in baseball history. The year before, Cap Anson of Chicago had batted .421, beating out Detroit's Dennis Brouthers, who had batted .419.

With the inception of the American League (AL) in 1901, baseball settled into a routine that was interrupted dramatically only once, by the emergence of the short-lived Federal League in 1913. The National League/American League World Series started in 1903, with the Red Sox beating the Pirates in the best-of-nine series. Leading the way for manager Jimmy Collins' Red Sox were veteran pitchers Bill Dinneen, who won three games, and Denton True "Cy" Young, who won the other two of his team's five World Series victories. Dinneen had finished the season with 21 wins, Young with 32.

The next 20 years in baseball were dominated by five teams, New York and Chicago in the National League and Boston, Detroit, and Philadelphia in the American League. The names of managers John J. McGraw, Connie Mack, Frank Chance, and Hugh Jennings were tops among the game's big winners. Wealthy clubs like the Giants had developed a stranglehold on talent by paying top salaries to top players.

Not until Branch Rickey took control of the St. Louis Cardinals in 1919 did a team other than the traditional leaders dominate both leagues. A mediocre player and a so-so manager, Rickey established his genius as a general manager when he convinced owner Sam Breadon to stop buying talent and to start *growing* it. The resulting "farm system" paid dividends when six years later a crop of fine young players, among them Rogers Hornsby, led St. Louis to five pennants and three World Series championships in nine years.

Hornsby, the player-manager, won it all in 1926. Bill McKechnie's crew repeated with a pennant victory in '28, Gabby Street's in '30 and '31. And Frankie Frisch's "Gashouse Gang" won it all in 1934. Cardinal dominance continued into the '40s, further illustrating the value of the farm system and underscoring baseball's symbiotic relationship between field managers and general managers.

The interdependence of their relationship perhaps is best illustrated by a young pitcher who hit his first home run in 1915 and was traded to the New York Yankees in 1920. The next year, now a *former* young pitcher, Babe Ruth hit 59 home runs for the Yanks, and his former Red Sox manager, Eddie Barrow, found himself in the front office. Ruth went on to hit 60 homers in 1927 to lead manager Miller Huggins' "Murderer's Row" to its fifth pennant in seven years and a World Series championship. He already had led them to their new home in 1923, appropriately nicknamed "The House that Ruth Built."

Ruth may have "built" Yankee Stadium, but his three accomplices in "Murderer's Row" helped fill it up. Bob Meusel, Tony Lazzeri, and Lou Gehrig joined with the Babe to achieve a baseball slugging record of .489 in 1927. Opposing pitchers wanted to avoid the Yankee "Hit Men." Meusel that year batted .337, Lazzeri .309, Gehrig .373, and Ruth, in addition to his Olympian 60 home runs, hit .356. Oklahoma football coach Barry Switzer told me once that "great players make great plays." Yankee manager Miller Huggins learned much earlier that they also make a lot of runs.

Manager Leo Fohl and pitcher Hub Pruett of the St. Louis Browns, however, remained unimpressed with Ruth's statistics. A mediocre catcher during a short-lived playing career, Fohl must have helped Pruett find the Babe's weakness—a secret he shared with no one. With an unimpressive lifetime earned-run-average of 4.63 and an equally unimpressive record of 29 wins and 48 losses, Pruett managed what no other pitcher in history could accomplish. Of the 24 times he faced Ruth, he struck him out 20.

The Yankee dynasty, however, had been born. In 1929, manager Joe McCarthy celebrated with the Cubs the first of his nine league pennants. The remaining eight were with the Yankees, from 1932 to 1943, including four consecutive World Series championships.

In 1953, the Braves and manager Charlie Grimm stole a few headlines when they became the first major league franchise to switch cities, from Boston to Milwaukee. Although the Milwaukee Braves and new manager Fred Haney gave the Beer City two pennants and one Series in '57 and '58, it was the Yanks who again dominated major league baseball.

This time it was Casey Stengel, the so-so manager of Brooklyn for 3 years and Boston for six, who, though he never finished higher than fifth place with either team, rode the Yankee wave from '49 through the 50s, winning 10 pennants and seven World Series championships, five of them consecutively. He so dominated baseball during the entire decade that "The Old Perfessor's" knowledge of the game remained unquestioned in spite of his pre-Yankee record.

Stengel's last year with the Yanks was 1960; they lost the World Series to Danny Murtaugh's Pittsburgh Pirates by one game. Stengel was succeeded by Ralph Houk, former Yankee catcher, who won three more pennants and two World Series championships, then by Yogi Berra, perhaps the greatest of all Yankee catchers, who won another pennant in 1964. Never before had baseball experienced such consistent dominance. Only the Giants and the Cubs of the early 1900s, Walter Alston's Dodgers of the '50s and '60s, and the resurgent victory streaks of Connie Mack's Athletics have come close to the Yankees' viselike grip on pennants and World Series trophies.

8  Men's Sports

Although AL teams in the past 20 years have won as many World Series championships as the NL, AL attendance failed to meet owner expectations in the late '60s and early '70s. As a result, the league passed the "designated hitter" (DH) rule on January 11, 1973. A pinch-hitter for the pitcher, the DH provided more offensive punch; although the rule was introduced for a 3-year trial period, it is still used today.

The change reflected baseball's search for self-renewal and affirmed the wisdom of its leaders. In each instance, whether it was the Athletics' Connie Mack, resplendent in suit, tie, and topper (the Grand Old Man of Baseball was the most obvious of just a few managers not to wear his team's uniform), or the Yanks' Casey Stengel and Yogi Berra, muddling the otherwise precise English language, the game of baseball has been in good hands.[1]

As Yogi once indicated, "Baseball is 90% mental; the other half is physical!" In his inimitable way, however, Yogi made sense. Whatever the proportions of mental and physical commitment, the great managers in baseball have always found the right combinations in their players and, in the process, have established themselves among America's greatest coaches.

---

[1] To settle the recurring question of why managers wear their team's uniform: Rule number 1.11(b) specifies that *all* team members must wear uniforms. Burt Shotton of the Dodgers and Connie Mack of the Athletics were the only two not to wear uniforms.

# HIGH SCHOOL BASEBALL

## America's Greatest High School Baseball Coach

### Vince Meyer

Coach Vince Meyer accepted the head job at St. John High School in Bancroft, Iowa, in 1935. Forty-six years later, having touched the lives of countless young athletes with his special grace, Coach Meyer retired from the game as one of the two or three winningest high school coaches in any sport, with a record of 1,105 career victories. His teams advanced to the state tournament 32 times, returning home with the state championship six times.

An English teacher, Coach Meyer also found time to coach basketball and to serve as St. John's athletic director for several years. He also was active in parish programs, having served for 12 years as the only layman on the Diocesan Board of Education. For his selfless commitment to his school and community, Coach Meyer was elevated by Pope John XXIII to the rank of St. Gregory. Six years later, he was inducted into the Iowa High School Baseball Hall of Fame.

Honors continued to accrue to Coach Meyer. In 1976, the Iowa High School Athletic Association presented him the Lyle T. Quinn Award for outstanding service to interscholastic athletics. At about the same time, Coach Meyer received another very special honor. One of his former players, Denis Menke, made it to the big leagues, eventually to play for the Houston Astros and the Cincinnati Reds.

In 1981, Coach Vince Meyer retired from his teaching position and from baseball. He died three months later. Coach Meyer is the only baseball coach to be inducted into the National High School Hall of Fame.

---

## Other Qualifiers

**Murl Bowen.** The head baseball coach at Asher High School in Oklahoma from 1961 to 1980 and again from 1981 through 1986, Coach Bowen has earned a record of 1,244 wins against only 246 losses, a national record. One of only a few coaches to devote a 36-year career to just one school, Coach Bowen won the Oklahoma state title five consecutive times from 1970 through 1974.

**Jack Curran.** With a 672-172 record and a winning percentage of .800, Coach Curran has dominated New York City's Catholic High School Athletic Association. His teams have won the city title 13 times and have been runners-up 8 times. Coach Curran has spent his entire 29-year career at Archbishop Molloy High School in Briarwood, New York.

**Winston Havenstrite.** A man who devoted 28 years to four different schools, Coach Havenstrite headed up the baseball programs at Drummond, Oklahoma City Northeast and Northwest, and Del City high schools. During that time, he coached some of the finest baseball players in the state of Oklahoma and earned a win/loss record of 663-247, the fourth highest in the country.

**Joseph Kasberger.** Coach Kasberger is another coach who has devoted his entire career to one school. Coach Kasberger was with St. Benedict's High School in Newark, New Jersey, from 1931 to 1969 and developed some of the finest baseball players in New Jersey. Coach Kasberger's teams earned a total record of 610-150.

**Jack Kaiser.** Coach Kaiser has coached for 35 years at Oak Park and River Forest High School in Illinois and is still at the reins, having led his school to 1,022 wins and 440 losses. Counting both his spring and summer records, Coach Kaiser has won 25 league titles, 24 district championships, and five state titles. A member of the American Baseball Coaches Association Hall of Fame, Coach Kaiser has won Coach of the Year honors five times and has been involved in clinics, advisory councils, and committees far too numerous to mention. A man dedicated to his sport, Coach Kaiser has been pleased to twice see his teams ranked in the nation's top 20.

**Ronald Klein.** The second high school coach selected into the American Baseball Coaches Association Hall of Fame, Coach Ron Klein has spent his entire 27-year career at New Trier High School in Winnetka, Illinois. With a record of 733 wins and 363 losses, Coach Klein has earned his five-time recognition as Coach of the Year, and his contributions extend well beyond the baseball diamond. Klein has been president of the Illinois Baseball Coaches Association as well as a member of several selection committees and executive boards. A recent recipient of the first Presidential Award of the Illinois High School Baseball Coaches Association, Klein continues to coach at New Trier.

**James Phipps.** The first high school coach inducted into the American Baseball Coaches Association Hall of Fame, Coach Jim Phipps has watched more than 100 of his players play in college and six make it to minor league baseball. Coaching at Niles West in Skokie, Illinois, and Lake Havasu City in Arizona, Phipps compiled a record of well over 500 wins, including two state championships and three runners-up. A veteran of 42 years' experience and nearing 70 years of age, Phipps will return to the diamond once again next year.

**John Schwartz.** Coach Schwartz is another successful baseball coach from the Sooner state, and during his 26-year career at Moore High School in Oklahoma he has earned a distinction that most coaches can only imagine. He is the third-winningest coach in the history of high school baseball. When Coach Schwartz's career ended in 1977, he had achieved the enviable career record of 758-211-2.

**Dick Seltz.** Coach Seltz has distinguished himself on the baseball diamond with a current record of 509-165 and a winning percentage in excess of .750, in addition to winning the state title once and earning runner-up status twice. He has also contributed his time and energy beyond the field of play to assist the Minnesota High School Baseball Coaches Association as both a member of the board of directors and its president. He also has served for the National Federation of High School Leagues as a member of the Rules Committee.

## COLLEGE BASEBALL

### America's Greatest College Baseball Coach

**Raoul "Rod" Dedeaux**

That a man with one of the most outgoing personalities in all of sports would advocate having a little fun is not surprising. Says Dedeaux of his coaching philosophy: "First, you have to play smart baseball. If you learn to do things right all the time, it doesn't matter who you're playing. Secondly, stay loose. When we work, we work hard; but we have fun, too. A little clowning always helps."

Whatever the Dedeaux success formula, whether clowning or working hard—or finding a way to do both—no one can question his results. During his 45 years with the USC Trojans, Coach Dedeaux recorded 1,332 victories against only 571 losses for a winning percentage of .699. Even more impressively, he won an unprecedented 11 national titles, including a string of 5 in a row. No other coach in the history of college baseball has won more than four national championships, and none has won more than *two* consecutively. His teams also have won 28 conference crowns and have made 27 appearances in the NCAA tournament.

The accomplishments of truly great coaches are measured in terms of the lives they touch. Coach Dedeaux has touched hundreds with his genius, and much of it has rubbed off. Tom Seaver played for Coach

Dedeaux's Trojans, as did Freddie Lynn, Dave Kingman, Ron Fairly, Roy Smalley, Steve Kemp, Rich Dauer, and Don Buford. In fact, scores of Coach Dedeaux's players earned All-American status and went on to play professional baseball.

Just a short time ago, when the All-Star game was held in Seattle's Kingdome, Coach Rod Dedeaux experienced what no other college baseball coach has enjoyed. Four of his former players (Fred Lynn, Dave Kingman, Roy Smalley, and Steve Kemp) played in the game. Said Coach Dedeaux after the game, "I don't think any other school's ever had that many All-Stars. I know it was one of the proudest moments of my life."

Proud moments became routine in Coach Dedeaux's career. He was named Coach of the Year six times by the American Baseball Coaches Association and was inducted into their Hall of Fame in 1970. Finally, in 1984, he was selected by the United States Olympic Committee to coach the U.S. baseball team in the 1984 Summer Olympics. The team won a silver medal.

## Number Two

**Cliff Gustafson.** Coach Gustafson just as easily could have been listed among America's greatest high school baseball coaches as well as the top five college coaches. While at South San Antonio High School from 1955 through 1967, Coach Gustafson established a win/loss record of 344-85-5 and led his team to seven state championships and a winning percentage of .798. His two consecutive state titles during his last two seasons caught the eye of the powers-that-be at the University of Texas, and Coach Gustafson joined the Longhorns as head baseball coach in 1968.

He took them immediately to a 23-11 record and a fifth-place finish in the NCAA tournament. In 1969, the Longhorns won 40 and lost only 6 for an .870 winning percentage. A friend once said to Coach Gustafson jokingly, "Well, you can't win 'em all"—to which he replied: "You can if you're good enough." It was this philosophy that led Texas to a record of 1,030 wins and 215 losses under Gustafson. His career winning percentage of .824 is the best of any coach in the history of college baseball, and it eventuated in two NCAA titles, two second-place finishes, six third-place finishes, and three fourth-place finishes.

Coach Gus, as his players call him, has won 18 Southwest Conference Championships in his 20 years at the helm and has been selected by the American Baseball Coaches Association twice as their Coach of the Year. He has coached 26 first-team All-Americans, and more than 95 of his players have gone on to sign professional contracts. Their level of dedication is as pronounced as their coach's and may be explained best by Coach Gus' capsulized philosophy: "I have always believed that you play games to have fun. But I have never seen anybody have fun when they lose." It's a philosophy that brought him to the top of his profession: one of only three coaches to win more than 1,000 games and the best win/loss percentage of any coach in the game's history.

## Number Three

**Dick Siebert.** Jerry Kindall's college coach and an inductee into the American Baseball Coaches Association Hall of Fame during the year in which Kindall was winning his first NCAA championship, Coach Richard Siebert is an institution in the Big Ten. Himself a winner of three NCAA championships, Coach Siebert also led the Gophers to a record of 754 wins, against only 361 losses, and 11 Big Ten championships. His 1977 Big Ten championship team concluded its home campaign that year with an incredible record of 26-0.

Seasons such as these contributed to Coach Siebert's career record, which ranks him among the top seven or eight coaches in the country to win more than 700 games at a major university. The "home field advantage" was one of many pluses that Siebert's Gophers brought to each contest. The advantage was especially pronounced, however, because "The Chief," as his players and fellow coaches called him, *designed* the field.

Now deceased, Coach Siebert has been immortalized by the many friends and fans who have contributed their time and energy to dedicate in his name the very stadium he designed and to acknowledge him as one of the great names in college baseball.

## Number Four

**Jerry Kindall.** A shortstop for eight years in the big leagues, Jerry Kindall earned the reputation of being one of baseball's best infielders before retiring in 1965 to return to his alma mater, the University of Minnesota, to coach basketball and baseball. In 1973, he took over the head baseball job at the University of Arizona and took the Wildcats to a second-place finish in their conference. Four years later, Coach Kindall and his Wildcats concluded the season with a 56-17 record and their coach's first NCAA championship. It would not be his last.

Coach Kindall led Arizona to a second NCAA championship in 1980 and a third in 1986, making him one of only four coaches to win three or more NCAA championships. His total record of 635-340-3 makes him one of the winningest coaches in the country. During his 17 years with the Wildcats, Coach Kindall has been instrumental in the development of 15 All-Americans and 84 players later to sign professional contracts. He has been acclaimed the National Coach of the Year three times (1976,

1980, and 1986) and has been named the PAC-10 Coach of the Year as well as the *Sporting News* Coach of the Year.

While at Minnesota as an undergraduate, Kindall played shortstop for the legendary Dick Siebert and was a key element in the team's 33-9 record and NCAA crown in 1956. When Coach Kindall later won the NCAA title at Arizona, he became the only person in the history of college baseball to both play for and coach an NCAA championship team.

Kindall's philosophy is best summed up in his own words: "When a player has self-esteem and a good image of himself and those around him, he's free to play his best." It is a philosophy that has established Coach Kindall as one of the sports world's best motivators and one of college baseball's greatest coaches.

## Number Five

**Ron Fraser.** Leading the NCAA Division I active coaches in career victories with 1,069, Ron Fraser is only the second coach in Division I history to win over a thousand games. Honors accrue to Coach Fraser almost as quickly as victories. He has been inducted into five halls of fame, most recently the American Baseball Coaches Association Hall of Fame in 1986. He has been named Coach of the Year on 10 different occasions and has watched proudly as 118 of his former players have gone off to play professional baseball.

Coach Fraser has led the Miami Hurricanes to the NCAA tournament 17 consecutive times and has established a play-off record of 49-20 for a winning percentage of .710. In 1974, Coach Fraser led the United States team to its only world championship. For the accomplishment, he was selected as the World Amateur Baseball Coach of the Year. In 1987, Fraser was selected as the International Baseball Association Coach of the Year, the first American ever to be so honored. And in 1982 and again in 1985, Coach Fraser led his Hurricanes to two NCAA Division I championships. Considerable accomplishments in only 25 years of coaching.

## Other Qualifiers

**David Brazell.** The head baseball coach at Grand Canyon College from 1953 through 1980, Dr. David Brazell established a record of 728-385-8 for a winning percentage of .649. In National Association of Intercollegiate Athletes (NAIA) competition, he won the district championship eight times and the area championship four times. In 1980, his last with the 'Lopes, Coach Brazell took Grand Canyon to the NAIA national championship with a record of 56-14-2. He left his successor with such outstanding talent that Grand Canyon won the national championship in 1981 and 1982 as well. The NAIA Coach of the Year in both 1979 and

1980, Dr. Brazell was inducted into the NAIA Baseball Coaches Hall of Fame in 1974 for outstanding contributions to the sport.

**Ed Cheff.** As head baseball coach for 12 years at Lewis and Clark State College in Idaho, Coach Cheff has compiled an NAIA record of 375 wins against only 47 losses. In the last four seasons, the Lewis and Clark Warriors won the NAIA national championship three times. Cheff teams have played for the championship for six consecutive years. Under Coach Cheff, 23 Warriors have earned NAIA All-America honors and only four failed to graduate at the end of that current school year. Cheff has watched 56 of his players sign professional contracts, and he has earned Coastal Division Coach of the Year four times and NAIA Coach of the Year twice. Cheff also finds time each year to volunteer his services to work with one or more NAIA coaches committees.

**Ken Dugan.** Nearing his 30th season as head man of the baseball Bisons, Coach Dugan has led Tennessee's David Lipscomb College to two NAIA national championships (1977 and 1979). In 1984, the Bisons went on to develop the NAIA's second-longest win streak in history, 34 games. Dugan's teams also have won three Volunteer State Athletic Conference (VSAC) championships, 14 NAIA district titles, and five area championships. The author of two best-selling books on baseball, Coach Dugan also has coached Pan Am and World Games teams and still holds the batting average and slugging percentage records of his alma mater, David Lipscomb College. His win/loss record of 858-308 makes him one of the winningest coaches in America. For his accomplishments, Coach Dugan has been inducted into the NAIA National Coaches Hall of Fame and the American Baseball Coaches Association Hall of Fame.

**Clint Evans.** The coach of the University of California/Berkeley from 1930 through 1952, Coach Evans compiled a record of 509 wins and 327 losses with six ties. His teams won seven California Intercollegiate Baseball Association (CIBA) championships and tied for two others during his 22-year tenure with the Bears. His philosophy, "Be a good loser, but don't lose," led California to a national championship in 1947 with a 31-10 record. In addition to his nine first-place finishes, Evans' teams finished second six times and third four times. During his 22 years with the Bears, Evans' teams finished lower than third only four times. In recognition of such noteworthy accomplishments, Coach Clint Evans was inducted into the American Baseball Coaches Association as a charter member in 1966.

**Joe Hicks.** Although Coach Joe Hicks is a member of the American Baseball Coaches Association Hall of Fame, his most cherished accomplishment involves his 500th career victory as the head coach of the

Vikings of Long Beach City College. His victory that day was won by his son, who was pitching for the team—and his *other* son, who was catching. During his 22 years with the "Vikes," Coach Hicks won 13 conference championships and four state championships, making him one of the winningest coaches in collegiate baseball.

**Marty Karow.** As head baseball coach at Ohio State University for 25 years, from 1951 through 1975, Coach Karow led the Buckeyes to almost 500 victories, five Big Ten championships, and in 1966, the NCAA crown as the nation's best team. That same year, he was named College Baseball Coach of the Year, and just one year later was asked to coach the U.S. Pan American team. A former All-American fullback for the Buckeyes in 1926, Karow went on to play professional baseball for the Boston Red Sox before returning to Ohio State, where he coached such future greats as Galen Cisco and Frank Howard. In recognition of his coaching record and several contributions to the game, Coach Karow was inducted into the Ohio State University Sports Hall of Fame and, in 1970, into the American Baseball Coaches Association Hall of Fame.

**Demie Mainieri.** The head coach of Miami-Dade Community College for 28 years, Coach Mainieri is one of the winningest coaches in collegiate baseball, with over 900 career victories. In addition to an enviable win/loss record, Coach Mainieri took his teams to the NJCAA national championship once (1964), the runner-up spot three times, and a third-place finish once. He was chosen FJCC Coach of the Year three times and District Coach of the Year twice and served as president of the NJCAA Baseball Coaches Association. Mainieri was inducted into the American Baseball Coaches Association Hall of Fame in 1988.

**Mark Marquess.** Another sure bet for the American Baseball Coaches Association Hall of Fame, Coach Marquess has made significant achievements during his 12 seasons with Stanford University. Under his direction, Stanford has never had a losing season, has advanced to the NCAA regionals for the past seven years, has appeared in the College World Series four times in six years, has won four of the last five PAC-10 Southern Division championships, and has won two NCAA championships (1987 and 1988). A graduate of Stanford in 1969, coach Marquess has earned a win/loss record of 497-251-4 and a winning percentage of .663. He has been the PAC-10 Southern Division Coach of the Year three times in the last five years and, most recently, led the United States to its first gold medal in baseball at the 1988 Summer Olympics in Seoul.

**John Scolinos.** The winningest active collegiate baseball coach, with 1,129 victories, Coach Scolinos has coached for 41 years, the last 27 with California Polytechnic in Pomona. Enormously successful during his tenure with California, Scolinos has won his conference crown six times and has taken the Broncos to the NCAA Division II title three times, in 1976, 1980, and 1983, each time being selected as the Division II Coach of the Year. In 1980, the year of his second NCAA crown, Coach Scolinos was selected Coach of the Decade by *College Baseball* newspaper. A short time later, he was chosen by USC coach Rod Dedeaux to be the pitching coach for the 1984 U.S. Olympic team. His contributions to the game were acknowledged even before his NCAA championships when he was elected in 1974 to the American Association of College Baseball Coaches (AACBC) Hall of Fame.

**Gil Stafford.** Coach Gil Stafford is the successor to Dave Brazell at Grand Canyon College, and in eight short years he has won five area championships and three NAIA national titles. His win/loss record of 379-161 ranks among the highest of young coaches, and his winning percentage of .702 is among the best of all of America's great collegiate baseball coaches. Another sure bet for the American Baseball Coaches Association Hall of Fame, Coach Stafford is one of only two coaches at Grand Canyon College since 1953 to establish one of the nation's top programs there.

# PROFESSIONAL BASEBALL

## America's Greatest Professional Baseball Manager

### John J. McGraw

A tough little man dealing with tough big men in baseball's early years, John Joseph McGraw played professional baseball for 17 years, mostly in the National League with Baltimore and New York. His managerial career started in 1899, as a player/manager with Baltimore, and continued through the 1906 season with the New York Giants. Effective in both capacities, McGraw already had won a World Series championship in 1905 and earned a lifetime batting average of .334 by the time he became a nonplaying manager in 1907.

Second only to Connie Mack for seasons managed (34) and career victories (2,840), "Little Napoleon" leads all managers with pennants won (10) and is fifth on the World Series list with three championships. In addition, his career winning percentage of .589 ranks among history's greatest. Beyond the statistics, it was McGraw who introduced the hit-and-run to baseball. He also conceived the drag bunt, double steal, squeeze, cutoff defense, and relief pitcher. For such contributions, baseball officials in Washington, DC, at a centennial dinner in 1970, enshrined the name of John J. McGraw as "The Greatest Manager of All Time."

A contentious 120-pound third baseman during his early playing days with Baltimore, "Muggsy" became a contentious manager with New York years later. He was a martinet of the first order and had few superstars on his teams. Although he did claim Christy Matthewson, Bill Dinneen, and a few others, McGraw made it to the top of the major league heap by driving himself and his players with relentless energy.

McGraw was scarred for life by the death of his mother when he was only 12 and the death of his first wife after only two years of marriage. That he had never recovered was particularly apparent as he aged, childless, and approached the end of his career. Yet he remained sensitive to the needs of his players and always found a place in his organization for those who had grown old.

John J. McGraw died on February 25, 1934, near New Rochelle, New York, a victim of internal hemorrhaging. He was enshrined in the Baseball Hall of Fame in Cooperstown four years later, firmly established as baseball's greatest manager.

## Number Two

**Connie Mack.** Cornelius McGillicuddy, one of the pioneers of professional baseball, began his playing career in 1886 as a catcher with Washington. A fair player for eight years, Mack's career was cut short by a broken leg. He became a player/manager for Pittsburgh for three years but was fired after placing sixth in the league. Mack then joined forces with Milwaukee of the Western League and managed them for four seasons. When the Western League was transformed by Commissioner Ban Johnson into the American League, Connie Mack assumed control of the Philadelphia franchise, receiving 25% interest in the team.

Says Mack of his first year in Philadelphia: "I came to Philadelphia in the winter of 1900-01 with a franchise but no players, no park, and no partner. By forgetting that sleep is an essential to keeping a man alive, I had a park, a team, and a partner by opening day." Mack won the American League pennant in 1905 but lost the Series in five games to McGraw's New York Giants. He would go on to win seven more pennants, winning five World Series championships in 1910, 1911, 1913, 1929, and 1930. Mack was always a dapper presence at his games, in suit and tie and tophat. Even though baseball rules require that *all* team members (including coaches) wear the team's uniform at games, Mack preferred to be a bit more resplendent. (As did Burt Shotton of the Dodgers in his day, apparently the only other coach not to wear his team's uniform.)

In February of 1930, the year of his last World Series championship, Connie Mack received what he called his greatest honor: He was awarded the Edward Bok prize for being the Philadelphian who did the most for his city the previous year. The award carried an embossed scroll, a gold medal, and $10,000 in cash. Said Mack of the award, "It was the proudest moment of my life when I received it."

Connie Mack continued to manage Philadelphia until 1950, having established the longest managerial tenure in professional baseball—53 years. He also won more games than any other manager (3,776), including five World Series championships. Connie Mack died in 1956, history's last link with baseball's formative years.

It would be 22 years before the Athletics, now in Oakland, would win another World Series championship, so indelibly had Mr. Mack made his imprint on the club. His imprint on baseball was no less indelible. Connie Mack was inducted into the Baseball Hall of Fame in 1937.

## Number Three

**Casey Stengel.** Charles Dillon Stengel was an outfielder for 15 years in the major leagues, playing for five different teams and earning the respectable lifetime batting average of .284. Born in Kansas City, Missouri, he picked up the nickname "Casey" from the first two letters of his hometown.

Although the first nine years of his managerial career were mediocre, when Stengel joined the Yankees in 1949, he walked almost immediately into sports immortality, establishing records with the Yankees that are unparalleled. Joe McCarthy's record of four consecutive Series victories lasted only 10 years. From 1949 through 1953, Casey's first 5 years with the team, the Yankees won the world title every year. They finished in second place in 1954 but returned to the World Series for the next four consecutive years, winning it twice. They returned to the World Series once more in 1960, losing to Pittsburgh in seven games. Within a 12-year period of time, the New York Yankees, under the direction of Casey Stengel, played in the World Series 10 times, winning it seven.

Some sports buffs claim that "The Old Perfessor" had little to do with the Yankees' dominance of the Series in the fifties, asserting that anyone could have won with the aggregate of superb talent fielded by that team. Casey himself refutes the argument in his autobiography: "Everybody knows we had a lot of playing talent when I was managing the Yankees, but a lot of people don't realize how fast the talent kept wearing out. By the time of my fourth World Series in 1952, only two of the regulars that had started for me in the first Series game in '49 were still around—Rizzuto and Berra."

Therein lies the Stengel genius—the ability to find and coordinate talent and to earn the respect of all his players. Said Elston Howard, the first black to play for the Yanks, of Stengel's genius: "He had a technique of two-platooning his men. He worked guys like myself, Mickey Mantle,

Tom Tresh, Bobby Richardson, and Tony Kubek gradually until we became major leaguers. This way he carried a continuous supply of good talent.''

Stengel's knowledge of baseball was overshadowed only by his ability to mangle communication. Asked once to describe the future of young catcher Greg Goosen, Casey reported: "He's just 20 years old and in 10 years he has a chance to be 30.'' But good advice was Stengel's greatest strength, and it didn't necessarily involve baseball. Said Casey to a friend of the press: "When you drink, drink in the hotel bar and put your room key in your shirt pocket. Then, if you fall off the stool, the bartender will see your key and call a bellboy and get you to your room safe. If you're out drinking and you fall off the stool, somebody will take your key and slip into your room and steal all your money when you're asleep.''

The inimitable Casey Stengel is perhaps remembered best by ex-Baseball Commissioner Bowie Kuhn: "There has never been anyone like him and never can be. Casey was irrepressibly himself. But Casey left a nation that adored him and a host of memories so vivid and marvelous that we really can't ever lose him.''

## Number Four

**Joe McCarthy.** Joseph Vincent McCarthy, was a no-nonsense taskmaster who demanded and received the best each of his players had to offer. One of the few managers in the majors never to play in a big league game, McCarthy spent 13 years in the minors before assuming the head job of the Chicago Cubs in 1926. During his five years with Chicago, he took the team, which had finished eighth the year before his arrival, to no lower than a fourth-place finish and to the World Series in 1929, losing to Philadelphia in five games.

Two years later, McCarthy joined forces with the New York Yankees, much to the dissatisfaction of Babe Ruth, who had expected the manager's job. After a second-place finish his first year, McCarthy took the Yankees to the World Series championship in 1932. Four years later, he took the Yanks to the World Series again to initiate the first of four consecutive world titles. In all, Joe McCarthy's teams played in nine World Series, winning seven, a record that is second only to his career winning percentage of .614, the highest in baseball history.

When asked by sportswriter Ed Fitzgerald if he was expecting to win in 1946, McCarthy removed the cigar from his mouth and said: "Why else would I be here? What would anyone play for except the championship?" Such was the relentless drive of the man who spent most of his managerial career with the Yanks, and such as the determination that provoked pitcher Joe Page to remark after McCarthy's death in 1978: "I hated his guts—but there never was a greater manager."

## Number Five

**Walter Alston.** Walter Emmons Alston was another of baseball's committed few who never made it as players but established themselves as legends after winning games as managers. Having established himself as an outstanding minor league manager with Montreal, Alston joined the Brooklyn Dodgers in 1954 and in one year led them to a World Series championship over the Yankees in seven games. They returned to the World Series in 1956, this time losing to the Yanks in another seven-game series.

Alston continued his winning ways with the Dodgers after their move to Los Angeles. He won World Series titles in 1959, 1963, and 1965. He took the Dodgers to the World Series twice more in 1966 and 1974 but lost both times, once to Baltimore and once to Oakland. Following two second-place finishes in '75 and '76, Alston retired from major league baseball. He was inducted into the Hall of Fame in 1983.

During his 23-year career with the Dodgers, Alston claimed seven pennants and became the sixth manager in history to win 2,000 games. Only two men, John McGraw and Connie Mack, remained with one team longer than "Smokey" Alston, and only three managers have won more World Series championships than Alston's four. In addition, during his 23 years Alston led the Dodgers to a first- or second-place finish 15 times, for a total record of 2,042-1,615 and a winning percentage of .558, the eighth highest in the history of baseball.

A man who himself appeared in only one major league game, striking out in his one at-bat for the St. Louis Cardinals in 1936, Walter Alston has become a Hall of Famer and ranks fifth on the all-time win list, with 2,042 wins in his 23 years. Although he was described by some as colorless, Walter Alston stands today, several years after his death, among the giants of the game.

## Number Six

**William McKechnie.** William Boyd McKechnie began his playing career in 1907 with the Pittsburgh Pirates and concluded it 13 years later after playing with eight different teams. He started his managerial career with Pittsburgh in 1922 and led them to a World Series championship in 1925. In 1928 he switched to St. Louis and immediately brought the

Cards to a world title. The 1930 season found "Deacon" Bill McKechnie in Boston, where he earned respectability but no trips to the World Series.

McKechnie concluded his managerial career with Cincinnati from 1938 through 1946. One year after joining the club, he led the Reds to the World Series, where they lost to the Yankees in a four-game sweep. The very next year, however, McKechnie took Cincinnati once more to the World Series, where his team beat the Detroit Tigers in seven games.

The number-five manager on Bill Deane's list of "turnaround geniuses," McKechnie established himself as a legend of the game and was inducted into the Hall of Fame in Cooperstown in 1962.

## Number Seven

**Leo Durocher.** Leo Ernest "Lippy" Durocher started his playing career with the New York Yankees and Babe Ruth in 1925. Fondly dubbed "Huggins' Boy" by his teammates, Leo the Lip learned much from his diminutive mentor before he was traded to Cincinnati and then to St. Louis, where he played with Frankie Frisch's Gashouse Gang from '33 to '37. He finished his playing career six years later with the Brooklyn Dodgers, where he was a player/manager since 1939.

During his final season as player/manager, in 1941, Durocher led Brooklyn to the World Series, losing to the Yankees in five games. Ten years later, having switched to managing the New York Giants, Durocher took his team to the World Series again, losing once more in a six-game series. Three years later, however, the Giants were back, this time to beat the Cleveland Indians in a four-game sweep. Leo remained with the Giants for one more year and then took an 11-year leave from the managerial ranks. He returned to lead the Chicago Cubs from the National League cellar to second- and third-place finishes during his 7-year tenure with them.

From Chicago, Durocher went to Houston for two years. At the end of the 1973 season he retired from baseball. Relishing his reputation of being a fighter, Leo does a better job than anyone else of summing up his personality with the following story. Describing how badly he wanted to win, he said, "If I were playing third base, and my mother was rounding third with the run that was going to beat us, I would trip her. I'd pick her up and I'd brush her off, and then I'd say, 'Sorry, Mom, but nobody beats me.'"

Traveling home shortly after making that comment, Leo was greeted by his mother at the door: "You said that about your own mother? You'd trip me, Son, your own mother?!" Leo denied it at the time, but years later admitted: "For the rest of my visit, she walked around with an injured air. And I guess she had a right to. God rest your soul, Mom, I'm afraid I would have."

## Number Eight

**Billy Martin.** The on-again, off-again genius of the Yankee dugout, Billy Martin stands alone among Bill Deane's "turnaround geniuses" as the most consistent miracle worker in the majors. Alfred Manuel Pesano, otherwise named "Billy Martin," was the fair-hitting but feisty second baseman of the New York Yankees from 1950 through 1957 and a journeyman infielder for one club per year for the remainder of his 13-year career as a player. As a manager he was every bit as nomadic.

Martin began his managerial career with Minnesota in 1969, taking the Twins from a seventh-place finish the year before to a record of 97-65, a winning percentage of .599, and an American League West championship. He traveled to Detroit in 1971, remaining with them for three years and leading them to a division title in 1972. From Detroit, Martin went to Texas and prodded the hapless Rangers from 100+ losses the previous year to a 84-76 record in 1974. In 1975, midway through the season, Martin joined the New York Yankees for the first of a series of appearances with them. The next season he took the Yankees to the World Series, only to lose to the Cincinnati Reds. One year later his Yankees won the Series over the Los Angeles Dodgers in a 4-2 victory.

In 1980 Martin joined forces with the Oakland Athletics, taking them from over 100 losses the previous year to a respectable 83-79 record in 1980 and a Western Division title in 1981. Back with the Yankees in 1983, Martin revived them once again from a fifth-place finish the year before to a 91-71 record in 1983. Fired once again by Yankee owner George Steinbrenner in 1988, Billy Martin certainly would have managed again. His life, however, was tragically cut short in an automobile accident in 1989.

## Number Nine

**Whitey Herzog.** Ninth on Bill Deane's list of "turnaround geniuses" and first on *Sports Illustrated's* list of baseball's greatest active coaches, Dorrel Norman Elvert "Whitey" Herzog, according to *SI* staff writer Peter Gammons, is "win or lose, the best around." A marginal ballplayer for four clubs during his 9-year playing career, Herzog started his managing career with Texas in 1973 with an inauspicious win/loss record of 47-91. In 1975 he accepted the head job with the Kansas City Royals and after one year took them to three consecutive West Division championships.

In 1980, Whitey was hired by St. Louis to revive the sagging fortunes of the Cardinals. In only two years Herzog took the Cards to a World Series title. He took them to the World Series twice more, losing in 1985 to Kansas City and in 1987 to Minnesota. With three World Series appearances and one world title under his belt, Herzog is baseball's greatest active manager.

To what does he attribute much of his success? Says Whitey: "The biggest difference between a successful manager and an unsuccessful one is getting a second chance." After completing his playing career, Whitey returned to his hometown of New Athens, Illinois, to be a labor foreman, where, he said, "I had 35 guys working for me on this job, and only about 15 of them wanted to work." Fed up, he accepted a scouting job in the majors and ultimately went with Texas, where he discovered more men who didn't want to work. Said Whitey with his characteristic bluntness, "I think they're the worst excuse for a major league team I ever saw."

Given his second chance, Whitey made history, claiming, "Managing is simple. You pick out your best players and try to get them out there in their positions as often as possible." His modesty notwithstanding, Whitey Herzog is certain to continue winning and to be one of Cooperstown's future inductees into the Hall of Fame.

## Number Ten

**Sparky Anderson.** George "Sparky" Anderson played 152 games at second base for the Phillies in 1959, hit .218, and then apparently disappeared from baseball. In fact, Anderson had moved to the minors, where he remained until 1969 when he became a coach with the brand-new San Diego Padres. He remained with them for a year and then in 1970 accepted the job of managing the Cincinnati Reds. Sparky took the Reds from a third-place finish the year before to a 100-game season and a trip to the World Series, where they lost to Baltimore. During his years with Cincinnati, Sparky finished fourth in the West Division only once, second three times, and first five times, playing in the World Series four times and winning it twice with back-to-back victories in 1975 and 1976.

Next he moved to Detroit, where ex-Yankee great Ralph Houk had been unable to restore the early Tiger greatness that had temporarily been revived by Billy Martin and Mayo Smith in the preceding years. The young man who had made sparks fly at second base in the minors embarked upon a five-year plan to bring the Tigers to the World Series. Doubting Thomases in the Detroit media scoffed at him, but in 1984, five years after his arrival, the Tigers won the World Series championship with a 4-1 victory over San Diego.

In 1984, Sparky Anderson became the first manager in big league baseball to win a World Series championship in both leagues, the first to win 100 or more games in both leagues, and the first to win the Manager of the Year award in both leagues. Four years later, he was selected by *Sports Illustrated* as the number two greatest active manager and the best with players and the media. With only one year of playing and 18 years of managing major league baseball, Sparky Anderson still claims: "The biggest break I ever got in the world was to be a part of major-league ball." Sparky has made the most of it and is destined for the Hall of Fame in Cooperstown.

## Other Qualifiers

**Lou Boudreau.** Lou Boudreau was only 24 years old when, in 1941, the Cleveland Indians' front office decided to appoint him manager. Almost immediately, Boudreau started turning the team around. Later to become a Hall of Fame shortstop, the player/manager for the Indians in six short years led them to a World Series championship in 1948. He batted .355 to lead the way and, at the end of the season, was selected by the nation's sportswriters as the American League's Most Valuable Player, beating out Joe DiMaggio and Ted Williams for the honor. During his 16 years with Cleveland, Boston, Kansas City, and Chicago, Boudreau won 1,162 games and lost 1,224 for a winning percentage of .487. Born in Harvey, Illinois, in 1917 and inducted into the Hall of Fame in 1970, Lou Boudreau is one of baseball's great names.

**Roger Craig.** After seven seasons as pitching coach for the San Diego Padres, Roger Craig was selected as the team's manager in 1978. The guru of the split-fingered fastball, Craig transformed also-ran pitching staffs into legitimate contenders, earning a .519 winning percentage with the Padres during his first year. It was at San Francisco, however, that Craig earned Manager of the Year honors by taking the Giants, who had lost over 100 games in 1985, to the National League West Division title in 1987.

**Joe Cronin.** Another of baseball's player/managers, Joe Cronin hit .309 in 1933 when he took Washington to the World Series championship. Playing for the Boston Red Sox throughout most of his career, Cronin hit a lifetime batting average of .302 to earn induction into the Hall of Fame in 1956. After being a player/manager for 13 years, Cronin restricted himself to the dugout in 1946, the same year he led Boston to another World Series championship—this time behind the bat of Ted Williams. It was Williams who said of Cronin: "I can't tell you how important he was to me. I had understanding from a wonderful man. He taught so many players so much. Joe Cronin was a great player, a great manager, a wonderful father. No one respects you more than I do, Joe."

**Jimmy Dykes.** Hall of Fame sportscaster Jack Brickhouse identified Jimmy Dykes as one of the finest managers he had ever seen. A player/manager for the first six of his 21 years as a manager, Jimmy Dykes had been an infielder for Philadelphia for 16 years before the White Sox's front office gave him the reins in 1934. Dykes had his greatest years in Chicago, leading the team to a record of 899-938 during his 13 years with them.

**Clark Griffith.** Bill Deane of the Baseball Hall of Fame identified the "Old Fox" as his third greatest "turnaround genius" of the century. One of the game's old-timers, Griffith started as a player for St. Louis and Boston in 1891 and eventually went with the Cubs, where he remained as a pitcher until 1900. A consistent 20-game winner for the Cubs, Griffith took over as manager for the White Sox in 1901, then for the Yankees in 1903, and later for Washington in 1912, where he remained until his retirement in 1920. Inducted into the Hall of Fame in 1946, Griffith's career as a player or a manager spanned 4 decades.

**Charlie Grimm.** With a baseball career that touched six decades, "Jolly Cholly" Grimm had his greatest years with the Chicago Cubs, where he advanced to the World Series four times: '32, '35, '38, and '45. Grimm lost all four Series, but in 1932 he helped lead the team to the National League title by playing first base and hitting a very respectable .307 in 149 games. Grimm later managed for Boston and Milwaukee and in 1960 returned to the Cubs for his final season.

**Bucky Harris.** The second-place manager on Bill Deane's 22-name list of "turnaround geniuses," Stanley Raymond Harris had been a major league ballplayer for only five years when, at age 27, he was named manager of the Washington Red Sox. During his playing days he was called the best clutch hitter Joe McCarthy ever saw. Bucky Harris won his first world championship as a rookie manager in 1924 with Washington. He drove in seven runs to lead them to the victory over "Muggsy" McGraw's New York Giants. Harris's Washington team won the pennant again in 1925. Twenty-two years later, when Harris was head manager of the New York Yankees, his team won another pennant and a World Series championship over the Brooklyn Dodgers. Inducted into the Hall of Fame in 1975, Bucky Harris retired after the 1956 season, having devoted 29 years to big league baseball.

**Ralph Houk.** A so-so catcher for the New York Yankees from 1947 to 1954, "Major" Ralph Houk took over as the Yankees' nonplaying manager in 1961, inheriting a team that had established five World Series records in 1960: highest batting average (.338), most runs (55), most hits (91), most total bases (142), and most runs batted in (54). They had nonetheless lost the Series to Pittsburgh, who hadn't won a world championship since 1925. Houk took over in 1961 and led the Yanks to a 4-1 Series championship. He repeated with another World Series title in 1962 by beating San Francisco four games to three, and in 1963 he lost the World Series title when the Los Angeles Dodgers shut out the Yanks in four straight games. In 1964 Houk moved to the front office as the team's general manager, where he made a behind-the-scenes contribution to one more American League pennant in 1964.

**Rogers Hornsby.** One of baseball's greatest hitters, with a lifetime batting average of .358, "Rajah" Rogers Hornsby was also one of the game's finest managers. Overshadowed by his playing accomplishments, Hornsby's managing record includes a World Series championship with St. Louis in 1926 and a National League pennant with the Cubs in 1932. A player/manager, Hornsby assumed his responsibilities with mixed feelings. During the two years preceding his first year as player/manager, "Rajah" batted .424 and .403 to lead the major leagues. While calling the shots for the Cardinals in 1926, he could manage only a .317, subpar by his own standards. After batting .224 during the 1932 pennant year, Hornsby abandoned managing the following year, but he resumed it again in 1933 and continued in that capacity intermittently throughout the rest of his career. Hornsby retired from baseball in 1953.

**Miller Huggins.** After playing nine years for Cincinnati and St. Louis of the National League as a second baseman, Miller James Huggins became a player/manager for St. Louis in 1913. In 1917 he became a nonplaying manager and in 1918 became the head manager of the New York Yankees. Nicknamed "The Mighty Mite" by his friends, Huggins discovered immediately that his athletic fortunes were tied closely to the majestic power of the Sultan of Swat. Babe Ruth's home run production and the sheer batting power of the Yank's "Murderer's Row" brought Huggins' crew to the World Series championship game six times in eight years, winning the world title in 1923, 1927, and 1928. Huggins' 12 years with the Yankees resulted in a win/loss record of 1,067-649 for a winning percentage over .600. Only 5 feet 4 inches and 140 pounds, Huggins battled bigger men most of his life—and oftentimes won. On September 29, however, a few days before the completion of the 1929 season, he died of blood poisoning. In 1964, the little man named "Hug" by scores of admiring players was inducted into the Baseball Hall of Fame.

**Al Lopez.** A respected catcher in the major leagues for 20 years, Alfonso Ramon Lopez learned his trade well with three different teams—Brooklyn, Boston, and Pittsburgh—before becoming the manager of the Cleveland Indians in 1951. In three short years he took his team to the American League pennant, losing the World Series to the New York Giants. Two years later, Lopez went to Chicago, where he led the White Sox to their first pennant in 40 years, breaking the Yankee stranglehold on the American League. He remained with Chicago for eight more years and retired in 1969, later to be inducted into the Baseball Hall of Fame.

**Tom Lasorda.** Thomas Charles Lasorda literally spent most of his baseball career in the minors. After graduating from Norristown High School in Pennsylvania, he signed his first contract with the Philadelphia Athletics and a short time later pitched for Schenectady in the Canadian/American League, where he led all players in wild pitches (20). He later played for Montreal in the International League before being brought up to play with the Dodgers for two years. A year later he was traded to Kansas City where he played for one year, but in three big league seasons and 58 pitching appearances, he was 0-4 with an earned run average of 6.52.

His lackluster playing career, however, only served to emphasize, by contrast, the brilliance of his managerial career. As a manager in the minor leagues, he won five league titles through 1972 before becoming the Dodgers' third-base coach. In 1976, he was picked by Chairman of the Board Walter O'Malley to succeed Walter Alston. In 13 years, Lasorda has brought the Dodgers to the league championship game five times, winning it three times, and to a World Series title in 1981. With a win/loss record of 928-807 and a winning percentage of .535, Tommy Lasorda is one of baseball's great active coaches.

**Danny Murtaugh.** A man selected by both Jack Brickhouse and Bill Deane as deserving special recognition for his ability to get a team to not only turn around but also repeat as champions, Daniel Edward Murtaugh broke into baseball in 1941 as a second baseman for Philadelphia. During his first year, he played in 85 games and batted .219. In 1951 he played his last game, this time for the Pittsburgh Pirates; six years later, he was chosen to manage the team. Murtaugh remained with the Pirates, off and on, for 14 years. During that time, the Pittsburgh Pirates improved steadily. The year before Murtaugh joined the team, they had a 62-92 record; within three years they had won their first World Series championship in 33 years with a win/loss record of 95-59. After finishing in third place the year before, with Murtaugh's return the Pirates found themselves playing for the National League pennant, losing to Cincinnati in three games. The next year, however, Pittsburgh won their second World

Series under Danny Murtaugh. Murtaugh again left but returned a year later to lead the Pirates to two more pennant championship games, losing both, one to Los Angeles and the other to Cincinnati. Murtaugh retired after the 1976 season, having led his team to another 92-70 record.

**Steve O'Neill.** A catcher for the Cleveland Indians throughout most of his big league playing career, Stephen Francis O'Neill ranks sixth on Bill Deane's list of "turnaround geniuses of the century." O'Neill started his managing career with the Cleveland Indians in 1935, leading them to three consecutive winning seasons. In 1943 he jumped to the Detroit Tigers, a team that had suffered two back-to-back losing seasons. Within three years O'Neill molded the Tigers into world champions, winning a close 4-3 victory over the Chicago Cubs. O'Neill remained with the Tigers until 1948, spent two years in Boston in 1950-1951, and then concluded his career with the Philadelphia Phillies in 1954.

**Chuck Tanner.** Another of Jack Brickhouse's favorite big league managers, Charles William Tanner was an itinerant outfielder for four teams during his nine-year playing career. He started with Milwaukee in 1955 and concluded with Los Angeles in 1962. He accepted his first management job with the Chicago White Sox in 1970, leading them to their first second-place finish in six years. Three losing seasons with the Sox, however, led to his transfer in 1976 to the Oakland Athletics, where he remained for one year. He then established himself and his reputation as a manager with the Pittsburgh Pirates. After only two years with the Pirates, Tanner led them to the world title in 1979. A utility outfielder who achieved a lifetime batting average of only .261, Chuck Tanner has established himself as one of baseball's great managers. He is currently with Atlanta.

**Earl Weaver.** In 1966, with the leadership of manager Hank Bauer, the Baltimore Orioles won their first World Series championship since 1944, when they had been the St. Louis Browns. The '44 world title had been their only one in the team's 43 years of existence. In 1966, Hank Bauer brought them their second. In 1967 they slipped back to a tie for sixth, and in 1968 Earl Weaver was brought in to restore respectability to the Oriole franchise. He did just that. He joined the team midway through the 1968 season and led them to a 91-78 win/loss record. In 1969, 1970, and 1971, the Baltimore Orioles played for the World Series championship, winning in 1970 with a lopsided 4-1 victory over Cincinnati. They finished first again in the East Division in 1973 and 1974 and again in 1979, when they played for the world title, losing a close Series to Pittsburgh. Weaver's last year with the Orioles was 1982, finishing second in the division with a win/loss record of 94-68. In all, Earl Weaver led the Baltimore Orioles to five World Series, winning twice, five seasons of 100 or more wins, a win/loss record of 1,397-956, and a winning percentage over .600. Weaver retired after the 1982 season, a sure bet for Hall of Fame honors.

**Dick Williams.** Fourth on Bill Deane's list of "turnaround geniuses," Dick Williams is one of baseball's most well-traveled managers. As a utility infielder/outfielder in major league baseball from 1951 through 1964, Williams played for Brooklyn, Baltimore, Cleveland, Kansas City, and Boston. His playing career ended with Boston in 1964. Three years later, Williams became the Red Sox manager. The Red Sox had finished in ninth place in the two preceding years, a trend that in one year Williams reversed into a trip to the World Series, in which the Sox lost to St. Louis in a close seven-game battle. Four years later, Williams was with Oakland, leading them to their first 100+ game season in the 40 years since Connie Mack had led the then Philadelphia Athletics to the World Series in 1931. The next year, in 1972, Williams led Oakland to the world title over the Cincinnati Reds. His team repeated as world champions in 1973 with a 4-1 World Series victory over the New York Mets. From Oakland, Williams traveled to Anaheim where he managed the Angels for two seasons, then to Montreal for five more, on to San Diego for two, and finally to Seattle, where he currently is manager of the Mariners. With three trips to the World Series and two world titles, Williams has established himself as one of baseball's best.

**Harry Wright.** Born in 1835 in Sheffield, England, William Henry Wright is credited as being major league baseball's first manager. In 1869, he took baseball's first professional team on a 66-game tour and lost but one game. Two years later, more teams having joined the professional ranks, Wright moved to Boston, taking the Red Sox name with him, and played in the outfield, pitched, and caught in addition to managing his team to six championships in his first seven years. Wright remained with Boston until 1881, moved to Providence for two years, and then moved to Philadelphia for the last 10 years of his long career. Wright had but five losing seasons during his 23 years leading major league teams and was inducted into the Baseball Hall of Fame in 1953.

# Chapter 2

# BASKETBALL

A loose interpretation of the origin of basketball traces it to the excavations of the Mayan and Toltec ball courts in Mexico, the largest of which is in Chichen Itza near Cancun. The field on which the Mayan game was played is 480 feet by 120 feet and is enclosed at each end by two high walls, each of which holds at the center, some 25 to 30 feet above the ground, a vertical stone ring. The almost impossible object of the game was to *kick* a hard rubber ball through scores of opposing players and then through one of the rings, ending what sometimes was *days* of competition. Although the game had a ball and a "hoop," its comparison to basketball as originated by Dr. James Naismith in 1891 is more romantic than real.

The comparison might make sense, however, when we realize that the captain of the losing side was beheaded by the captain of the winning side. The "do-or-die" and "win-at-all-costs" philosophies of some present-day basketball fans and players, particularly in the game's regional hotbeds, cause the figurative demise of coaches every year. Fortunately, most of them agree with Dean Smith, North Carolina head coach: "If you make every game a life or death proposition, you're going to have problems. For one thing, you'll be dead a lot."

Certainly, James Naismith did not conceive of his new activity as a life-or-death proposition when he accepted the challenge at Springfield College to create a game that could be played indoors. Nor did he ever indicate that the Mayans or the Toltecs influenced his thinking. In fact, Naismith created his game by methodically selecting activities that could be played indoors and that would give a maximum of exercise and enjoyment to his PE students (Brasch, 1970). In his own words:

> [I] began to think of the fundamental principles of *all* games. I soon discovered that in all team games some kind of a ball was used. . . . The next step was to secure some kind of a goal through which the ball could be passed. . . . It then occurred that if the ball be thrown

in a curve it would not be necessary or advisable to put too much force on the ball. I decided that by making the goal horizontal, the ball would have to be thrown in a curve, minimizing the severe driving of the ball. . . . It would be placed above [the players'] heads, so that once the ball left the shooter's hands, it was not likely to be interfered with. (Basketball Hall of Fame souvenir book, 1987)

Naismith decided on peach baskets suspended on the balcony of each end of the gymnasium. The height of the balcony was exactly 10 feet, the height of today's baskets. Tradition is reflected further in the number of players on each side. At first the number was unlimited, and mob scenes resulted after the initial tipoff. In 1895, Naismith reduced the number to five, where it remains after almost a century of play.

In many sports it is difficult to identify the first coach; in basketball, however, the honor must go to Naismith, although a fellow coach at Springfield in 1891 comes close to sharing it. Amos Alonzo Stagg, an inductee into the basketball as well as the football halls of fame, received his initial coaching assignment at Springfield and played with Naismith in history's first public basketball game, the Springfield students versus their teachers. Youth won out over limited experience and the students won 5-1, with Stagg scoring the only basket for the faculty. Stagg went on to introduce the game to the Midwest when he left the same year to coach at the University of Chicago.

Naismith hadn't been much of a threat to the students. He played in only two games during his entire association with the sport he created—"Just didn't get around to playing." Stagg *had* been a threat—to life and limb, his own as well as the students'. The former All-American football player for Yale got a black eye in the game and earned guarded praise from Naismith: "I wish Lonnie could have made the point without fouling everybody." Naismith was just as candid about himself: "Once I even used a grapevine wrestling clamp on a man who was too big for me to handle" (McCallum, 1978).

Naismith's creation may not have been a work of art that day, but it worked. It publicized the new game and lured hundreds of curiosity seekers into the gym to watch the internecine warfare that was Springfield "basket ball." Crowds became so engrossed that ultimately, as the sport reached other schools, the playing areas had to be separated from the spectators by large screens of chicken wire. The activity on both sides of the wire was so frenzied in those early days that the wires weren't removed until 1929.

Even chicken wire was scant containment for the rough and tumble that was turn-of-the-century basketball. Coaching strategy capitalized on brute strength and, when possible, batting shots away from the basket; goaltending was legal in those days. Although the sport attracted specialists, many of the players were football and baseball players who regarded basketball as a way to stay in shape during the winter—including Lou Boudreau at Illinois, Jackie Robinson at Southern Cal, Otto Graham at Northwestern, and Bob Zuppke at Wisconsin, later to become one of college football's toughest and most successful coaches.

While Zuppke was earning his basketball letter as a "scrub" at Wisconsin, a youngster destined for greatness in the sport was growing up on the plains of Halstead, Kansas. Born in 1901, Adolph Rupp, the man who won more basketball games (875) than anyone in history, later revealed that he had never heard of James Naismith until he entered one of his PE classes at the University of Kansas in 1920.

That destiny's winningest basketball coach would cross paths with the game's creator may not be too surprising. Interesting is the fact that Rupp would *play* basketball for the game's *second*-winningest coach (770 career victories), "Phog" Allen, who also was one of Naismith's apprentices. It doesn't take too much imagination to envision the game's creator sitting in the stands in 1924 watching Kansas win a national championship, unaware that two of his protégés—Allen, the coach, and Rupp, the player—would be his game's two winningest coaches.

Not much, however, would have surprised Naismith. In just four years, his peach baskets dangling at opposite ends of the gymnasium during an intramural rivalry in Springfield, Massachusetts, were transformed into "nets" in the auditorium that housed the first women's intercollegiate game in California. Just a year later, the first professional basketball game was played in Trenton, New Jersey. And in 1898, the first professional league was formed, consisting of teams from Trenton, Camden, the Pennsylvania Bicycle Club, the Hancock Athletic Club, and the Germantown Club.

All of these teams had coaches, some very successful. One of the first, Frederick Burkhardt, coached the Buffalo Germans in 1895. He took his team of six players on barnstorming tours as far away as the Midwest and eventually compiled a record of 792-86, winning 111 straight at one stretch. In fact, Burkhardt's Germans participated in the exhibition tournament at the 1904 Summer Olympics in St. Louis and probably were instrumental in the growth of professional basketball as well as the eventual inclusion of the sport as an Olympic event in 1936.

As successful as the game had been in early amateur circles, it was initially unsuccessful as a professional sport. Professional basketball didn't realize its golden era until the 1920s. The development of the American Basketball League in 1925 helped give the game the boost it needed by drawing upon the knowledge and organizational skills of players and coaches, some from other sports. The league included teams from New York, Philadelphia, Detroit, Cleveland, and Chicago. Visionaries saw a good thing and hustled to get in on it. The owner of the Chicago franchise was none other than George Halas, the motive force behind professional football.

With the nationwide acceptance of basketball on an amateur as well as a professional level, fans everywhere started asking the inevitable question: "What's the best team in the country?" America's first National Invitational Tournament (NIT) provided the answer in March of 1938 when Temple defeated Colorado 60-36 with Byron "Whizzer" White, football All-American and future Supreme Court justice, leading the way for the Buffalos.

One year later, Coach Howard Hobson's Oregon team beat Ohio State 46-33 to win the first NCAA basketball championship. The championship was played at Northwestern University in front of a small but raucous crowd of 5,000. The crowd doubled the next year when the championship was played at Kansas City's Municipal Auditorium. Ten thousand people watched two teams take the floor, both of which already had become basketball legends.

Branch McCracken's Indiana Hoosiers and "Phog" Allen's Kansas Jayhawks each had coasted to the championship game. The game was expected to be a Midwestern shoot-out and it was not a disappointment. However, it was not the close match-up that experts had expected. Following a 32-19 halftime lead, largely the result of McCracken's fast break, Indiana cruised to a 60-42 victory.

The tournament enjoyed a profit of almost $10,000 that year; each coach received a $750 check for his team's efforts. More importantly, the fast break changed the game and challenged already outdated traditions. Just as importantly for NCAA officials, the tournament established itself as a legitimate drawing card, and for basketball fans everywhere the incurable fever called "March Madness" became America's annual epidemic.

One reason for the fever was basketball's growth into a fast-paced, high-scoring frenzy that owed much of its excitement to coaches like Frank Keaney at Rhode Island, Branch McCracken at Indiana, and Piggy Lambert at Purdue, along with a legion of fast-break artists who thought the center jump after every score was about as exciting—and probably as old-fashioned—as pulling balls out of peach baskets almost half a century earlier.

These coaches and players fought to eliminate the center jump—and did battle with an army of traditionalists, among whom was Naismith, who saw both suspense and strategy in the center jump and who reasoned, some of them anyway, that its elimination would heighten both the pace of the game *and* the incidence of heart failure among its players. No athlete, they thought, no matter how well conditioned, could sprint from baseline to baseline without the relief of a center jump. No sport in America involved such *sustained* exertion. But progress, not love, makes the world go round. The center jump was eliminated in 1937 and the 10-second clock was introduced—and no one collapsed from the strain.

The strain of *competition* took its toll a few years later, however, when in 1951 over 30 players were arrested for cheating so their teams would win by fewer points than the gamblers' "point line." The scandal touched only New York schools at first but eventually spread to the Midwest. Coach Nat Holman, former standout guard for the Original Celtics in the '20s, watched his CCNY team be among the first to be hit. Just one year earlier, Holman had helped them win the NCAA *and* NIT championships, the only team in history to win both during the same season—both against Bradley and both in Madison Square Garden.

But the game rebounded quickly—thanks to players and coaches like John Wooden, who introduced a self-control and commitment that overshadowed the '50s scandal. The only person to be enshrined in the National Basketball Hall of Fame in Springfield as both a player (Purdue/'60) and a coach (UCLA/'72), Wooden introduced a coaching style that brought discipline and spontaneity to UCLA. It led the Bruins to 10 NCAA championships, seven of which were consecutive from 1967 to 1973.

Pro basketball progressed on a parallel course. Starting with teams like the Original Celtics and the New York Rens, basketball's first all-black team, pro basketball moved quickly into the national spotlight. Twenty years earlier, the first professional league appeared and disappeared almost as fast as its paying customers. In the '20s and '30s, however, Celtic players like Joe Lapchick and Nat Holman, later to become coaches, and "Tarzan" Cooper and "Wee Willie" Smith of the Rens traded in buses and barnstorming for publicity and paychecks.

Having taken the game to the people for so many years, the people were now coming to the game. They continue to come. The Wilt Chamberlains, Michael Jordans, and Larry Birds help; so do coaches like Ray Meyer, Red Auerbach, and Pat Riley. During the 1982-1983 season, NBA attendance was just under 10 million. By 1987-1988, it had grown to 12,654,374, an average of 13,419 per game. The Detroit Pistons alone passed the one million mark, averaging over 26,000 fans per game. One third of those fans were women (Sachare, 1988).

The game now has universal appeal. Excitement, commitment, and astonishing stats are not the exclusive province of the pros—nor even of the college ranks. Good friend Nelson Campbell recently published a book entitled *Grass Roots and Schoolyards* (1987) that illustrates the broad popularity of the game in high school across the country and highlights its elevated position in the social hierarchies of even the smallest rural communities.

Do the pros have all the high-scoring games? In New Mexico in 1970, high school coach Ralph Tasker's Hobbs Eagles *averaged* almost 115 points per game. Winning streaks? Coach John Wooden's UCLA streak of 88 games pales before the record of Coach Ernest Blood's Passaic Wonders. The New Jersey high school reeled off a string of 159 consecutive wins from the years 1919 to 1925. And dedication? Well, what team is more dedicated than the high school from Barrow, Alaska? With a student population of a few more than 100, they spend an annual $100,000 to travel 27,000 miles to play basketball and six other sports. The nearest competitor is 500 miles away. Dedication.

Basketball has it all, and it owes much to the visionaries who introduced the three-point shot in the old American Basketball League in 1961 and to the NCAA for finally introducing it to college basketball in 1986. It owes a debt to the early "giants" of the game like Wilt Chamberlain and to recent phenoms like "Air" Jordan, who made the slam dunk basketball's most spectacular play. And it owes much to Naismith and a succession of coaches who could mold such changes into solid strategy that established basketball as a national fever and themselves as legends of the game.

# HIGH SCHOOL BASKETBALL

## America's Greatest High School Boys' Basketball Coach

### Vergil Fletcher

Coach Fletcher extended his impact on basketball well beyond the gymnasium. At a time when most coaches couldn't find the time to contribute to the advancement of their sports, Coach Fletcher was a member of both the Illinois Coaches Basketball and the Illinois Coaches Football halls of fame because of his impressive record as well as his involvement in state and national organizations.

He was president of the Illinois Coaches Association and director of the Illinois Basketball Coaches Association. Coach Fletcher also is a member of the National High School Hall of Fame and, to round out his unparalleled contributions to the sport, is a founder and lifetime member of the Basketball Hall of Fame. Coach Fletcher has been among the most active in his profession as a clinician and speaker for many years.

Coach Fletcher molded the Collinsville Kahoks in Illinois into one of the nation's powerhouses, establishing a lifetime coaching record of 794-216. During his 32 years at Collinsville, he won 20 conference championships and two state championships, and he was among the final four another three times. His coaching career produced over 20 wins in all but five years, and over 30 wins five more times.

One of Coach Fletcher's most significant accomplishments as a high school basketball coach was to introduce the zone press defense in 1960, revolutionizing the game. During this time, he also coached football, winning 100+ games, and he led his track squads to numerous district championships. Coach Vergil Fletcher is an excellent example of greatness being found in the total impact of a man on the success of his teams as well as in the advancement of the sport he loves.

## Number Two

**Ernest Blood.** Coach Blood's record of 1,296 wins against only 165 losses is the highest in high school history. During his first nine years of coaching, according to the National Basketball Hall of Fame, Blood's teams never lost a game. During his next nine years, he established a record of 200-1 with his Passaic High School "Wonder Team," including a string of 159 consecutive victories, a record that still stands. "Prof" won 12 state championships during his 55 years of coaching and has been inducted into the Basketball Hall of Fame in Springfield, Massachusetts.

## Number Three

**Dolph Stanley.** All great coaches supplement championship victories with their own personal trophy case filled with precious memories. Some have only a few championships to show for their efforts; their greatness inheres in a complete dedication to the game that is reflected not just in the record books but in the minds and hearts of their athletes. Dolph Stanley is such a coach. Although championships are not foreign to him, they fail to define the dimensions of his greatness.

Coach Stanley dedicated himself to high school and college basketball for 52 years, mostly in a half-dozen Illinois high schools. He won close to a thousand games and established offensive and defensive strategies (the zone press, quick-passing offense, "four-corner" offense, full-court press, "tipping-zone" defense, and even the pregame handshake) long before they were credited to men who followed him. Though he led several teams to the state play-offs, his finest year came in 1944 when he took Taylorville High School to the state championship with a perfect 45-0 record and had a 23-point victory margin in the title game.

Coach Stanley concluded his career in 1987 at Keith Country Day School at the age of 82.

## Number Four

**Walt Shublom.** Coach Shublom's 14-year career with the Wyandotte Bulldogs in Kansas City, Kansas, has resulted in a 296-26 record for a .919 winning percentage. Shublom collected 10 state championships, five consecutively, and finished second in the state three times. His influence has resulted in 17 state championships at Wyandotte, the national high school record. A coach committed to his sport, he also founded the "Clinic of Champions," one of the Midwest's largest and most informative clinics for high school coaches.

**Morgan Wootten.** With 31 years' experience, a record of 819-113, and a winning percentage of .863, Coach Wootten is one of the most accomplished and respected coaches in the history of high school basketball. He has been head coach at DeMatha High School near Washington DC for 30 years and has won more than his share of championships. Perhaps his most notable impact on the game, however, has been the significant number of players he has sent to major colleges: Adrian Dantley, Kenny Carr, Sid Catlett, Adrian Branch, Bob Whitmore, Danny Ferry, and others. Another accomplishment? It was Wootten's DeMatha that snapped Lew Alcindor's (Kareem Abdul-Jabbar's) 71-game win streak in high school.

## Number Five

**Ralph Tasker.** Another member of the National High School Hall of Fame, Coach Tasker has earned an overall career record of 910-235, including 10 state championships in New Mexico. Five of the nation's top eight single-season scoring performances have been recorded by Coach Tasker's teams. Eleven of his former players have been drafted by the NBA, and more than 100 have gone on to play college ball. Coach Tasker was selected twice as the National Basketball Coach of the Year and is the subject of the book *Living Legend*.

## Other Qualifiers

**Tom Barringer.** Coach Barringer has established an enviable 433-132 record during his 25 years of coaching in Pennsylvania. A role model to his players, Coach Barringer has led his teams to 17 Erie County and six PIAA district championships.

42  Men's Sports

**C.H. Blanchard.**  A truly remarkable coach, Coach Blanchard already is in the National High School Hall of Fame for football, but during his 35 years' experience in Wyoming he also led Rock Springs, Casper, and Cheyenne high schools to a total of 13 state championships in basketball while earning a record of 708-126

**Jennings Boyd.**  Coach Boyd has accomplished what no other high school coach could do—a national-record eight consecutive state championships, with the Northfolk Blue Demons in West Virginia. During his 25 years as coach, he won nine state championships and earned 307-62 record, for a winning percentage of .832.

**Jimmie Bryan.**  Coach Bryan has coached basketball in Virginia for 27 years and has earned a 478-94 record, for a winning percentage of .836. He has won 22 district and four state championships and is the executive director of the Virginia High School Basketball Association. Coach Bryan also is a member of the National High School Hall of Fame.

**Everett Case.**  Coach Case led his teams to a record of 467-124 and four Indiana state championships before taking the reins at North Carolina State University. He is a member of the Basketball Hall of Fame in Springfield, Massachusetts.

**Leslie Gaudet.**  Coach Gaudet has accomplished in Louisiana what most coaches dream of—a record of 1,026-353 in 28 years.

**Lofton Greene.**  Coach Greene has achieved a 711-200 record, including a remarkable 12 state championships and five second-place finishes. The head man at Michigan's River Rouge High School for 38 years, Coach Greene has been named High School Basketball Coach of the Year and is a member of the National High School Hall of Fame.

**Tom Stanton.**  Coach Stanton is one of the most dominant figures in Missouri sport history. His 44 years of coaching produced a lifetime mark of 793-191 and, while at Beaumont High School, his winning percentage of .831 produced 11 public school and five state championships. He is a member of the National High School Hall of Fame.

**Eric Staples.**  Coach Staples has earned a truly enviable record of 924-198 during his 32 years of coaching in Georgia.

**Arthur Trout.**  Coach Trout established the best record in Illinois history during his 37 years of coaching. Leading the Centralia Orphans against a variety of schools in the state's one-class system, Coach Trout earned a record of 809-334, three state championships, and six finishes among the final four. Coach Trout is a member of the National High School Hall of Fame.

**Walter Van Huss.**  Coach Van Huss has accomplished a remarkable 923-275 record during his 33 years in Tennessee.

**Paul Walker.**  Coach Walker started his career in Kentucky, but it was at Middletown High School in Ohio that he established a record of 564-137, winning 17 district, eight regional, and five state championships. While earning a career record of 696-163, Coach Walker was twice named High School Coach of the Year. He is a member of the National High School Hall of Fame.

## COLLEGE BASKETBALL

### America's Greatest College Men's Basketball Coach

John Wooden

The only man in basketball history to be inducted into the Basketball Hall of Fame as both a player and a coach (as player for Purdue, in 1960, and as a coach, in 1972), Coach Wooden established records at UCLA that may never be matched. During his 27 years at the school, he registered 620 wins against only 147 setbacks. From 1964 to 1975, the Bruins won 10 NCAA national championships, seven in a row (an NCAA record), and put together consecutive win streaks of 88 during the regular season and 38 during NCAA tournament play.

"The Wizard of Westwood" started his coaching career at Dayton High School in Kentucky and Central High School in Indiana, compiling a 218-42 record for a winning percentage of .830. Then he moved to Indiana State University, where he established a 47-14 record before moving to UCLA in 1948. During his tenure at UCLA, Coach Wooden was named Coach of the Year six times.

Coach Wooden ranks sixth among winningest coaches and fourth among best percentages (.803). Such prodigious coaching accomplishments have overshadowed a playing record that most athletes only dream of. While at Martinsville High School in the late '20s, John Robert Wooden won All-State honors for three consecutive years. While playing for Piggy Lambert's Purdue Boilermakers, he earned All-Big-Ten and All-American honors during the 1930, 1931, and 1932 seasons, receiving the College Player of the Year award in 1932.

In 1953, John Wooden was named to the Helms All-Time All-America team. Eleven years later, he was inducted into the Indiana Basketball Hall of Fame, named the Coach of the Year, and selected by Californians as their "Father of the Year." John Wooden's illustrious career, which was interrupted only once when naval lieutenant Wooden served during World War II, had a fitting conclusion in 1975 when Wooden coached his last game—an NCAA tournament championship.

*Author's note:* A couple years ago, I joined Coach Wooden in an educational workshop at a high school south of Chicago. During one discussion, Wooden enunciated the essence of his philosophy of discipline: "Make the rules clear and the penalties severe—and always be fair." In a few short minutes, I understood the essence of the man.

## Number Two

**Adolph Rupp.** A standout player on "Phog" Allen's 1924 Kansas national championship team, Adolph Rupp holds the distinction of being college basketball's winningest coach. His record of 875 victories against only 190 losses established a winning percentage of .822, the third highest in history, and a reputation of legendary proportions.

A decent and enormously popular man, Coach Rupp, during his 41 years at the University of Kentucky, led his teams to one NIT title and four NCAA championships while winning 24 Southeast Conference titles. In addition to coaching scores of All-Americans and future professionals, Coach Rupp led the 1948 Olympic basketball team to a gold medal. While earning four Coach of the Year awards, Adolph Rupp the man also managed to find the time to be one of his community's most prominent civic leaders.

Coach Rupp was inducted into the Basketball Hall of Fame in 1968.

## Number Three

**Forrest Clare "Phog" Allen.** The number two winningest coach in basketball history, with a 770-223 record for a percentage of .768, "Phog" Allen is the prototype of the coach who has contributed far more to the game of basketball than a remarkable win/loss record. Closely associated with James Naismith throughout his early career at Kansas, Coach Allen worked hard through the years to realize success for his teams and to advance the game of basketball. During his 39 years of coaching, his teams won three national championships, including one NCAA.

Perhaps more importantly, Phog cofounded the National Association of Basketball Coaches (NABC), serving as its first president. He also served extensively on the research, rules, and Olympic committees. It was Coach Phog Allen who provided the biggest push for basketball as an Olympic sport. He also was a member of the NABC committee that initiated the NCAA tournament.

The coach of such future greats as Adolph Rupp and Dean Smith, Coach Allen was one of the first men to be inducted into the Basketball Hall of Fame.

## Number Four

**Bob Knight.** *Volatile* is only one of the many words to describe Coach Bob Knight. *Demanding* and *innovative* are two of the others. No other coach in basketball history has been more committed to individual excellence, in himself as well as in his players, than Coach Knight. The "search for perfection" is not a catchphrase in his coaching vocabulary but the standard against which he judges his own efforts and the performance of his teams.

Though never reached, perfection is something that Coach Knight's teams have come close to. During his 22 years of coaching, Knight has earned a 468-169 record for a .735 winning percentage, one NIT championship, and three NCAA championships, a list of accomplishments that suggests continued success for Coach Knight teams and a probable higher ranking for Bob Knight as one of America's greatest coaches.

## Number Five

**Dean Smith.** Consistency is the hallmark of the Dean Smith era at North Carolina State. By 1985, as the head coach of the Tar Heels, Coach Smith had accumulated 17 years of being either first or second in the ACC, 11 years of 25 victories, a string of thirteen 20-win seasons, and, most recently, a 611-175 career record with the fifth-highest number of wins in history.

A model of self-control and professional integrity, Coach Smith has been named the NCAA Coach of the Year three times (in 1977, 1979, and 1982), has reached the NCAA final four seven times, and is one of few coaches to have won the "Triple": a NCAA championship in 1982, a NIT championship in 1977, and an Olympic gold medal in Montreal in 1976. He served as the NABC president in 1981-1982 and is a member of the Basketball Hall of Fame in Springfield, Massachusetts.

## Other Qualifiers

**Clair Bee.** With a 410-86 record, Coach Bee has the highest winning percentage (.827) in NCAA history. During his first five years at Rider College, from 1925 to 1930, his teams lost only seven games. During the next 20 years at Long Island University, his teams won 95% of their games, including one string of 43 straight. His 1939 team was undefeated and the winner of the NIT championship.

Coach Bee originated the 1-3-1 defense and was primarily responsible for the 3-second rule. He also wrote extensively, authoring 21 expository books as well as 23 volumes of the "Chip Hilton" fictional series for juveniles.

**Denny Crum.** With a record of 388-128 and two NCAA championships, Denny Crum is one of the premier coaches in college basketball. Employing pressing defenses and fast-break offenses, Coach Crum's Louisville teams are annual challengers for the NCAA crown.

**Ed Diddle.** Coach Diddle joined Western Kentucky University in 1922 and stayed for 42 years. One of the first coaches in the nation to use the fast break, Diddle's teams won 32 conference titles and participated in three NCAA and eight NIT tournaments. His record of 759-302 ranks as the fourth-highest win total in NCAA history.

**Clarence "Bighouse" Gaines.** With the third-highest total number of victories in basketball history and eight Central Intercollegiate Athletic Association (CIAA) Coach of the Year awards, Clarence Gaines ranks as one of the game's finest coaches. "Bighouse" put Winston-Salem on the map with his 769-354 record and 11 CIAA titles, and his activities outside of basketball made him a deserving recipient of the Paul Robeson Award for Contributions to Humanity.

**Nat Holman.** A distinguished professional career with the Original Celtics while coaching CCNY to a 423-190 record marks the 37-year career of Nat Holman. Perhaps Holman's most distinguished coaching accomplishment occurred in 1950 when his "Cinderella" CCNY Beavers won both the NIT and the NCAA titles, the only team in basketball history to have won both during the same year.

**Henry Iba.** When Coach Iba moved to Oklahoma State University (at the time, Oklahoma A & M) in 1934, a legend was born. Within 12 years, his Aggies won two consecutive NCAA championships, and they were runners-up three years later. Coach Iba's accomplishments include 767 wins, the third-highest total in NCAA Division I history, and winning two Olympic gold medals when he coached the Olympic basketball teams in 1964 and 1968.

**George Keogan.** Coach Keogan worked at several high schools and universities before moving to Notre Dame in 1923. He proceeded to lead the Fighting Irish to a 385-117 record, for a winning percentage of .767, the seventh highest in NCAA Division I history. Coach Keogan created the shifting man-to-man defense and coached many All-Americans, but his coaching career was cut short when he died unexpectedly during the 1943 season.

**Mike Krzyzewski.** The winningest coach in Duke University history, Mike Krzyzewski has compiled a record of 231-101 at Duke and a career record of 304-160, including his five years with the United States Military Academy at West Point. A perennial favorite for the Atlantic Coast Conference (ACC) title, Krzyzewski has won it twice during his ten years with the Blue Devils (1986 and 1988), and has been selected for NCAA tournament play every year since 1984. Within one five-year period, Krzyzewski led Duke to the NCAA Final Four four times, earning a tournament record of 21-7, the best percentage among active coaches and tenth on the all-time list.

**Al McGuire.** As the fiery and outspoken head coach of the Marquette Warriors, Al McGuire established a 405-143 record for a winning percentage of .739. During his tenure at Marquette he won an NIT championship, and he concluded his brilliant career with an NCAA victory in 1977.

**Frank McGuire.** With a career that spanned championship seasons in high school, college, and professional coaching, Frank McGuire holds an enviable place in the record book. He's the only coach to win 100 games at three different colleges and the only coach to reach the NCAA finals with two different universities, winning the NCAA tournament in 1957 while coaching the North Carolina Tar Heels. In addition, Coach McGuire was named Coach of the Year three times and is a member of the Basketball Hall of Fame.

**Ralph Miller.** Basketball's winningest Division I coach prior to his retirement, Coach Miller currently has a record of 632-351 to rank eight on the all-time list for NCAA Division I teams. Coach Miller's teams have appeared in the NCAA tournament eight times and in the NIT six times. Miller has been named Conference Coach of the Year six times and National Coach of the Year twice. The mentor of the Oregon State Beavers, Miller set at least 20 players to the NBA and was a perennial challenger for the PAC-10 title. He retired in 1988.

**Ray Meyer.** An institution with the DePaul Blue Demons, "Coach" earned the fifth-highest win total in NCAA Division I history with a record of 724-354. During his 42 years at DePaul, Coach Meyer led 22 teams to the NCAA and NIT tournaments, winning the NIT in 1945. Starting with George Mikan and progressing through scores of other outstanding players, "Coach" has introduced many players to the NBA. He is a member of the Basketball Hall of Fame.

**Jerry Tarkanian.** One of the most charismatic college coaches in the game today and a man who brings his Nevada–Las Vegas "Running Rebels" into the top 10 in the country almost every year, Coach Tarkanian has established himself as a towel-chewing, run-and-gun motivator who has earned wide respect and a record of 473-100 for a percentage of .825, the second highest in NCAA Division I history; he earned his first NCAA National Championship in 1990.

**John Thompson.** A towel *carrier* and a man who commands respect not only because of his size (he's 6 feet 10 inches and weighs close to 300 pounds), but because of his ability to relate to his players, Coach Thompson, in his relatively brief 15 years of coaching, has established a record at Georgetown of 350-120 in one of the toughest conferences in the land and has won one NCAA championship. He has sent innumerable players to professional basketball and was the coach of the 1988 Olympic team.

# PROFESSIONAL BASKETBALL

## America's Greatest Professional Men's Basketball Coach

**Arnold "Red" Auerbach**

With a cigar in one hand and a trail of NBA championships in his wake, Coach "Red" Auerbach has made his name synonymous with professional basketball. Formerly team captain and a three-year regular at George Washington University, Coach Auerbach spent three years coaching high school basketball after completing college in 1940. In 1946, he joined the newly formed NBA and led the Washington franchise to 143 wins. In 1950, Red joined the Celtics and proceeded to make history.

He led the Celtics to nine NBA championships, including eight straight from 1959 through 1966, an NBA record. Including his playoff victories, Coach Auerbach won 1,037 games with the Celtics, making him the only professional coach in history to win over 1,000 games. His regular season record of 938-479 ranks highest among NBA coaches for total wins, and his winning percentage of .662 places him among the finest coaches in the history of the game.

When he finished his coaching career, Red moved to the front office where he traded in his whistle and clipboard for the team president's desk and the challenging task of putting championship teams on the floor.

Coach Auerbach's eye for talent and his relentless energy to not only *be* the best but to *get* the best resulted in Celtics teams that combined the best of ability and team play.

Celtics tradition is rich with the names of basketball greats: Larry Bird, John Havlicek, Bill Russell, Kevin McHale, Bob Cousy, Bill Sharman, Dave Cowens, Don Nelson, Paul Silas, Bill Walton, Tom Heinsohn, and many others who have been touched by the undeniably insistent hand of Red Auerbach. Having first established himself as professional basketball's premier coach and then as one of this country's great corporate leaders, it is not surprising that Coach Arnold "Red" Auerbach was selected by Pro Basketball Writers Association (PBWA) as the "Greatest Coach in the History of the NBA."

## Number Two

**Pat Riley.** In 1980 the Los Angeles Lakers had won only two NBA championships since their move from Minneapolis in 1960. During the preceding decade, they had won four. One year after Pat Riley arrived in 1981, the Lakers beat the 76ers to win the NBA championship in six games. During Riley's next seven years, the Lakers would win it twice more and three times be the NBA runner-up. Only twice during his 8 years with the Lakers has Coach Riley failed to bring his team to the NBA championship game.

Winning 60 games during the regular season is one of professional basketball's major accomplishments. Bill Fitch and K.C. Jones each had done it three times in a row with the Celtics. Pat Riley's 1988 season marked the Lakers' fourth consecutive 60-game season, an accomplishment unparalleled in the sport. Pat Riley's tenure in professional basketball is relatively short; his impact on the game, however, has been little short of remarkable—with only continued success in sight.

## Number Three

**Red Holzman.** Coach William "Red" Holzman's long and distinguished career got better with each passing year. A two-year All-American at CCNY, Red went on to star for the professional Rochester Royals. His first coaching job was with the Milwaukee Hawks, soon to become the St. Louis Hawks (and later the Atlanta Hawks). Coach Holzman remained with the Hawks for four years, one year as a player/coach.

Later he served as an assistant coach for the New York Knicks, assuming the head coaching job in 1968. During his 14 years with the Knicks, Coach Holzman compiled a 560-424 record, two NBA championships and one runner-up, and the distinction of being named the NBA Coach of the Decade in 1970. In 1981 Coach Holzman was the first recipient of the NBA Coaches Achievement Award, and he was inducted into the Basketball Hall of Fame as a coach in 1985.

## Number Four

**K.C. Jones.** After helping lead the University of San Francisco to back-to-back NCAA championships in 1955 and 1956 and coaching briefly in the college and professional ranks, K.C. got his first NBA head coaching job with the Capitols, soon to be the Washington Bullets, where he achieved a record of 155-91. In 1978, Coach Jones rejoined the Boston Celtics as an assistant coach under Tom Sanders.

After a poor showing in the 1983 play-offs (the Celtics lost four straight to the Milwaukee Bucks), K.C. was given the head coaching job and proceeded to lead the Celtics to four consecutive NBA championships games, winning two of them in 1984 and 1986. His career record of 406-168, although remarkable, is outshone by a home-court record with a winning percentage close to .900. In addition to his two NBA titles, Coach Jones's teams have been NBA runners-up three times. What is most amazing is that as both a player and a coach, K.C. Jones has had a hand in 12 world championships, 11 with the Celtics.

## Number Five

**Tom Heinsohn.** A Scholastic All-American in high school and an Academic All-American for Coach "Buster" Sheary's Holy Cross Crusaders, Coach Tom Heinsohn had the physical and the intellectual ability to lead one of the best Celtics teams of all time. After starting on eight NBA championship teams for the Celtics and averaging 18.6 points per game throughout his career, Heinsohn became the Celtics coach in 1970 and earned a record of 427-263 in regular-season play for a winning percentage of .619. In play-off competition, he led the Celtics to a record of 47-33 and two NBA championships (in 1974 and 1976).

## Other Qualifiers

**Billy Cunningham.** Elected to the Basketball Hall of Fame as a player in 1985 and a protégé of Tar Heel coach Dean Smith, Coach Cunningham led the Philadelphia 76ers for eight years, achieving a record of 454-196 for a winning percentage of almost .700. A dynamic and knowledgeable young coach, Cunningham coordinated the talents of such

All-Pros as Moses Malone and Julius Erving, taking Philadelphia to an NBA championship in 1983.

**Joe Lapchick.** A professional basketball player at the age of 17, Joe Lapchick used his 6-foot 5-inch frame to earn money for his immigrant parents in Yonkers, New York. During his 19-year tenure, he earned the reputation of being the best center of his time. He also learned much about the game. Following his professional career, Coach Lapchick led St. John's University to four NIT championships before coaching the New York Knicks to a record of 427-263, a winning percentage of .619, and three NBA runners-up. Lapchick was inducted into the Basketball Hall of Fame in 1966.

**John Kundla.** The head coach of the Lakers when they were situated in Minneapolis and while they were enjoying the services of big man George Mikan, Coach Kundla led the dominant team of his era to a record of 423-302 and five NBA championships.

**Dick Motta.** One of the winningest coaches in the NBA, coach Dick Motta coached the Chicago Bulls to one of their most respectable records during his eight-year tenure. He did much the same with the Dallas Mavericks within a similar time frame. His cumulative win/loss record of 808-750 is the third highest number of wins in professional basketball.

**Jack Ramsay.** Well-traveled and well-versed in professional basketball, Coach Jack Ramsay has been with the Pacers, the Clippers, the 76ers, and the Trailblazers, earning one NBA championship and a career record of 826-732, the second-highest number of wins in the history of the NBA.

**Bill Russell.** One of the all-time dominant figures in professional basketball, both as a player and a coach, Big Bill Russell, in just seven years of coaching with the Celtics and the Supersonics, established a record of 324-249 and won two NBA championships as a player/coach. In 1980, the PBWA chose Russell as the "Greatest Player in the History of the NBA." He also is one of its greatest coaches.

**Gene Shue.** Associated with two of the winningest franchises in the NBA, Coach Gene Shue contributed greatly to their success. During his 16 years as head coach of the 76ers and Washington Bullets, Coach Shue earned a win/loss record of 757-768—the fourth-highest number of wins in NBA history—and two second-place championship finishes.

# Chapter 3

# FOOTBALL

No one in sports is indispensable. Coaches have been shouting it for decades, backed by experience. Consider June 1, 1925. Wally Pipp, one of baseball's finest hitters, sustained an injury. Pipp had been the Yankee first baseman for 10 years and had averaged .306 batting in the previous four, hitting .329 in 1922. His injury wasn't serious, but it was expected to sideline him for a while. "Indispensability" suffered one of its biggest setbacks when Pipp, the irreplaceable Yankee first baseman, was replaced by backup infielder Lou Gehrig. Gehrig the "Iron Man" kept his new job for 2,130 consecutive games—14 years, a major league record.

The story is the same in all sports, for all participants. "Indispensable" players nurse wounds while "no-names" lead teams to victory. Head coaches are replaced by assistants who win championships. In football's formative years, for example, coaches were *so* indispensable that teams didn't *have* them. When Princeton and Rutgers squared off on the Common between College Avenue and Sicard Street in New Brunswick, New Jersey, on November 6, 1969, team captains controlled history's first intercollegiate football game. Amos Alonzo Stagg explained the captain's authority: "He chose the team . . . and was not above playing favorites. Once elected, he was answerable to no one" (Stagg, 1924).

For almost a quarter of a century, football teams placed their athletic destinies in the hands of a single player, his role more one of leader than of strategist. Certainly the Camps, Woodruffs, and Warners of the early game contributed formations and trick plays as captains, but sophisticated game strategy had to await full-time coaches who had the time to refine and complement the accumulated knowledge of their predecessors. Princeton decided to hire coaches in 1883, Yale in 1888 (Stagg, 1924).

The evolution of the game during the decades preceding Princeton's decision had been marked by the growing tendency to run with the football as well as kick it. Prompted by 21-year-old Walter Camp, the decision to replace the rugby "scrum" with a line of "scrimmage" introduced exciting strategies that paved the way for more running and, eventually, passing. Coaching became increasingly important as the two elements combined to introduce a strategic complexity that overshadowed the original game.

The scrum had been little more than two piles of bodies opposing each other for possession of a ball few of the players could see. Rugby fans had grown accustomed to it, but American players and spectators expected more excitement. The congestion created by the scrum left the players winded and the spectators bored. One of those spectators, Andrew Dickson White, the president of Cornell, was *so* bored that he refused a student request to play Michigan on a site half-way for both schools. Said White: "I will not permit 30 men to travel 400 miles merely to agitate a bag of wind!" (Danzig, 1956). Camp's recommendation to establish a line of scrimmage and to alternate possession of the ball may not have excited President White, but it gave football the boost it needed to establish itself as a legitimate crowd-pleaser.

In the same year, 1880, Camp pushed for the reduction of players from the rugby-dictated 15 to a more workable 11. Only 13 years earlier, the number on each side had been 25; six years later it had been 20; and by 1876, 1 year after rugby had been introduced to America, it was reduced to 15. The year 1880, therefore, thanks to young Walter Camp—soon to become Yale's first official football coach—was pivotal in the development of American football. It also highlighted the need for full-time coaches to handle strategy and team activities.

Camp must be considered one of the game's first coaches, maybe *the* first (Yale, 1888), but even *he* later acknowledged a debt to Yale's 1876 captain, Eugene V. Baker. Said Camp: "He taught me when I was a freshman the best part of football, as I know it" (Danzig, 1956). Thanks to Camp, however, a knowledge of the fundamentals of *kicking* a football was being complemented by an understanding of *running* with it. Eleven of Camp's colleagues were the first coaches hired by major universities (Twombley, 1976). Camp's intuitive grasp of what football needed contributed more than anything to the spectacle that grew almost immediately into one of the foremost sport activities on college campuses.

Coaching also helped. Apparently unnecessary during football's infancy, coaches soon became a guiding hand through its formative years. Wrote Stagg in his book *Touchdown!* (1924): "It was a poor player who could not find a job as coach in the early 90s." Many did. Stagg himself started his 57-year head coaching career at Springfield College in 1890. Two years later, he established one of football's great programs at the University of Chicago in the Western Conference (WC), later to become the Big Ten. Glenn Scobey "Pop" Warner started his 44-year coaching career at the University of Georgia in 1895 for $34 a week and later moved to Carlisle for $1,200 a year, where the blend of his knowledge and the talents of players like Frank Mt. Pleasant, Albert Exendine, and the immortal Jim Thorpe established Carlisle's reputation among the all-time greats.

Henry Williams, one of history's winningest coaches, graduated from Yale in 1891 and immediately settled into a coaching job at Army, where he helped establish the Army-Navy rivalry, one of the oldest in football. Fred Folsom (Dartmouth '95) started his 19-year career with Colorado during the same year and established a career winning percentage of .779. By this time, collegiate football had spread across the country, but the Eastern Big Three—Yale, Harvard, and Princeton—still dominated the statistics.

This may have been due to their early recognition of the value of coaching. Although Harvard continued to practice team captaincy, Princeton acknowledged the need for a guiding hand by appointing a committee of three coaches, each a graduate and former player, in 1883. Walter Camp was appointed the Yale coach in 1888 and led the school to its ninth consecutive undefeated season.

George Woodruff, Yale's captain in 1886, established the University of Pennsylvania as a power in the early 1890s and earned himself the reputation as one of football's all-time great coaches with history's third-best winning percentage (.846). But few men at the time underscored the strategic contributions of coaches any better than Fielding "Hurry Up" Yost at Michigan.

Michigan was the first school in the Midwest to play football, and under the direction of team captains it felt its way through its first 23 seasons. However, in 1901, Yost's first year as head coach, the Wolverines went undefeated and claimed the national championship. The following year, Yost's team again was undefeated, concluding the season by humiliating Stanford in the first Rose Bowl, 49-0. That coaching makes a difference, however, was *most* evidenced by Michigan's statistics during Yost's first five years: 2,746 points scored by the Wolverines to 40 for their combined opponents.

Yost and his fellow coaches across the country were accelerating the game's evolution by creating new formations and strategies and by acknowledging advancements that happened by accident. One of the most exciting of these serendipitous advancements was the forward pass. During the 1876 Yale-Princeton game it was none other than Walter Camp who, being tackled, threw the ball forward to a teammate for a touchdown. When Princeton protested, the referee established precedent in the fairest way possible. He flipped a coin to determine the legality of the play and awarded the touchdown to Yale (Danzig, 1956).

Almost 20 years elapsed, however, before the forward pass figured prominently in the outcome of a game. In 1895 while coaching at Auburn, John Heisman watched a North Carolina fullback, standing in punt formation, throw the ball forward to a teammate standing outside his end.

The play went for 75 yards and a hotly contested touchdown. From that moment, realizing the offensive potential of throwing the ball, Heisman pushed to legalize the forward pass. With the help of Dr. Harry Williams, a member of the Rules Committee, and Paul Dashiell, the coach of Navy, Heisman saw it written into the rule book in 1906.

A decade later, on October 7, 1916, *Coach* John Heisman, the namesake of college football's most prestigious award, used the forward pass as Georgia Tech's coach to lay waste to Cumberland College. Placed on the field *against their will*, 15 law students filled in for their disbanded football team to salvage the $3,000 in forfeit money Cumberland had guaranteed a couple years earlier to schedule the game with Tech. Southern hospitality suffered a serious blow when Georgia Tech, led by contemporary football's model of athletic excellence, rolled over Cumberland 222-0 in football's most lopsided game.

Ironically, when Heisman years earlier had watched North Carolina throw one of history's first forward passes, the opposing coach at Georgia had been "Pop" Warner. Pop was one of the most innovative coaches of all time and usually was the one to shock opponents with bold, new strategies. The loss to North Carolina may have been the reason why he later referred to the forward pass as "a bastard offspring of real football" (Warner, 1927). His opposition to the forward pass was as bold as his innovations: "The rules committee will have to curb its use . . . to prevent it from dominating the game at the expense of rushing or kicking the ball and to keep the game from being considered 'pass ball' instead of football."

The forward pass may have *saved* football in addition to revolutionizing it. The year 1905 was so brutal that President Roosevelt called representatives of Yale, Harvard, and Princeton to the White House to tell them "to clean up their act" if they wanted to save the sport. Thirty-three players had died that year, and 246 had suffered debilitating injuries. The Rules Committee hoped to counter the violence of football's mass formations by writing the forward pass into the rules before the next season.

The new strategy, however, was slow to catch on. Pop Warner, never one to be out of step with the times, was one of only two or three coaches to be credited with the development of the technique. Athletic folklore likes to attribute the spiral forward pass to Knute Rockne and Gus Dorais at Notre Dame in 1913, but Warner used it with success in 1907, the year he returned to Carlisle from Cornell. While Rockne and Dorais were just starting high school, Eddie Cochems, the head coach for St. Louis University in 1906, had refined the spiral forward pass. In fact, he had written about it in a 1907 book on football fundamentals.

The credit *Warner* received also may have been mistaken. Pop left Carlisle after 1903 to return to Cornell for three seasons. Before his return to Carlisle in 1907, the year quarterback Frank Mt. Pleasant used the spiral forward pass with such success, George Woodruff, formerly of Penn, had directed the Indians. He stayed for only 1 year, 1905, and was succeeded in 1906 by Frank Hudson, an 1899 third-team All-American at Carlisle, and Bemus Pierce, a perennial bloomer who logged more than 30 years of collegiate (Carlisle captain '96) and professional football.

History may have overlooked their contributions to the development of the spiral forward pass; Warner admitted that Mt. Pleasant had mastered the technique before the 1907 season. Probably no one will know for sure. What is a certainty is the proof provided by Rockne and Dorais in 1913 that the forward pass could win games and the growing contributions of coaches as the game evolved. Of particular interest is the almost fatalistic mix of athletic and strategic talent at key times in that evolution.

In 1912 the last of the early changes were made that dramatically affected football coaches. The Rules Committee decided in 1912 to award 6 points for a touchdown. In 1897, touchdowns and field goals had both been worth five points, the safety two, and the goal after touchdown 1. Only 3 years earlier, the TD had been worth 4 points, the goal after TD 2, and the field goal 5. And a year before that, in 1883, when Walter Camp introduced the idea of numerical scoring, the touchdown had been worth 2 points, the safety 1, the goal from touchdown 4, and the goal from field 5.

The 29 years of numerical scoring saw significant changes in the game, and most of the coaching strategy was a direct reflection of the number of points awarded the touchdown. It is ironic that Pop Warner, the man so responsible for the popularity of the forward pass, was so opposed to its introduction into the rules of the game.

It also is ironic that the six-point touchdown and its emphasis on *running* the ball would be introduced by a man experts still consider to be the world's greatest runner. Babe Ruth, baseball's greatest power hitter, introduced the "live" ball in 1920, and Jim Thorpe was at Carlisle to introduce the six-point touchdown. In fact, he scored more touchdowns in 1912—twenty-five—than any major college player for the next 76 years. Pop Warner deserves a lot of the credit. His intelligence was complemented by the common sense to see opportunity in every phase of the game—and in every absence of a rule. The Rules Committee in 1907, for example, met hastily to declare illegal Warner's tactic of blocking the defensive halfback *before* the offensive receiver caught the ball!

Warner also was responsible for the development of the three-point sprint stance, the cross-body block, and the double-wing formation. His association with Jim Thorpe established both of them as key players in the unfolding drama that was American football.

While he was coaching at Georgia and Cornell, Warner also played professional football, most notably with Syracuse in 1902, teaming up with Bemus Pierce, the meandering journeyman who captained Carlisle in 1896 and who would play for Coach Jim Thorpe's Oorang Indians in 1923. Although men like Pierce and Warner brought color to the early years of professional football, the game originally enjoyed only passing popularity.

Even the antics of established baseball moguls like Connie Mack failed to push pro football into the spotlight. While Warner played for Syracuse, Mack organized the Philadelphia *football* Athletics, touting stars like playboy pitcher Rube Waddell and the ubiquitous Bemus Pierce. He claimed the world championship after handing Pittsburgh and its fullback/linebacker Christy Matthewson one of Christy's few defeats. The experience must have renewed Christy's love of baseball; he won 30 games in each of his next three years with Muggsy McGraw's New York Giants.

Not until Ohio provided the battleground for Canton and Massillon in the mid-1910s did professional football establish itself within the spectrum of American sports. When coaches like George Halas, Ted Nesser, and Jim Thorpe contributed their names and talents to the fledgling American Professional Football Association (APFA), soon to become the National Football League (NFL), professional football rivaled its collegiate counterpart for a share of the "sportlight."

In the 1920s football dominated the college scene. The East's Big Three, although still respectable, surrendered national championships to teams across the country: Illinois, Notre Dame, Alabama, George Tech, and Stanford. Their coaches became household words: Sutherland, Rockne, Zuppke. And when Red Grange, after scoring a touchdown each of the first four times he touched the ball against Michigan, made the jump to the Chicago Bears and George Halas, professional football entered its golden era. The smallest crowd to watch the Bears during Grange's first year was 28,000 in Columbus, Ohio; the largest was 73,000 in New York.

Football had arrived, a matchless combination of player talent and coaching genius that guaranteed excitement. Unique to the United States, football has continued to evolve as a national passion, piqued by the creativity of coaches and the performances of players. With the increase in performance and the growing availability of talented athletes, the platoon system of substitution replaced the "sixty-minute player." Special teams were soon organized, reintroducing the strategic value of kicking the ball.

Specialists in all phases of the game, situation players, and the new strategies they provide, attest to football's sophistication and underscore the need for more coaches per team to develop players as well as game plans. Even some high school programs have as many as 10 to 16 coaches. The game has grown well beyond the days of one player/captain. Some say it has grown too big, and maybe it has. But the coaching genius that nurtured it is undeniable and still ranks among the sport world's most dramatic accomplishments.

# HIGH SCHOOL FOOTBALL

## America's Greatest High School Football Coach

**Gordon L. Wood**

In the hotbed of Texas prep football, Coach Wood stands alone. His current win/loss record of 405-88-12 represents the greatest number of wins of any high school football coach in the game's history—and he's still coaching. He is the only coach in high school history to record over 400 victories and has a winning percentage of well over .800. Coach Wood has spent his 43-year career at seven different high schools in Texas but has been at Brownwood High School for the past 23.

Coach Wood's impressive credentials are highlighted by 24 district championships, 9 state titles, and four undefeated seasons. Coach Wood has been named Coach of the Year four times, and Brownwood's football stadium has been named in his honor. Coach Wood's on-the-field accomplishments are unmatched in the history of the game.

His off-the-field contributions to the sport are equally impressive. He has been a member of the Texas High School Coaches Association for 50 years, serving as vice president, president, and director. He also has lectured widely and is a member of the Texas Sports Hall of Fame as well as the Texas State High School Coaches Association Hall of Fame.

Coach Wood was inducted into the National High School Hall of Fame in 1983.

---

## Number Two

**Julius W. "Pinky" Babb.** The second-winningest coach in the history of high school football, Coach Babb spent almost all of his 39-year career at South Carolina's Greenwood High School. His record of 336-81-23 is the nation's best record at a single school, and his winning percentage of .806 is among the tops in the country. Coach Babb's teams were undefeated five times and recorded 10 or more victories 14 different times.

Coach Babb's matchless win/loss record and his team's eight state championships resulted in a myriad of honors. He was named Coach of the Year several times during his career and was inducted into the South Carolina Athletic Hall of Fame in 1973. In addition, Coach Babb is a member of the National High School Coaches Association Hall of Fame, Furman University's Hall of Fame, and the National High School Hall of Fame.

## Number Three

**Win Otto Brockmeyer.** If names presage personal destiny, Coach Brockmeyer's parents are responsible for his remarkable football coaching career. Win Brockmeyer, during his 34 years with Wausau High School in Wisconsin, seemed almost incapable of *losing*. His record with the Lumberjacks was 230-33-9 for an exceptionally high winning percentage of .875 and 26 championships in the Wisconsin Valley.

During one six-year period, Brockmeyer's charges drove to a state-record 46 consecutive victories. In that time, the Lumberjacks, led by future Hall of Famers Elroy "Crazylegs" Hirsch and Jim Otto, outscored their opponents by a margin of 744 to 41. During the 1942 season, coach Brockmeyer's team averaged 32 points per contest while allowing its opponents *none*. While coaching at Fairibault, Minnesota (1934-1936), Brockmeyer coached Heisman trophy winner Bruce Smith in addition to assuming several other coaching responsibilities. Even with the Lumberjacks a few years later, Brockmeyer coached a total of seven sports, three of which—football, basketball, and track—he had lettered in while attending Mankato High School.

Brockmeyer played his college ball at the University of Minnesota where he shared backfield duties with the immortal Bronco Nagurski. He captained the Gophers during his senior year. Coach Win Brockmeyer, now deceased, is enshrined in the National High School Hall of Fame.

## Number Four

**C.H. Blanchard.** Similarly honored in this book as one of high school basketball's greatest coaches, C.H. Blanchard has established himself as even a greater football coach. With a career record of 144-42-3 and a winning percentage of .774, Coach "Okie" Blanchard spent most of his 35-year career in Cheyenne, Wyoming, where he produced five undefeated football teams and eight state championships, three of which were consecutive.

Coach Blanchard's 1947 team won the state championship by a score of 27 to 0 and earned recognition among the nation's sportswriters as perhaps the best high school team in the country. "The best" is a term that rested easily with Coach Blanchard. The head coach of basketball and track as well as football, he gained nationwide recognition during his career as the coach who won an unprecedented 31 state championships and 57 district titles in three different sports.

In the middle of his career, Coach Blanchard assumed duties with the University of Wyoming, but after a 2-year stint, decided to return to the high school level. Coach Blanchard's 31 state championships are a high school record and have earned him a spot in the National High School Hall of Fame.

## Number Five

**Joe Coviello.** The man responsible for introducing the Wing-T offense to the state of New Jersey, Coach Coviello modeled its effectiveness by recording a lifetime record of 243-51-10 and a winning percentage of .827 while winning 20 conference crowns and seven state titles. Dividing his time among three schools, Coviello established his coaching greatness at Memorial High School in New Jersey, where he directed the team to a state-record 40 straight victories and an unparalleled record of 117-18-3.

During his tenure at Memorial, Coviello went head-to-head with a man who later was to be acknowledged a football genius. Coviello's team won the game against Englewood, New Jersey's St. Cecilia High School, winning by a score of 43 to 6 and earning the respect of St. Cecilia's head coach—Vince Lombardi. The victory occurred in 1946, the same year that Coviello brought the Wing-T offense into statewide prominence.

For his many accomplishments, Coviello was named Hudson County Coach of the Year eight times, and he received the state's Football

64 Men's Sports

Sports Award once. A man dedicated to his sport, Coach Coviello has been a member of the Executive Committee of the New Jersey State Interscholastic Athletic Association, the chairman of the football rules and policy committees, and one of the men responsible for implementing the New Jersey state play-off competition.

Coach Coviello is a member of the National High School Hall of Fame.

## Other Qualifiers

**Paul Adams.** Coach Adams has been the head coach of Deerfield High School in Illinois for 23 years and has led the Warriors to a career record of 177-47 for a .740 winning percentage and 11 trips to the state play-offs. Coach Adams has dominated his conference, one of the toughest in the country, with 14 conference titles and one state championship. He has had three runners-up to the state crown. He has enjoyed two undefeated teams (1973 and 1975), has coached several high school All-Americans, and has sent players to universities like Iowa, Notre Dame, and Minnesota. Adams is a member of advisory councils and has been inducted into his state's high school football coaches association hall of fame.

**Pete Adkins.** Coach Adkins has devoted his entire 36-year career to two high schools in Missouri (most recently, Jefferson City High School) and has earned an enviable lifetime record of 308-55-4.

**A.W. Bazemore.** One of the winningest coaches in the history of Georgia football, Coach Bazemore, while at Valdosta High School, earned a record of 290-43-6 for a remarkable winning percentage of .855. Equally remarkable, his teams won 18 regional and 15 state championships. Coach Bazemore is a member of the Georgia Hall of Fame and the National High School Hall of Fame.

**Walt Braun.** Coach Braun has spent most of his 32 years of coaching at Marysville in Michigan and has earned a career win/loss record of 221-70-3, including one state, four regional, and 19 conference championships. In addition, he has served for 14 years with his state high school football coaches association.

**Ed Buller.** In terms of career victories, Coach Buller is the fourth-winningest coach in the history of high school football. During his 44-year career in Kansas at Bucklin, Agenda, and Clyde high schools, Coach Buller's teams have won 335 games while losing only 78.

**Sid Cichy.** Shanley High School in North Dakota enjoyed Coach Cichy's services for 30 years and watched its reputation grow from local to national prominence as its football teams established a record of 231-38-3 for an unparalleled winning percentage of .859 and 16 North Dakota state championships. Coach Cichy's teams were never beaten in state championship play. He has earned several Coach of the Year awards and is a member of the National High School Hall of Fame.

**Ralph Cummins.** As the head coach of Clintwood High School in Virginia for 33 years, Coach Cummins has earned a record of 261-84-15, along with three state championships and two runners-up. Coach Cummins also joins that legion of coaches who extend themselves beyond the playing field; he has been a board member and executive, including president, of the Virginia Coaches Association and has served on several other advisory and study committees.

**E.B. Etter.** Another of several coaches who have devoted 40 years of their lives to high school football, Coach Etter divided his time between two Tennessee high schools, Chattanooga Central and Chattanooga Baylor, and earned a career mark of 324-102-13.

**Gerry Faust.** The ex-bossman of the Fighting Irish at Notre Dame, Coach Faust first established himself as one of high school football's premier coaches. His 18-year career at Cincinnati's Moeller High School resulted in a win/loss record of 174-17 for the unheard-of winning percentage of .907 and five state championships.

**John McKissick.** Tied for the second-winningest coach in the history of high school football, Coach McKissick has spent his entire 34-year career in Summerville, South Carolina, and has earned a record of 346-62-13.

**Chuck Moser.** Another example of commitment beyond the football field, Coach Moser devoted 16 seasons to high school football in Missouri and Texas, earning a career mark of 141-29, a winning percentage of .828, and three state championships. His record in Texas, one of the hotbeds of high school football, is most remarkable—a record of 78-7-2 and three consecutive state titles. Moser also served as president of his state's high school coaches association and was appointed by the Governor as a member of the Texas Commission for Physical Fitness.

**Pat Panek.** Coach Panek proved his ability to develop winning programs by spreading his talents among five high schools in Colorado and Nebraska (most recently at Fullerton, Nebraska). In the process, he earned a career win/loss mark of 328-117-29.

**Mike Pettine.** The head coach of Central Bucks West High School in Doylestown, Pennsylvania, since 1967, Coach Mike Pettine has earned over 200 career victories, including a Pennsylvania state winning-streak record of 54 consecutive victories. Within that time, Coach Pettine has won 14 league championships and had 12 undefeated seasons. Central Bucks West was ranked the state's number one team four times and was ranked among *USA Today's* top 25 high school football teams in 1985, 1986, and 1987. Coach Pettine also is president of the Pennsylvania High School Football Coaches Association.

**William Boyce Smith.** Coach Smith spent his entire 44-year career at Tennessee's Springfield High School and established both himself and the school as first local and then statewide legends. His win/loss record of 288-116-34 ranks fourth among the nation's high school coaches who coached at one school. Featured in *Ripley's Believe It or Not* for his "point-a-minute-offense," Coach Smith at one time led his team to 30 consecutive victories and 10 state titles. In addition, he has worked tirelessly to promote recreational activities in the Springfield community. Coach Smith is a member of the Tennessee and the National High School Halls of Fame.

# COLLEGE FOOTBALL

## America's Greatest Division I College Football Coach

### Knute Rockne

Wrote Pop Warner in the *Saturday Evening Post* on October 6, 1934: "No one ever asked me to pick the greatest football coach of all time, but if I were asked I would unhesitatingly name Rockne." That is quite a tribute coming from a man others have called the greatest, but it is undoubtedly an accurate selection. No one made his mark on college football as indelibly as the "Rock."

Rockne's record of 105 wins against only 12 losses resulted in a winning percentage of .881, the best Division I percentage in the history of the game. The young man who worked in Illinois as a railroad brakeman to pay his college tuition at Notre Dame and who later taught chemistry at his alma mater before becoming head football coach sought excellence in himself and, later, a commitment to perfection in his teams.

Even as a player and captain with the Notre Dame football team Rockne touched the game with his special genius. Mistakenly credited by some sport historians as inventing the forward pass, Rockne actually combined with teammate Gus Dorais to *perfect* it, so much so that on November 1, 1913, the Fighting Irish used it to defeat a superior Army team, 35-13.

It is interesting to note that Rockne joined with Dorais again only a few years after graduating from Notre Dame, and while coaching football there, to play with the Massillon Tigers against Jim Thorpe and the Canton Bulldogs in a part of the country that ultimately became the cradle of professional football.

While playing with Massilon in 1919, Coach Rockne coached Notre Dame to an undefeated season. He would have four more—1920, 1924, 1929, and 1930. His successes resulted not simply from innovations such as the Notre Dame Shift, a piece of strategy that confused the defense, but from a personal magnetism that attracted even the most recalcitrant football players. Said teammate Gus Dorais of Rockne's ability to motivate players: "Rockne was the greatest inspirational coach ever in the business. He was a dean of men to all the athletes, and they would break their necks for him."

The essence of Knute Rockne probably is best expressed in his own words: "Football teaches a boy a sense of responsibility—responsibility as a representative of his college, responsibility to his teammates, responsibility in controlling his passions—fear, hatred, jealousy, and rashness. Football brings out the best there is in everyone." Certainly it was the medium through which Knute Rockne expressed the best of what he was.

One of Rockne's "Four Horsemen," Harry Stuhldreher, described best Rockne's impact on his players when he wrote of it in his book *Knute Rockne: Man Builder*. In one section he describes an afternoon practice session. The team had been told to gather around Coach Rockne to start the practice. Wrote Stuhldreher: "They have experienced it before. Every day at quarter to four it gets them. It sets their jaws a little firmer; it flexes their muscles and stiffens their backbones; it makes the blood run faster in their veins. Subjected to the electric flow of his personality, they become as supermen."

As supermen, the Fighting Irish had won 10 and lost none during Rockne's final season with Notre Dame. They had won their third national championship. In the spring of the following year, Knute Rockne died in an airplane crash. In one terrifying moment, Bonnie Rockne and her children lost a husband and father. Notre Dame lost a son whose open love of football and decency graced the campus with a unique spark that energized everyone. And the world of athletics lost a human being whose inspirational impact as a legend would be no less than what his impact had been as a man.

---

## Number Two

**Paul "Bear" Bryant.** Prowling the sidelines in his checkered hat, Coach Bryant dominated college football for 38 years. His record of

323-85-17 ranks second among college football coaches, and his bowl record of 29 games and 15 wins ranks first. Each of the seven times he brought the Crimson Tide to the Sugar Bowl, he won the game. A standout player for Alabama years before he became the Tide's head coach, Bryant played right end for three years ('33, '34, and '35) and upon graduating became an assistant coach for four more.

He left Alabama to coach the line at Vanderbilt but left after two years to join the Navy during World War II. Discharged as a lieutenant commander, the Bear signed on as head coach of Maryland, stayed for one year, and transferred to Kentucky. He stayed at Kentucky for only two years, then switched to Texas A&M in 1954. He moved to Alabama in 1958 and remained with his alma mater until 1982, where he never had a losing season and he won the national championship five times.

The coach of such notable NFL quarterbacks as Richard Todd, Kenny Stabler, and Joe Willie Namath, Coach Bryant also has the distinction of having recruited the first black athlete in Alabama's history. Only one month after he retired from coaching, Coach "Bear" Bryant died of a heart attack. The man who had earned his nickname by wrestling a bear to win a bet of $1 had contributed more than he would ever realize to the rich tradition that is college football.

## Number Three

**Pop Warner.** One of football's most innovative minds, Glenn Scobey "Pop" Warner not only coached some of football's best players, such as Jim Thorpe and Ernie Nevers, but he is credited with introducing and certainly with refining many of the game's lasting strategies. Pop Warner gave football the single- and double-wing formations, the crouch start, refinement of the spiral forward pass, the cross-body block—originally called the "Indian block" because it originated at Carlisle—and the reverse play.

There is no question that Warner ranks among the game's greatest coaches when it comes to win/loss record and longevity. He coached at six schools for a total of 44 years, compiling a record of 313-106-32, the fourth highest in the history of college football. He ranks second to none, however, in imagination and originality. In one four-year period of time, his Stanford teams played in the Rose Bowl three times, winning once and tying once.

Said Lloyd Jordan, who played under Warner and later coached with him at Pittsburgh: "Pop was one of the grandest creative geniuses in football. He was very patient in his coaching, and the men who played under his direction respected and loved him as a man as well as a coach." Perhaps the ultimate tribute for Coach Warner came from no less a sport world luminary than Grantland Rice, who wrote: "It would be difficult to say which coach had the greatest influence on college football. . . . Pop undoubtedly was the greatest inventive genius. His single and double wing still have a big place in any football offense—still remain as one of the most effective offenses football knows."

*Author's note:* I feel a special affection for Coach Warner. It was Warner who discovered my grandfather, Jim Thorpe, at Carlisle and who helped him become the "Greatest Athlete of the First Half-Century."

## Number Four

**Amos Alonzo Stagg.** Coach Amos Alonzo Stagg started his career as a player for Yale in 1885, where he earned All-America honors as a senior. His coaching career started in 1890 at Springfield College in Massachusetts and ended 57 years later at the College of the Pacific in 1946. During that time Stagg spent most of his time with the University of Chicago and the old Western Conference, the forerunner of the Big Ten. Following his retirement as a head coach in 1946, he returned to the game as an assistant to his son at Susquehanna University from 1947 to 1953.

A man of strong character and simple honesty, Coach Stagg in his youth was as good at baseball as at football, once pitching for Yale and striking out 20 batters. He turned down a major league baseball contract to coach for Springfield, where he remained for two years, met James Naismith, and carried the new game of basketball to his second coaching assignment at the University of Chicago. His efforts with basketball were so pronounced that he is a member of the Basketball Hall of Fame as well as the Football Hall of Fame.

Coach Stagg's record of 314-199-35 places him third on the list of winningest coaches, and his contributions to the Rules Committee from 1904 through 1932 identify him as one of the game's most influential men. He also was one of its most innovative. Coach Stagg is credited with the development of the tackling dummy, the huddle, men in motion, the end around, and several other innovations.

Said Grantland Rice of Stagg in 1943: "Lonnie Stagg, at 81, can speak with Victor Hugo: 'The snow of winter may be on my head, but the sunshine of eternal spring is in my heart.' " It was the boundless energy of eternal spring that made the Grand Old Man of football one of this country's greatest.

## Number Five

**Joe Paterno.** Coach Joe Paterno's career is best summarized by his own words: "I think if it's a question of winning and losing, football is a silly game. That's why I'm coaching. I think I can do some good for young people. I would prefer to be thought of as an educator rather than a coach." It was this attitude and the resultant academic accomplishments of his players that identifies Coach Paterno as one of history's five greatest.

During his career at Penn State, Coach Paterno has had 19 first-team Academic All-Americans, 10 Hall of Fame scholar-athletes, and 13 players who have won NCAA postgraduate scholarships. Said Joe Radecic, the center on Penn State's '86 team: "He emphasizes the books—or you don't play. Football or school, he wants everything done right. He won't settle for anything done halfway."

In an age when football players are exploited for their beef and not their brains, Coach Paterno has used both to elevate Penn State to a position of one of the best in the country. During his 22 years with the Nittany Lions, Paterno has won 207, lost 48, and tied 2. His teams have participated in 19 bowl games, a record second only to that of Alabama's Bear Bryant, and have won 12, again second only to Bryant.

He has been in the Cotton Bowl twice and has won it twice. He has been in the Orange Bowl four times, winning it three times. And every time he appeared in the Fiesta Bowl (four times), Penn State won it. In addition, he has won the NCAA national championship twice in the last six years and has sent well over 100 players into the NFL. One of his national championships came in 1986, the year he was selected Coach of the Year, Kodak Coach of the Year, and *Sports Illustrated's* Sportsman of the Year, an honor shared by only one other college coach, John Wooden of UCLA.

Said Georgia Tech coach Bobby Dodd of Paterno: "He graduates players. He treats 'em good. He has a good football team every year, and he's a class guy. He also stands for something in football that I stood for: honesty. He'd never buy a football player in a million years." Joe Paterno is college football's best example of a coach who plays according to the rules and with a solid ethical code—and wins. That's why he's among America's greatest.

## Other Qualifiers

**Walter Camp.** If American football had a father, his name was Walter Camp. Camp was the first football coach at Yale, and his contributions to the game extend well beyond win/loss records. It was Walter Camp who played for Yale when they defeated Harvard in the first American rugby game with only 11 players on each side. It was Walter Camp who first suggested that safeties count as scoring plays. It was Walter Camp who eliminated the rugby "scrum" and created the line of "scrimmage," thereby giving possession of the ball to one of the teams. With predictable possession of the ball, teams emphasized strategy and soon realized the need for coaches. And it was Walter Camp who introduced downs and yards to gain, signals, and numerical scoring.

Player, coach, organizer, innovator—Walter Camp is the first name in American football.

**Bob Devaney.** Soft-spoken and unyielding in his demands for personal excellence, Coach Bob Devaney first led the University of Wyoming to respectability, then moved to the University of Nebraska where he molded one of college football's most enduring powerhouses. When Devaney arrived in 1961, Nebraska was at best a mediocre representative of the Big Eight; under Devaney's leadership, it has become one of the sport world's premier programs.

A win/loss record of 136-30-7, two back-to-back Associated Press national championships, and a winning percentage of .806 establish Coach Devaney as one of the finest coaches in the college game.

---

*Author's note:* I played fullback for Coach Devaney when he first arrived at Nebraska in the early sixties. In only one year, he pushed the Cornhuskers into the top 10 teams in the country, and he did it with a quiet insistence that we all do our jobs. I never heard him yell, but we all learned early in our relationship with him that we had better perform to the best of our ability, or else. We did and the Cornhuskers still do; that's what makes for winners.

**Woodrow "Woody" Hayes.** A tackle for Denison University for 3 years, Woody Hayes returned to his alma mater in 1946 as head football coach. In three years he had two undefeated teams. He continued his winning ways at Miami of Ohio for two more years and in 1951 began an illustrious career at Ohio State University. Under Hayes, the Buckeyes won two NCAA national championships and appeared in the Rose Bowl eight times, winning four times. Hayes completed his career at Ohio State with a lifetime winning percentage of .759 and a total of 238 wins.

**Lou Holtz.** A name suddenly synonymous with the legendary football traditions at the University of Notre Dame, Coach Holtz began his career at William and Mary in 1969. He remained there for three years, then transferred to North Carolina State, where he served for four years and earned a 33-12-3 record, four bowl appearances, and three final rankings among the nation's top twenty teams.

In 1977 Coach Holtz moved to Arkansas, where in his first year he guided the Razorbacks to an 11-1 record, an Orange Bowl victory over Oklahoma, and a number three ranking in the final AP poll. He led Arkansas to two more top ten finishes and five more bowl appearances in the next six years before moving to the University of Minnesota in 1984. In just his second year with the Golden Gophers, Coach Holtz led them to an appearance in the Independence Bowl and their first winning record in years.

In 1986 Coach Holtz took over a faltering Notre Dame program, suffered a losing season his first year, but re-established the Fighting Irish as a national powerhouse the very next year with a record 8-4, a Cotton Bowl appearance, and a final ranking of 17 in the AP poll. In 1988, only his third year at the helm, Coach Holtz led Notre Dame to a perfect 12-0 record and a national championship victory over West Virginia in the Fiesta Bowl.

A man who immerses himself in challenge, Coach Holtz ranks among the top ten active coaches for career victories and is rapidly establishing himself as one of the coaching legends in Notre Dame football history.

**Frank Leahy.** Once a standout lineman on one of Knute Rockne's teams, Frank Leahy, in 1941, as Notre Dame's head football coach, found himself able to enlarge upon the football mystique of the Fighting Irish. At Notre Dame for only 11 years, Leahy's record of 87-11-9 and winning percentage of .887 rank second only to Knute Rockne in Notre Dame's long and storied history. His record of four NCAA national championship teams, two consecutively in 1946 and 1947, is an accomplishment few coaches can claim.

**Tom Osborne.** A perennial contender for the national championship, Tom Osborne's Cornhuskers boast one of college football's best records. After being an assistant to Bob Devaney for 8 years, Osborne took the reins at Nebraska in 1973 and since then has won almost 150 games and has a winning percentage of .807.

**Ara Parseghian.** Ara Raoul Parseghian, the 24-year-old rookie for Paul Brown's Cleveland Browns, found his professional playing career ended by a hip injury, so he moved immediately to Miami of Ohio as an assistant coach to Woody Hayes. He eventually took over the program when Hayes moved to Ohio State. Only 26, he was an immediate success, and in five years moved to Northwestern, where he brought the roar back to Wildcat football.

A career record of 74-41-2 attracted the attention of Notre Dame decision makers, and Coach Parseghian was hired by the Fighting Irish. Two NCAA national championships later, with one of the highest winning percentages in Notre Dame history, Coach Parseghian retired from football.

**Bo Schembechler.** With well over 200 wins, Bo Schembechler, like Woody Hayes and Ara Parseghian, started his coaching career at Miami of Ohio before moving to Michigan in 1969. A record of 207-57-7 and a winning percentage of .777 have distinguished Coach Schembechler as one of college football's great coaches. He has appeared in bowl games 14 times, wining three, two of which were Rose Bowl victories, one in 1981 by a score of 23-6 over Washington, the other in 1989 over Southern Cal.

**Charles "Bud" Wilkinson.** High on the all-time win list, Coach Wilkinson established at the University of Oklahoma a remarkable record of 145-29-4 for a winning percentage of .826 and three NCAA national championships. Under Wilkinson, the Sooners were the Big Eight representatives to the Orange Bowl five times, winning four times. Wilkinson also added two Sugar Bowl victories to a career that spanned 17 years.

**George Woodruff.** One of football's earliest coaches, George Woodruff began his career with the University of Pennsylvania in 1892 and remained there until 1901, winning in 1895 and 1897 what were considered at the time two national championships. An 1889 graduate of Yale and a Phi Beta Kappan, Coach George Washington Woodruff introduced guards and tackles coming out of the line to run interference for ball carriers. He also practiced law while coaching, ultimately giving up coaching in 1901 to become assistant attorney general of the United States. During this time, he still found time to coach football, once at Illinois in 1903, again at Carlisle in 1905. With a record of 142-25-2 and a winning percentage of .846, George Woodruff is among college football's greatest coaches.

**Fielding "Hurry Up" Yost.** With exhortations of "Hurry up" and "Hustle," Coach Yost propelled his players to history's first Rose Bowl victory, a 49-0 win over Stanford in 1902, and a career record of 196 wins with a percentage of .828, twelfth on the all-time list. It was at Michigan that Yost realized his most remarkable success, in his first 4 years winning 55 games and losing only once, to Amos Alonzo Stagg's University of Chicago. Yost's record at Michigan of 164-20-10 is one of the most envied in all of sports.

# SMALL COLLEGE FOOTBALL

## America's Greatest Small-College Football Coach

### Eddie Robinson

The names Eddie Robinson and Grambling University are synonymous in the history of college football. The winningest coach in college football's history with 336 career victories, Coach Robinson has been a welcome fixture at Louisiana's Grambling University for 44 years—and he's still going strong. With a total record of 336-113-15 and a winning percentage of .740, Coach Robinson has established Grambling University as one of college football's premier programs.

Anyone who knows Coach Robinson or has even a passing relationship with him understands the reasons for his success. He does everything with a touch of class. In 1985, when Prairie View A&M succumbed to the Grambling attack to record the victory that would make him the winningest coach in college football history, Robinson accepted the nation's praise with characteristic humility: "All I want is for my story to be an American story, not black and not white. Just American. I want it to belong to everyone."

It was typically American. In fact, it was an American favorite—rags to riches. Coach Robinson's introduction to Grambling football had him mowing the field, marking the lines, taping ankles, transporting injured players to the hospital, even writing up the game summaries for the local papers. Forty years later, he exceeded the total number of career victories of Paul "Bear" Bryant to become the winningest coach in the college ranks. Only 3 years earlier, he had accepted from Coach Bryant the Walter Camp Foundation's 1982 Distinguished American Award.

Former players joined him for the celebration. Pro football's "Tank" Younger, former Green Bay great Willie Davis, and present-day standout Doug Williams were all there. In fact, the auditorium was teeming with NFL greats. Eddie Robinson and Grambling University have sent more than 200 players to the NFL, more than any other school including Southern Cal and Notre Dame. Coach Robinson has touched lives, not just the record books.

Coach Robinson's greatness inheres in his ability to relate to his players and secure maximum performances from them. That's why his records will not fade. Most records are footprints in the sand, washed away by time. Eddie Robinson's mark, however, is etched by successive generations of Grambling football players on the monument that is college football.

## Number Two

**Alonzo "Jake" Gaither.** Retired from football in 1969, Jake Gaither spent his entire 25-year career at Florida A&M University in Tallahassee. His accomplishments were sizable. First of all, his win/loss record of 203-36-4 ranks twelfth among all four-year college coaches. More significantly, his winning percentage of .844 places him in the select company of the top five college coaches of all time. Coach Gaither is in the company of George Woodruff of Yale and Frank Leahy and Knute Rockne of Notre Dame.

In addition, Coach Gaither was selected in 1969, the final year of his career, as the NAIA Coach of the Year.

## Number Three

**Bob Reade.** Coach Reade of Augustana College in Rock Island, Illinois, stands tall among football coaches everywhere. He has reached a coaching plateau that is reserved for few people. During his nine years of coaching, he has won almost 100 games but, amazingly, has achieved a win/loss percentage of over .900. Coach Reade simply does not know how to lose.

In a very competitive school setting that boasts a fine academic program and that graduates a significantly high number of its athletes, Coach Reade has combined the intellectual and physical abilities of his athletes into a widely respected program that has won four consecutive NCAA Division III championships. It is a record unparalleled in the history of collegiate football.

## Number Four

**John Merritt.** A graduate of Kentucky State in 1950, Coach Merritt waited only three years for his first head coaching assignment. He began his distinguished career at Jackson State University in Mississippi, remained there for nine years, and then accepted the head coaching position at Tennessee State in 1963. Nineteen years later, Coach Merritt had established a career record of 232-65-11 for a winning percentage of .771.

Coach Merritt's 232 career victories rank eight on the all-time list of coaching victories, and he is in some very good company. Sixth on that list is Woody Hayes of Ohio State, and 10th on the list, two places behind Coach Merritt, is Bo Schembechler of Michigan.

## Number Five

**John Gagliardi.** Having already dedicated 39 years of his life to coaching football and still coaching at St. John's University in Minnesota, John Gagliardi has won almost 250 games and has earned a winning percentage of .737. After coaching for four years at Carroll College in Montana, Coach Gagliardi transferred in 1953 to St. John's University, a 2,400-acre campus of woodlands and lakes a few miles northwest of Minneapolis.

Among his Division III counterparts, Coach Gagliardi has the highest number of wins and was selected in 1965 as the NAIA Coach of the Year. Among all football coaches in NCAA history, Coach Gagliardi ranks fifth, several wins ahead of Woody Hayes at Ohio State.

## PROFESSIONAL FOOTBALL

### America's Greatest Professional Football Coach

Vince Lombardi

In 1958 the Green Bay Packers had a 1-10-1 record, the worst in the club's 40-year history. The picture was indeed bleak. They hadn't had a winning season in 10 years, and they hadn't won a division title since 1944. Coach "Scooter" McLean's 1958 edition of the Green Bay Packers carried such names as Jim Taylor, Bart Starr, Paul Hornung, Dan Currie, Forrest Gregg, "Hog" Hanner, Jerry Kramer, and Ray Nitschke—and finished the season at the bottom of the Western Conference.

Club president Dominic Olejniczak learned of Lombardi's reputation for leadership with the New York Giants and contacted him, ultimately agreeing to a five-year contract with Vince as the team's coach and general manager. To even the most optimistic Green Bay fan, the task seemed an impossibility. But with the words "I have never been on a losing team, gentlemen, and I do not intend to start now," Lombardi transformed the first team meeting into a one-man ultimatum that established a football dynasty in Green Bay, Wisconsin.

No team so clearly reflected the personality of its head coach as the Green Bay Packers. After the 1959 season, his rookie year as a head coach,

Lombardi, at the age of 46, was named the NFL Coach of the Year. The honor, and the season's record of 7-5, resulted from a matchless combination of football knowledge and personality strength that showcased Vince's determination. He would accept from himself and from his players nothing short of their absolute best.

His team's skills were grounded in the basics and a firm belief in the Lombardi philosophy. Marie Lombardi, Vince's wife, said it best:

> When Vince is challenged to try to make a great one out of a ballplayer, I can only feel sorry for that player. Vince is just going to make a hole in his head and pour everything in. When it starts, the player hasn't any idea what he's in for, and he hasn't got a chance. He'll get hammered and hammered until he's what Vince wants him to be. You can't resist this thing. You can't fight it. But it's more than I want to watch!

The fans in Green Bay watched, and they danced in the streets. They watched quarterback Bart Starr grow in confidence until he became one of the best in the NFL. They watched the Green Bay "power sweep" rival the Oklahoma Land Rush for territory gained. As executed by Fuzzy Thurston, Jerry Kramer, Paul Hornung, and Jim Taylor, the Packer power sweep became the ultimate extension of Lombardi's fascination for running the football.

Most importantly, they watched the sheer power of Lombardi's will mold the lowly Green Bay Packers into one of the NFL's strongest teams. From cellar-dwellers in 1958, the Packers, driven by Lombardi's relentless energy, earned a record of 11-3 in 1961 and went on to beat the New York Giants in what became a lopsided contest, 37-0. They would go on to win two more NFL championships and the NFL's first two Super Bowl games. Said Earl Blaik of his former assistant at Army:

> If I had to pick one reason for Vince's enormous success, it would be that he has magnetism. This applies to almost all the great leaders, and Vince has certainly been a great leader. He may have learned a few things during our years together, but he didn't learn that magnetism at West Point. You don't put magnetism into people.

From West Point, Vince had gone to the New York Giants as an assistant, then to Green Bay. Although he had hungered for a head coaching position for years, his experiences as an assistant had brought him into closer contact with the athletes, where strategy is translated into action and where good teaching is essential. Said Sid Gillman of Vince the teacher: "He's got great knowledge of football, and he's got the ability to impart that knowledge, and anytime you put these two things together, you've got a helluva football coach."

Still a "helluva football coach," Vince retired from the sidelines at Green Bay to run the front office, but in 1969, wearied of watching from up top, he got back into the trenches, this time as the head coach of the Washington Redskins, a team that hadn't posted a winning record in 14 years. During Vince's first year, the Skins posted a 7-5-2 record and the promise of better things to come.

Now they were dancing in the streets in Washington. In September of 1970, however, a few days before the opening of what the fans expected to be a great season, a *Lombardi* season, Vincent Thomas Lombardi died of cancer. The courage he had demonstrated during his illness proved that, even in death, Vince was a winner. His own words, delivered to his players so many times in the past, illustrate his power to inspire: "You never lose, but sometimes the clock runs out on you."

The clock may have run out on him, but the spirit of Vince Lombardi's devotion to God, to family and friends, and to generations of players yet to come lives on. He once said, "The will to excel and the will to win, they endure. They are more important than the events that occasion them." The Lombardi philosophy transcended football; it embraced all of life, uncomplicated but powerful. It was and *is* undeniable—and it made Vince Lombardi America's greatest professional football coach.

## Number Two

**Paul Brown.** A motive force behind professional football's newest league in 1946 and one of the biggest reasons for its demise four years later, Coach Paul Brown led the Cleveland Browns to the All-America Football Conference (AAFC) championship four consecutive seasons, compiling a 47-4-3 record in the process. He so dominated the new league that fans eventually lost interest in the other teams, and the league soon folded—but not before history had been made.

During the league's first year, Cleveland, with a record of 12-2, won the title from the resurgent New York Yankees, who were coached by Ray Flaherty. At the conclusion of the league's second year, the Browns had a 12-1 record and again beat the Yankees for the AAFC title. The Browns won the title again in 1948 with a perfect 14-0 record and a victory over the Buffalo Bills in the title game. Finally, in the AAFC's final year, the Browns again clinched the title with a 21-7 win over the San Francisco 49ers coached by "Buck" Shaw.

In 1950, the AAFC merged with the NFL. Several teams, including the San Francisco 49ers, Cleveland Browns, Buffalo Bills, and Baltimore Colts, suddenly found themselves playing established NFL franchises with the nationwide expectation that now they would learn what professional football "was really like." In his first year in the NFL, Brown took Cleveland to a 10-2 record and an NFL championship when the team beat the Los Angeles Rams by a score of 30-28.

The season was no fluke. Cleveland again was in the title game at the end of the 1951 season, having earned a record of 11-1. They lost the game but returned again next year to play Detroit for the NFL championship. Again they lost, but in 1953 Brown took Cleveland to the championship game an unprecedented fourth time, losing by one point, again to Detroit (17-16). At the conclusion of the 1954 season, however, Paul Brown's Cleveland Browns would defeat Detroit by a score of 56-10 to clinch their second NFL championship. They would win it again in 1955 with a win over Los Angeles in the Coliseum.

During the first 10 years of Coach Brown's 21-year career, his teams won a league or a division championship every year. That is an accomplishment unparalleled in the history of professional football. Coach Brown retired from Cleveland at the completion of the 1962 season but returned to football 6 years later with the Cincinnati Bengals. The Bengals were an expansion club at the time, but in 2 short years Brown guided them to the Central Division championship of the AFC and a play-off berth.

Coach Brown's success at Cincinnati was a fitting conclusion to a career with a 222-112-9 record and a winning percentage of .660. It was at Cleveland, however, that Paul Brown established himself as one of the legends of the game. His use of notebooks, statistical studies, and sideline play-calling and his 158-48 record identify Paul Brown as one of pro football's all-time great coaches.

## Number Three

**Tom Landry.** At this writing, Coach Tom Landry is tied with Green Bay's Curly Lambeau for the second-longest tenure as an NFL coach—29 years. Most coaches come and go like soldiers in a parade. Some pass so quickly, they are indistinguishable in the crowd. Not so with Tom Landry. Even disinterested parties, most of whom artlessly disdain the Sunday afternoon ritual in front of the tube, recognize the well-dressed and superbly controlled former Cowboy head coach.

Why wouldn't they? Thomas Wade Landry was the only head coach of the Cowboys for their predictably successful first 29 years in existence. In a game where the words "head coach" become a death knell for aspiring careers, Landry outlasted even the most tenacious; and he did it with decency and obvious good charm.

Born in 1924 in Mission, Texas, Coach Landry has had his share of success. He enjoyed a solid family life as a child and became an A student in high school, earning election to the National Honor Society. He was president of his class, an All-Area fullback, and one of the school's most gifted all-round athletes.

Upon graduation, Tom was escorted directly into the Eighth Air Force, flying 30 missions over Europe as a 19-year-old bomber pilot. During one of his missions, his B-17 ran out of gas over Belgium. Calmly guiding the plane between two trees that sheared off its wings, Landry saved the lives of its crew. When asked about the experience, all Coach Landry says is, "A lot of planes were lost that night."

It is this same quiet confidence that characterized his demeanor as the Cowboys' head coach. He developed one of the most formidable football machines in the history of the game, a team that by its play reflected the strategic knowledge and the calm precision of its head coach. The winner of some 270 professional football games, Coach Landry qualified the Cowboys for play-off competition 18 times and won the Super Bowl twice, in 1972 with a 24-3 victory over Don Shula's Miami Dolphins and again in 1978 with a 27-10 win over Denver. His teams also were runners-up to the Super Bowl champions three times with a 20-16 record in play-off competition. His five appearances in Super Bowl competition rank second in NFL history.

A board member for the Fellowship of Christian Athletes, Coach Landry has received numerous awards, including the Vince Lombardi Dedication Award, a distinguished service award from the NFL Alumni Association, the *Football News* Man of the Year Award, and most recently the Distinguished American Award from the Walter Camp Football Foundation and the Paul Brown Award from the Touchdown Club of Columbus, Ohio.

Coach Landry's philosophy is best summarized in his own words: "Adversity and achievement build character. People striving, being knocked down and coming back—that's what builds character in a man. And character is the ability of a person to see a positive end to things." Tom Landry has character. His recent release by the new Cowboy ownership was accepted with characteristic good grace and signaled the end of one of pro football's grand eras.

---

*Author's note:* In 1960, as Marquette University's fullback when they dropped football, I received a phone call from the Cowboys offering a contract. I declined in order to play for the University of Nebraska, but little did I realize at the time that I would later write a biography of Coach Landry in *Commitment of Champions* or that he would consent to write the foreword for the book. I also asked him to serve on the selection panel for this book. In a beautifully written letter, he declined the offer, indicating that all of his time would be devoted to rebuilding the Cowboys. I miss his contributions to the book but recognize that he probably wouldn't be in it were it not for such dedication to pro football. The game will miss him.

# Number Four

**Don Shula.** Asked several years ago to describe himself as a head coach, Don Shula replied: "I'm just a guy who rolls up his sleeves and goes to work." The work has paid off. During 26 years of coaching in professional football, Coach Don Shula has rivaled Tom Landry for most career wins among the league's active coaches. Both are second only to George Halas for career victories. Shula's accomplishments, however, don't end there.

Coach Shula is the only coach in NFL history to guide a team through an undefeated season. In 1972, the Miami Dolphins were 17-0 and winners of the Super Bowl over Washington (14-7). He is the only NFL coach to reach the Super Bowl three consecutive seasons ('72, '73, and '74). He also is the only coach in history to reach the Super Bowl six times. Combine these statistics with the fact that Don Shula is the youngest coach in NFL history to reach the 100- and 200-game marks, and his greatness, well before his retirement from the game, is well established.

Of all his records, the one least likely to be beaten in his record of 32-2 during the 1972 and 1973 seasons, both of which ended with Super Bowl victories. Perhaps equally unattainable are his six unbeaten streaks of 10 or more games, four more than any other coach in the game's history. Such statistics have translated into the AFC East crown 14 of his 18 years with the Dolphins and a 31-game winning streak at home from 1971 to 1974, an NFL record.

Born in 1930 in Grand River, Ohio, Don Shula as a running back at John Carroll University gained 125 yards when his team upset the Syracuse Orangemen, 21-15. He later went on to star for the Cleveland Browns and the Baltimore Colts at right cornerback with 21 career interceptions. After four years of college coaching (at Virginia and Kentucky), he served as defensive coordinator for the Detroit Lions before succeeding Weeb Ewbank as the head coach of the Baltimore Colts.

One of professional football's best examples of contributions beyond the field of play, Coach Shula has been a member of the NFL Competition Committee since 1975 and has created scholarship funds at six Florida colleges and universities. He also has been active in the March of Dimes, Catholic Charities, the American Red Cross, United Way, and the American Cancer Society.

Coach Shula has been married for 30 years to the former Dorothy Bartish, and they have five children, two of whom are in football. Equally successful as a coach, a husband, and a father, Don Shula seeks perfection in everything he does. "I don't have peace of mind until I know I've given the game everything I can." He settles for nothing less for his family. The essence of the man reflects itself in his on-the-field as well as his off-the-field behavior. "I hope it will be said that my teams showed class and dignity in victory or defeat." We can attest that they did; so did he.

## Number Five

**George Halas.**  The winningest coach in pro football history, with a record of 325-147-31 and a winning percentage of .689, Coach George Halas was an institution well before he completed his 40th season with the Chicago Bears. The only person to be associated with professional football for 63 years, from its origins in 1920 until his death as owner in 1983, coach Halas was first in the NFL in several categories.

He was the first to schedule daily practice sessions, the first to use a tarpaulin in inclement weather, the first to broadcast his team's games on the radio, and the first to use his opponents' game films to plot strategy. Halas also was the first to perfect the T-formation with a man in motion. It has become the foundation for most of today's offenses and, according to Coach Halas before his death, his greatest accomplishment in more than half a century of professional football.

Born in 1895 in Chicago, George Stanley Halas played football for Bob Zuppke at the University of Illinois. After a short stint in the navy during World War I, Halas played baseball for the New York Yankees and then helped found what has become the National Football League. Owner of the Decatur Staleys in 1921, Halas moved the team to Chicago where they became the Bears. He coached and played end for the team until 1929, in one game against the Oorang Indians recovering a fumble on his own 2-yard line and racing 98 yards for a touchdown, an NFL record that stood for more than half a century. The player who fumbled the ball was Jim Thorpe.

When he retired as a player in 1929, Halas retired as the Bears' head coach long enough for him to miss the thrills of the game he created. In 1933 he was back at the helm for another stint as head coach, this time until World War II interfered. Following another hitch with the navy, Halas again returned to the Bears, only to fire himself again in 1955. Two years later, however, he returned for his fourth go-around with the club and remained for 10 years until in 1968, at the age of 73, he announced his retirement for the last time.

"Papa Bear" to some of the greatest names in professional football, George Halas recruited and coached greats like Red Grange, Bronco Nagurski, Sid Luckman, Mike Ditka, Bulldog Turner, Gale Sayers, and Dick Butkus. More of his players have been honored by the Pro Football Hall of Fame than any other NFL team. Coach Halas was similarly honored in 1963. The man personally responsible for so many NFL firsts became one of the game's first men to be inducted into the Hall of Fame.

*Author's note.* In 1982, seeking firsthand information about Jim Thorpe for a family biography I was writing, I called the Bears' front office. To my surprise, Coach Halas answered the phone, a man obviously unaffected by social conventions. He was very helpful to me and even over the phone evidenced a commanding presence. I wasn't surprised when doing research for this book that Vince Lombardi had once said of the Papa Bear: "There is only one man I embrace when we meet and only one I call 'Coach.'"

## Other Qualifiers

**George Allen.** He never experienced a losing season in 12 years. A man imbued with the American work ethic, Coach Allen sums up his philosophy with the words, "Every day you waste is one you can never make up." Fired by an all-consuming intoxication for his work, he is compelled by a quiet frenzy that wastes not even the smallest part of a day. In high school, for example, he played three sports, lettering three times in each of them. He went on to play end for Marquette University in Wisconsin and, after graduation, to coach at Morningside College in Iowa and Whittier College in California.

In 1957, Coach Allen jumped to the pros, initiating what was to become a tenuous relationship with the Los Angeles Rams. A short time later, he accepted an offer to coordinate the defense for George Halas's Chicago Bears, where his players led the NFL in 10 of 19 defensive categories. In 1965, he returned to the Rams as head coach and led them to an 8-6 record his first year and an 11-1-2 record a year later. Fired in 1968 and rehired a short time later, Allen led the Rams to two more winning seasons but was fired again in 1970.

His firing had little to do with his ability to innovate. George Allen is credited with being the first head coach in professional football history to hire a special teams coach. In fact, he is still the definitive source regarding special teams in football. His innovations, however, didn't end there. In 1966, Allen also initiated pro football's first anti-drug program. He also is the father of "situation substitution," the practice of substituting players to accommodate strategic needs during certain game situations.

When Coach Allen joined the Washington Redskins a short time later, the combination of prolific thinking and hard work resulted in his design and construction of Redskin Park, pro football's first facility to house three football fields and an all-weather track. The concept effectively made pro football a year-round sport and ultimately resulted in a 1972 Super Bowl appearance for the Redskins, where they lost to Don Shula's Miami Dolphins.

Throughout his career, Coach Allen has also found the time to write eleven books. His talents as a teacher are further evidenced in the fact that 14 of his assistants have become head coaches. Currently the head coach at Long Beach State University, George Allen continues to touch the game of football with his special brand of commitment, a dedication that combines hard work with innovative genius, a formula for success in anybody's book.

**Wilbur "Weeb" Ewbank.** With an eye toward the most minute details, Coach Ewbank in 1954 grabbed the reins of the Baltimore Colts and in five years gave them their first NFL championship in years. The 1958 edition of the Baltimore Colts, with names like John Unitas, Alan Ameche, John Mackey, and Ray Perkins, teamed up with Ewbank to stage what many fans consider the greatest football game ever played, with a last-second victory that gave the Colts a 23-17 overtime victory over the Giants.

One year later, Coach Ewbank repeated with a second NFL championship. Ten years later he joined the Colts in another championship game, but this time he was on the opposite side of the field, as head coach of the upstart New York Jets, led by an underdog but brash Joe Willie Namath, a third-year pro barely beyond earshot of Alabama's "Bear" Bryant. Coach Ewbank led the Jets that day to one of pro football's most staggering upsets, a 16-7 shelling of the Colts, and he gained the singular distinction of being the only coach in history to win titles in both the AFL and the NFL.

A member of the Pro Football Hall of Fame, Coach Ewbank started his professional career at the age of 47. He retired 20 years later with a record of 130-129-7, a misleading statistic that fails to account for his first few years with each franchise when rebuilding was the only priority. With a nickname that resulted from his younger brother's inability to pronounce Wilbur, "Weeb" Ewbank retired from football as a coach widely respected by fellow coaches and players alike.

**Sid Gillman.** Pro football's pundit of the passing game, Coach Sid Gillman, in a few short years with the Los Angeles Rams, established himself as the NFL's Red Baron of aerial warfare. With quarterbacks Norm Van Brocklin and Billy Wade launching the attack and Elroy "Crazylegs" Hirsch and "Tank" Younger with their receptions transforming enemy into occupied territory, the Rams' swift strikes led to a title game in Gillman's first year. Playing his last football game for the Cleveland Browns, Otto Graham led Coach Paul Brown's charges to a victory over Los Angeles, but Sid Gillman, in just one year, had established himself as a dominant force in the NFL.

Gillman remained with the Rams for three more years, then moved to the LA Chargers. During his first year with them, he helped move the team to San Diego and in the process exploited the skills of quarterback Jack Kemp to lead them to the AFL title game, where they lost to the Houston Oilers. Gillman led San Diego to the title game again during his second year with the team but lost by a score of 10-3, again to Houston.

In the next four years, Coach Gillman took San Diego to the title game three times, winning it in 1963 with a convincing 51-10 shelling of the hapless Boston Patriots, and losing twice to the Buffalo Bills and their fine coach, Lou Saban. In all, Coach Gillman's record with San Diego was a respectable 86-46-6 with five title games and one AFL championship. Like Weeb Ewbank, he had played in title games in both the NFL and the AFL, further distinguishing himself as one of pro football's finest.

**Bud Grant.** The rap on Coach Grant was that he was unable to win the big one. Four times he took his Minnesota Vikings to the Super Bowl, and four times he lost. What most people forget, however, is that during his 18-year career with the Vikings Coach Grant made the play-offs 12 times, won the Central Division championship 11 times, and won one NFL and three NFC titles. Winning football games had become a habit to Bud Grant.

Before joining the Vikings, Grant had spent 10 years with the Winnipeg Blue Bombers in the Canadian Football League. A player for the Bombers before becoming their head coach, Grant had been the team's top pass receiver and had led the league in receptions three different times. A defensive cornerback as well, Grant set a pro football record by recording five interceptions in one game. But it was as a coach that Bud Grant established himself as one of football's all-time greats.

With Winnipeg, Coach Grant established a regular-season record of 102-56-2 and a play-off record of 20-10-1, including six Western Conference titles and four Grey Cup championships. Coach Grant was Canada's first coach to record 100 victories during his first 10 years. With Minnesota, Grant earned a record of 161-99-5 for a total career record of 283-175-8, the second-highest number of victories in professional football history, only 42 wins behind pro football's winningest coach, "Papa" George Halas.

**Chuck Knox.** One of pro football's top 10 winningest coaches, Coach Knox has divided his career among the Los Angeles Rams, Buffalo Bills, and Seattle Seahawks. With 15 years of experience and a winning percentage of almost .650, Coach Knox has earned the reputation of being one of the finest of professional football's active coaches. His first five years as a head coach were spent in Los Angeles, where he led the Rams to a 54-15 record and renewed NFL respectability.

From Los Angeles, Coach Knox accepted the challenge of reviving the Buffalo Bills. He arrived in 1978 for a 5-11 season but brought the team to two back-to-back winning seasons in '80 and '81 with 11-5 and 10-6 records, respectively. The 1980 season ended in an AFC Eastern Division championship for Buffalo and the promise of better things to come. Following the '82 strike season, Coach Knox moved to Seattle to accept yet another challenge with the Seahawks.

During the past five seasons with the Seattle Seahawks, Coach Knox has not had a losing season and has compiled a record of 48-31, taking the Seahawks to the NFL play-offs in 1987 with a thrilling 23-21 overtime loss to the Houston Oilers. His five-year tenure with the Seahawks has established them as a legitimate contender for additional play-off and conference honors.

Coach Knox's career record of 146-91-1 places him in the number five position of active NFL coaches.

**Earl "Curly" Lambeau.** The Green Bay Packers have had just one name and have played in just one city longer than any other team in NFL history. From the pre-NFL founding of the Packers in 1919 until 1949, one man, and one man only, had been responsible for the team's stability as well as its success. Team founder and general manager/coach for the team's first 30 years, Curly Lambeau is a name synonymous with Green Bay's early history.

As a freshman at Notre Dame, Curly Lambeau started in the same backfield as the immortal George Gipp and learned from his coach, Knute Rockne, the techniques of player motivation and the strategies of offensive football, particularly of the passing game. His teams at Green Bay reflected this training. A player/coach for the first 10 years of his tenure, Lambeau modeled his expectations of player performance so effectively that near the end of his playing career he led the Packers to three consecutive NFL Championships (in 1929, 1930, and 1931).

Only one other coach in NFL history would duplicate such an accomplishment, and he would do it in Green Bay—Vince Lombardi won the NFL Championship in '64, '65, and '66 to share with his Packers predecessor one of professional football's most envied accomplishments. In all, Lambeau won six NFL Championships during his 33 years of coaching and compiled a record of 234-135-23. Only George Halas, Tom Landry, and Don Shula have won more.

**John Madden.** The Greek philosopher Heraclitus said centuries ago that a man's character is his fate. If Heraclitus is right, John Madden had no alternative but to be a highly charged and successful football coach. With Coach Madden, what you see is what you get, a red-hot shock of spontaneity that energizes everyone within range of his personality. The Madden personality created one of television's most magnetic commentators, and it stimulated one of professional football's most successful programs.

John Madden coached the Oakland Raiders from 1969 to 1976 and recorded one of the highest winning percentages in NFL history. His career record of 112-39-7 resulted in a winning percentage of .731, second only to Vince Lombardi. During his very first year with Oakland, Coach Madden earned a record of 12-1. His second year resulted in a record of 8-4-2 and a succession of play-off victories that concluded with a loss in the AFC title game to Baltimore.

During the next six years, he took Oakland to the NFC title game four more times, losing the first three and winning the fourth. This first and most impressive AFC title victory for Madden led to a Super Bowl championship over the Minnesota Vikings (32-14) and a record that year of 13-1. Madden coached for two more years, retiring after the 1978 season to pursue an equally successful career providing his unique brand of "color" for NFL telecasts.

**Chuck Noll.** Says Coach Noll of his personal philosophy: "Sometimes [people] forget the simple elements that make a thing work. The nice thing about football, though, is that you have a scoreboard to show you how you've done." During his 19 seasons with the Pittsburgh Steelers, Coach Noll has had the scoreboard on his side. With over 160 career victories and a winning percentage of .639, Noll ranks fourth among active coaches in percentage of victories and fifth for number of wins. His accomplishments with the Steelers have been truly remarkable.

His career with Pittsburgh had not always been that bright. When he joined the club in 1969, Pittsburgh won its first regular season game and then lost its next 13 in a row. The second year showed marked improvement, five wins and nine losses. Noll's efforts to rebuild the club paid off in 1972 when, after only 4 years with the team, he led them to their first division title with a 11-3 record.

By 1974, Coach Noll had registered three consecutive winning seasons, the first such run in the team's history. The season also marked the first of four Super Bowl victories. No team in NFL history had won more. Four Super Bowl victories in just six years earned Coach Noll AFC Coach of the Year awards, the NFL Coach of the Year in 1976, and, for the Steelers, the Team of the Decade award for the '70s.

**Steve Owen.** "Football is a game played down in the dirt and it always will be. There's no use getting fancy about it." With those words, Steve Owen, the captain and All-NFL tackle of the New York Giants, led his team to a championship that allowed their opponents only 20 points in 13 games, a record that still stands. Steve Owen the coach embraced the same philosophy

From the time he became the Giants' player/coach in 1931, Coach Steve Owen sustained a gut-level toughness that brought two NFL championships to the Giants and six divisional crowns. His emphasis on defense stymied the great Paul Brown teams of the era, and he introduced the "umbrella" defense in 1950, the forerunner of today's 4-3-4 alignment. Coach Owen also is responsible for the development of the "A" formation on offense, a strategy that has been in use since its birth in 1937.

Born in the late 1800s in Indian territory, now Oklahoma, Steve Owen played football for little Phillips University in Enid, Oklahoma, and in 1926 joined the Giants. Only a year old at the time, the Giant franchise saw head coaches come and go for its first six years. Only one, Earl Potteiger, remained for more than one. With Steve Owen at tackle, he led the Giants to an 11-1 record in 1927 but faltered in 1928 and was replaced by LeRoy Andrews in 1929. He had managed, however, to chase the New York Yankees football team out of existence after only two years in the league.

Owen took the reins in 1931 and retired just before the 1953 season. His record of 154-108-17 at the time ranked behind only George Halas and Curly Lambeau for career victories. Shortly after Owen's death in 1964, George Halas paid him perhaps his finest tribute when he said: "Every team strives to do today what Steve was doing 20 years ago."

**Hank Stram.** A standout high school halfback, Henry Louis Stram received a scholarship to Purdue where he earned four letters in baseball, three in football, and the Big Ten Medal for being one of the conference's outstanding student athletes. Immediately after graduation, Stram joined the Purdue coaching staff, working 8 years with head coach Stu Holcomb. During the next four seasons, he coached variously at SMU, Notre Dame, and the University of Miami, and in 1960 he became head coach of the Dallas Texans, the new AFL franchise owned by Lamar Hunt.

In only two years, Stram led the Texans to the AFL championship, beating the Houston Oilers by a score of 20-17 in history's second-longest football game, a six-quarter affair that ended with a Tommy Brooker field goal. Four years later, now the Kansas City Chiefs, Coach Stram's team again won the AFL title, defeating the Buffalo Bills 31-7 and earning the dubious honor of meeting the Green Bay Packers in Super Bowl I. The Chiefs lost the game 35-10, but Stram's winning tradition continued; in 1969 they both won the AFL crown and defeated the Minnesota Vikings in Super Bowl IV by a score of 23-7.

Coach Stram won AFL Coach of the Year honors three times and concluded his career with the New Orleans Saints. His 17-year career record of 131-97-10 currently ranks him ninth on the all-time win list. One of history's best-dressed football coaches, Stram once said, "All I want to do is be me, Hank Stram. Period. Whatever that is, then that's what I am." It spelled coaching greatness in professional football.

**Bill Walsh.** The head coach of the San Francisco Forty-Niners from 1979 through 1988, Coach Walsh graduated from San Jose State in 1959. After coaching briefly at Stanford and Cal Berkeley, and then with the Raiders and the Bengals in professional football, he moved to San Francisco. Walsh's first year with the Forty-Niners concluded with a 2-14 record, his second with a 6-10. They were his last losing years. Three years after his arrival, Coach Walsh and the Forty-Niners earned a Super Bowl title; 3 years later they earned their second title, and they won their third in 1988. Coach Walsh's career record with San Francisco was 92-59-1.

# Chapter 4

# GYMNASTICS

Olympic victories are contemporary American standards for athletic excellence. Japan and the Eastern bloc countries, particularly the Soviet Union, have dominated not only volleyball and wrestling but gymnastics as well. The Soviet women have had unusual success, winning every Olympic gold medal for which they have competed since their current team concept was introduced in the 1960 competition in Rome.

American women medaled for the first time in 1984 when, in the absence of the U.S.S.R., they won the gold in Los Angeles. The American men won the silver in the same competition. The women lost the bronze medal versus the best women gymnasts in the world during the 1988 Olympics but affirmed the growing excellence of the American gymnasts, due in large part to Coach Bela Karoly, the former mentor of Nadia Comeneci and later of Mary Lou Retton and scores of American hopefuls.

The sport that originated in Greece and Rome and had been advanced primarily by Europe since the development of the European Gymnastics Federation in 1881 found its way to the Eastern bloc countries, who went on to dominate competition, and more lately to the United States. Although the concept of gymnastics had been popular in the U.S. for many years, American schools encouraged activities more in line with the ancient Greek concept of gymnastics: any activity performed in a gymnasium, including running, jumping, and rope climbing.

Actually, the *world* shared this concept for many years. During the 1911 World Gymnastics Championships, pole vaulting, shot-putting, and rope-climbing were included in the competition. In 1922 swimming was compulsory, and as recently as 1948 the list of activities included the high jump. The competition has been more a mini-Olympics than what we know today as gymnastics. In the past several years, the United States has made the transition and has moved up to world standards, thanks to veteran coaches like George Szypula at Michigan State and younger ones like Francis Allen at Nebraska and Greg Buwick at Oklahoma.

Formerly a team of also-rans in the Olympics, the United States' squad now contends legitimately for the gold medal in almost every current international competition. Much of this recent success is attributable not just to college or even high school–level coaches but to the many across the country who work with thousands of youngsters every year to identify and to develop gymnastic talent. Unfortunately, their individual efforts cannot be acknowledged in a book of this type. Their contributions, however, are no less noteworthy.

# COLLEGE GYMNASTICS

## America's Greatest College Men's Gymnastics Coach

### Gene Wettstone

Longevity alone identifies Coach Wettstone as one of the nation's premier gymnastics coaches. For 38 years he led the Penn State Nittany Lions to national prominence, earning a career record of 201-38-11 and winning *nine* NCAA team championships. In addition, 17 of his teams claimed Eastern Intercollegiate Gymnastics League (EIGL) titles. He also developed 25 NCAA individual titlists and 103 EIGL champions. Nine of Coach Wettstone's athletes competed in the Olympics, and three won the Nissan Award in recognition of the nation's outstanding senior gymnast.

Coach Wettstone also coached the U.S. Olympic teams in 1948 and 1956 and the World Games in 1970. The winner of two Big Ten All-Around championships as a competitor at Iowa, Wettstone went on to bring international competition to the United States and created the double dual meet format for collegiate competition.

One of his greatest contributions to the sport, however, was organizing international meets with the greatest teams in the world: the Soviet Union, Japan, Bulgaria, Finland, Hungary, Great Britain, Norway, Sweden,

Switzerland, and West Germany. The competitions introduced world-class techniques and training strategies to the United States and prompted the nation's interest in gymnastics as an interscholastic and intercollegiate sport.

In fact, coach Wettstone is remembered for much more than his team's nine NCAA crowns. He is considered one of this nation's gymnastics pioneers.

## Number Two

**Bill Meade.** Coach Bill Meade's success story is summed up best in his own words: "My career is my fun." It is a career that has spanned 40 years, producing one of the nation's finest gymnastics programs. Coach Meade introduced gymnastics to the University of North Carolina in 1949 and, seven years later, moved to Southern Illinois University at Carbondale to reintroduce their program. The result was a series of remarkable accomplishments. After 6 years at the SIU helm, Coach Meade strung together 69 consecutive dual meet victories to contribute to his career record of 284-121-1. Within one 9-year period, his teams won four NCAA team titles (1964, 1966, 1967, and 1972).

In addition, Meade has coached 15 NCAA individual champions and 55 All-Americans. Two of his gymnasts were Nissan Award winners; four were Olympians; six went to the Pan Am Games; and four represented the United States in the World University Games. He has been named national coach of the year three times and, most notably, has been a strategic part of *six* Olympic Games. For his remarkable contributions to the sport, Coach Meade has been inducted into the National Gymnastics Hall of Fame.

## Number Three

**Charles P. Pond.** A marine paratrooper during World War II, Coach Pond received his discharge and joined the high-flying world of college gymnastics. He became the head coach of the University of Illinois program in 1948 and within two years dominated Big Ten competition by winning 11 consecutive conference crowns through the 1950s. Within that time, Coach Pond's Fighting Illini also claimed four NCAA team titles—1950, 1955, 1956, and 1958. During his 25 years as the Illini head coach, Pond earned a record of 149-79-1 and won 54 national and international championships.

In addition, he coached 20 individual national champions, including standout performers Don Tonry and Abie Grossfeld in the fifties and

Hal Holmes and Sharon Richardson in the sixties. Coach Pond was also responsible for the development of the sunken tumbling pit, an innovation that helped prevent injuries and that was first introduced to the world at Kenney Gym at the University of Illinois.

Coach Pond's contributions to the sport are as noteworthy as his record. He has served as the president of the National Association of Gymnastics Coaches, a judge in the 1956 Olympics, an executive committee member of the United States Gymnastics Federation, a member of the Pan Am Games Committee, and the director of his own summer camp in Michigan. In addition, Pond has contributed to two books, written 13 articles, and assisted with the production of three films on gymnastics. Coach Pond retired from coaching in 1962.

## Number Four

**Hartley Price.** The head coach at both the University of Illinois and Florida State University during his long and colorful career, Coach Price won six national titles while with the Fighting Illini and five more with Florida State. He led the Seminoles to the NCAA team titles in 1951 and 1952 and to Amateur Athletic Union (AAU) titles in 1951, 1953, and 1954. Not only an outstanding gymnastics coach, Dr. Hartley Price was awarded Fulbright lectureships to India and Colombia. He served for 20 years on the United States Olympic Gymnastics Committee and three times was honored by the National Association of College Gymnastics Coaches (NACGC), being inducted into their hall of fame. He also was inducted into the Florida State University Hall of Fame in 1978 and the Helms Foundation Athletic Hall of Fame in 1959. Price is widely recognized for his efforts to bring gymnastics to all parts of the country and to all ages.

## Number Five

**Abie Grossfeld.** The winner of seven Big Ten titles and four NCAA titles while a performer at the University of Illinois, Coach Grossfeld has taken Southern Connecticut State University to a career record of 211-55-1 and three NCAA Division II championships during his 25 seasons with the school. He has coached 29 individual NCAA champions, 126 All-Americans, and four Nissan Award winners.

Perhaps more remarkably, Coach Grossfeld has been the coach of the U.S. National team for seven years, leading them to a gold medal in the 1984 Olympics as well as the 1987 Pan Am Games. He also has coached five U.S. teams at the World Championships and the 1972 U.S. Olympic team. Sixteen of his own gymnasts have competed in more than 85 international meets. For his efforts, Coach Grossfeld has been selected as the Eastern Coach of the Year 10 times.

## Other Qualifiers

**Francis Allen.** The winner of the Big Eight parallel bars title in 1964, Francis Allen graduated from the University of Nebraska in 1965 and, after five years as a graduate assistant, became the Cornhuskers' head coach in 1969. By 1979, he brought Nebraska its first NCAA team title, then went on to win four consecutive titles. He placed fifth in 1984 and was runner-up to the national championship teams in '85, '86, and '87 before winning the NCAA title again in 1988.

During his 20-year tenure with the 'Huskers, Coach Allen has developed such standout gymnasts as Olympians Jim Hartung, Phil Cahoy, Larry Gerard, Jim Mikus, Scott Johnson, Kevin Davis, West Suter, and Tom Schlesinger.

**Greg Buwick.** A top 10 finisher nationwide since his first year with the University of Oklahoma in 1984, Coach Buwick has led the Sooners to the Big Eight crown twice and to no lower than an eighth in the NCAA standings in recent competitions. His winning percentage of .826 is one of the best in the nation, as is his 55-13-1 record. He has been named Coach of the Year twice and finds himself playing a vital role in the future of gymnastics as the secretary/treasurer of the Men's Elite Coaching Association.

**Hal Frey.** The coach of two Olympians, one of whom (Art Shurlock) qualified as one of gymnastics' greatest coaches, Hal Frey devoted 30 years to two schools, the Circle Campus of the University of Illinois and the University of California, Berkeley. His record includes well over 200 dual meet victories, one AAU team championship at Chicago Circle, and two NCAA team championships at Berkeley. Frey was captain of his gymnastics team at Penn State, and as a coach he went on to lead Berkeley to 10 undefeated seasons and 13 PAC-8 team championships. Coach Frey has been a member of the U.S. Olympic Committee, president of the College Gymnastics Coaches Association, a member of the US Gymnastics Federation, and recognized as Wrestling Coach of the Year three times. In 1969 he was inducted into the Helms Athletic Foundation Gymnastics Hall of Fame.

**Newt Loken.** Twice Big Ten champion and once the NCAA All-Around champion at the University of Minnesota, Loken moved to Michigan where he spent his 36-year coaching career with the Wolverines. Also an All-American cheerleader at Minnesota, Coach Loken, in addition to his gymnastics responsibilities, worked with the Wolverine cheerleaders. During his 36 years with the gymnastics team, Loken earned an overall record of 250-72-1 for a winning percentage of .776. His teams recorded 12 Big Ten titles, two trampoline titles, and two NCAA team crowns. Twice National Coach of the Year and a member of three different halls of fame, Coach Loken also boasted 71 individual Big Ten titlists and 21 NCAA titlists. He retired from coaching in 1983.

**Ralph Piper.** Longevity alone could highlight Coach Ralph Piper as one of this country's great gymnastics coaches. His 38 years at the University of Minnesota establish him as one of the deans of the sport, and his career record of 195-129-1 against the toughest competition in the country underscores his reputation. During his tenure at Minnesota, Coach Piper won six Big Ten crowns and produced eight All-Around and 32 Big Ten individual NCAA champions and one All-Around (Newt Loken) and six individual champions. Coach Piper also is the author of four books, two of which deal with folk and square dancing. Multi-talented and well-traveled (he has spent time in 51 countries and every state in the Union), coach Ralph Piper is one of the gymnastics world's Renaissance Men.

**Fred Roethlisberger.** The most recent in the Minnesota Gopher tradition of great gymnastics coaches, Fred Roethlisberger starred as a competitor in the '60s in the World Championships, the Pan Am Games, and the Olympics before assuming the head coaching position in 1972. In 16 years at Minnesota, Coach Roethlisberger's teams have won seven Big Ten titles and finished second four times. His gymnasts have won 28 Big Ten individual titles, and he has led scores of athletes to international competitions in locations as diverse as Barcelona, Taiwan, and South Africa. A coach completely dedicated to his sport, Coach Roethlisberger has served on the United States Federation of Gymnastics (USFG) Board of Directors and the USFG Men's Program Committee and is active in the U.S. National Team program.

**Karl Schier.** A former Air Force lieutenant colonel and member of the Strategic Air Command, Karl Schier coached at the Air Force Academy before requesting duty in Vietnam, where he clocked 622 combat flying hours and earned the Distinguished Flying Cross, Bronze Star, and Air Medal with seven oak leaf clusters. Returning to the Air Force Academy in 1969, he led the Falcons to the NCAA finals four times in four years.

His record at Penn State was even more impressive. In Schier's 12 seasons as head coach at Penn State, the Nittany Lions posted a dual meet record of 111-23-1, winning the NCAA Championship in 1976 and finishing second once, third four times, and finishing in the top 10 six more times. Coach Schier has earned a career record of 180-67-2 and boasts

15 All-Americans at Penn State. He has served on several national and international gymnastics committees and is a member of the National Gymnastics Hall of Fame.

**Art Shurlock.** A performer for Hal Frey at the University of California in the early sixties, Art Shurlock took over as the head man of the UCLA Bruins in 1964 and in only two years led them to a sixth-place finish in the NCAA tournament. During his 23-year career with the Bruins, he has led his teams to two NCAA crowns, two second-place finishes, and four other finishes in the top 10. He has won five PAC-10 titles, and his gymnasts have been honored as the Conference All-Around champions six times.

In the past several years Coach Shurlock's teams have compiled a dual meet record of 102-13, and three of his Bruin gymnasts—Peter Vidmar, Tim Daggett, and Mitch Gaylord—were instrumental in leading the U.S. to its first gold medal in world gymnastics competition during the 1984 Olympics. Coach Shurlock also is involved in numerous gymnastics organizations.

**George Szypula.** When George Szypula retired as head coach of men's gymnastics at Michigan State University in July, 1988, 41 years of history concluded. The only men's gymnastics coach in Spartan history, Szypula closed out his career with a record of 250-179-5, the Big Ten title in 1968, and a share of the 1958 NCAA team championship. Himself a winner of four straight national AAU tumbling titles and an NCAA crown in 1943, Coach Szypula led his gymnasts to 18 NCAA and 47 Big Ten individual titles. Coach Szypula is a member of the National Polish American Sports Hall of Fame and the Temple University and the U.S. Gymnastics halls of fame. He also served for several years with various gymnastics organizations, perhaps most prominently as the executive director of the National Association of College Gymnastics Coaches.

**Mike Willson.** When Coach Willson took over the gymnastics program at Ohio State University in 1977, the team was ranked 82nd in the nation. During Willson's 11-year tenure with the Buckeyes, they have compiled a dual meet record of 142-32 for a winning percentage of .816 and have claimed three Big Ten titles and one NCAA team crown. Coach Willson has produced 14 All-Americans, 21 Big Ten individual champs, and two NCAA individual champs. His teams have finished in the NCAA top 10 six other times.

In 1985, the coach of the national champions, Coach Willson, was selected as the National Gymnastics Coach of the Year. The owner of an amazing 204-35 dual meet record at Odessa Junior College, Coach Willson won seven national titles and was named the Junior College Coach of the Year three times. He also is the former vice president of the USGF and has been the gymnastics delegate to the United States Olympic Committee for four years. He has never finished lower than fourth in Big Ten competition.

**Dick Wolfe.** Coach Wolfe arrived at Cal State Fullerton in 1969 and within two years led the brand-new program to its first NCAA championship. His teams won two more national titles in 1972 and 1974. For his accomplishments, Wolfe was named College Division Coach of the Year and Division I Coach of the Year in the same year, 1972.

Coach Wolfe has served on the United States Foreign Relations Committee and has been the vice president of the NACGC (1983).

**Maxmillian (Max) Younger.** Born in Pilsen, Czechoslovakia, in 1886, Max Younger emigrated to the United States in 1904 and eventually did his undergraduate and graduate work at Temple University. In 1926, he began his coaching career at Temple and remained there for 30 years, producing 13 championship teams, one of which won the NCAA crown in 1949. For being one of the pioneers in the sport, Coach Younger was presented in 1954 with the first Annual National Association of College Gymnastics Coaches Award; the NACGC would be led several years later by one of Younger's former gymnasts, George Szypula. Coach Younger was one of the most popular instructors on the Owl campus and could still demonstrate on the apparatus shortly before his retirement in 1956. He was inducted into the Temple Hall of Fame in 1971.

# Chapter 5

# ICE HOCKEY

Our history books attribute the invention of ice skates to the world's northern countries as early as the 12th century. The game of ice hockey didn't appear in North America until 1830. It was introduced to the United States by the British and Dutch at approximately the time when two teams of McGill University students were squaring off in Montreal and a team from Her Majesty's Royal Canadian Rifles, stationed in Kingston, were playing hockey on a frozen harbor just outside their barracks (Fischler & Fischler, 1983).

Exactly which of the two sites is the *birthplace* of hockey in North America is still speculative, but Kingston did have the first hockey league. The league may have been moderately well-organized, concluding with a championship game (Queen's University won the first title), but the game itself had few rules and little strategy. The purpose of the game was, as it is today, to push the puck past the goalkeeper for a score; but it usually was accomplished with few plays, little technique, and unrestrained mayhem. Techniques improved and mayhem moderated with the development of hockey's first governing body, the Amateur Hockey Association of Canada.

The Association contributed to the game's development. Another significant spur to the game's growth was a simple incentive that grew into the sport world's most cherished awards. In 1893, the son of the governor general of Canada convinced his father to establish a way to recognize the year's best hockey team. The governor general responded by purchasing a silver mug valued at $48.67 and declaring that the winner of an annual play-off would have its name inscribed on the cup. Lord Stanley named the cup after himself.

While Canadians were vying for Lord Stanley's Cup, their game at first remained largely unknown in the United States. But thanks to the creation of artificial ice, hockey began to flourish in New Haven and Baltimore, where students at Yale and Johns Hopkins spearheaded a local competition that within a few years spread to other Eastern and Midwestern cities. By the turn of the century, hockey teams thrived in New York, Philadelphia, Pittsburgh, and Chicago. In 1904, the first professional hockey league was established by an American dentist, J.L. Gibson, in the copper country of Houghton, Michigan. A dentist's motives for starting professional hockey league may be suspect, but the game had received from Gibson the boost it needed to catch on.

By 1917, now a well-established and highly coveted trophy for all Canadian hockey players, the Stanley Cup traveled for the first time to the United States when the Seattle Metropolitans won the National Hockey Association play-offs. It would not be the last time a U.S. Team won the cup, nor would the game of hockey be restricted to North America. The game had become so prominent in Eastern bloc countries that negotiations have been underway between them and the National Hockey League (NHL) to establish a *world* play-off competition to identify the world's best hockey team—perhaps to become for one year the *international* caretaker of the Stanley Cup.

It is an exciting prospect and represents yet another opportunity to showcase the athletic talents and coaching genius of the American men and women who devote countless hours to sports that continue to fascinate millions of people every year. The achievements of many of these coaches are well known, even legendary, within their cluster of followers but may be unknown to most sports fans. We are pleased to provide them some well-earned recognition.

# HIGH SCHOOL ICE HOCKEY

## America's Greatest High School Ice Hockey Coach

**Cliff Thompson**

A pioneer of high school hockey and one of the winningest coaches in the sport's history, Coach Thompson started his career at Eveleth High School in Minnesota in the mid forties. According to the *National High School Sports Record Book*, Thompson won four consecutive state crowns between 1948 and 1951. He also holds the record for consecutive wins, with 79. During his tenure with Eveleth, Coach Thompson earned a career win/loss record of 536-26-9 for a winning percentage of .952, the highest in the nation.

A contemporary of Coach Oscar Almquist, Coach Thompson established Eveleth, Minnesota, as the high school hockey center of the nation. Like Coach Almquist, he was a charter inductee into the United States Hockey Hall of Fame in Eveleth, the only two high school hockey coaches in the nation to be so honored.

## Number Two

**Larry Ross.** The head coach of hockey at Falls Senior High School in International Falls, Minnesota, for more than 30 years, Coach Ross has established a win/loss record of 566-169 for one of the nation's highest numbers of career victories. He has won 14 Regional crowns and has walked off with the state title six times, three times consecutively (1964-1966). Coach Ross also has been runner-up to the state champs twice and has earned Coach of the Year honors 10 times, once as National Hockey Coach of the Year. Coach Ross also has found the time to be a Hockey Region representative and to be the President of the Minnesota High School Coaches Association.

## Number Three

**Serge Gambucci.** With a career record of 255-39 and a winning percentage of .850, Coach Gambucci has one of the best high school records in the nation. During his 15 years with Grand Forks Central High School in North Dakota, he won the state's first 10 consecutive state titles, a record that ranks him third in the *National High School Sports Record Book*. A graduate of St. Cloud State in 1949, Coach Gambucci started at Grand Forks in 1955, five years before North Dakota decided to initiate a state championship series.

A former player who qualified for the Olympics in 1948 and 1952, Coach Gambucci was selected Coach of the Year several times and was given an award of merit by *Sports Illustrated* for winning 10 consecutive state titles. He was inducted into the North Dakota Coaches Hall of Fame in 1985 and the St. Cloud State Hall of Fame in 1989.

## Number Four

**Oscar Almquist.** A native of Eveleth, Minnesota, Coach Almquist was one of the pioneers of high school hockey. One of the original members of the United States Hockey Hall of Fame in Eveleth, Coach Almquist coached at Roseau High School, a few miles away from Eveleth. He led his teams to a career record of 405-150-20 for one of the greatest win/loss records in all of high school hockey.

## Number Five

**Bill Bellisle.** From 1933 to 1987, Mt. St. Charles High School in Woonsocket, Rhode Island, won 22 state championships, a national record for most state titles. They also rank number three on the all-time list for consecutive state crowns, with 10. Coach Bill Bellisle is the man responsible for their consecutive string of victories.

## Other Qualifiers

**Louis Astorino.** The head coach at Hamden High School in Connecticut since 1960, Coach Astorino has won three state titles and has had three runners-up to the state champs. Coach Astorino's 1976 squad also enjoyed a national championship. For his accomplishments he has earned several Coach of the Year awards and was named one of the nation's outstanding coaches in 1983 by the National Federation of State High School Associations. Coach Astorino has been president of the Southern Connecticut Hockey Association, a committee member of the Connecticut Interscholastic Athletic Conference, and chairman of the Hartford Whalers/Gordie Howe Scholarship Fund.

**Art Crouse.** Thirty years of head coaching experience at West Haven High School in Connecticut have produced for Coach Crouse a total of 362 career victories, four state titles, three runners-up to the champs, and four district crowns. Coach Crouse has been named Coach of the Year three times, most recently as the National Hockey Coach of the Year by the National High School Athletic Coaches Association (NHSACA)/Wilson selection committee. He also has served as a member of the Connecticut High School Coaches Association and has chaired the High School Hockey Committee.

**Brother Leonard.** A cleric at St. Dominic's High School in Lewiston, Maine, Brother Leonard divided his time between his religious responsibilities and the needs of the hockey team after school. His hard work paid off. From 1947 through 1952, St. Dominic's won six consecutive state titles. Combined with their record under Brother Leonard's successor, St. Dominic's ranks second on the all-time list for consecutive state crowns, with 11. They also rank second on the all-time list for total state titles, with 20, one of the highest in the nation for any sport.

**Brother Leopold.** Brother Leonard's successor at St. Dominic's High School was Brother Leopold, who continued his school's winning ways in ice hockey by recording five more consecutive state titles. Coach Bob Boucher, St. Dominic's current mentor, won another state title in 1988, giving St. Dominic's a total of 20 state crowns to make Lewiston, Maine one of the two or three high school hockey capitals of the nation.

**Spat Roy.** With a hockey tradition that dates back to 1927, Waterville High School in Maine claims a total of 16 state titles. A coach who contributed significantly to that record is Coach Spat Roy, who led his teams to five consecutive state titles from 1969 to 1973, for sixth place on the all-time list of consecutive state championships. Coach Roy was not a teacher. He worked in a clothing store by day and worked with the high school hockey team at night.

# COLLEGE ICE HOCKEY

## America's Greatest College Ice Hockey Coach

### Vic Heyliger

Inducted into the United States Hockey Hall of Fame in 1974, Coach Heyliger retired that same year as the third-winningest coach in the history of college hockey. The mentor of such future greats as Amo Bessone (when Heyliger was at University of Illinois) and John MacInnes, Coach Heyliger established the University of Michigan as the nation's premiere hockey program during the early days of the NCAA tournament. In fact, Michigan won the first tournament, an 8-4 victory over Eddie Jeremiah's Dartmouth team, in Colorado Springs in 1948.

Under Heyliger's guidance, the Wolverines repeated with five more NCAA titles, three consecutively (1951-1953), and were runners-up to the national champs in 1958, Heyliger's final year of coaching. His career win/loss record of 229-60-13 computes to a winning percentage of .780, the best in the nation. Coach Heyliger also is credited with helping to found the Western Collegiate Hockey Association in 1948.

Coach Heyliger moved to Colorado Springs in 1958 but came out of retirement to help guide the hockey program at the Air Force Academy. In March of 1974, he retired from coaching altogether.

## Number Two

**John MacInnes.** With a career mark of 555-295-39, Coach MacInnes is among the winningest coaches in hockey history. He spent his entire career with Michigan Tech, posting 23 winning seasons, seven Western Collegiate Hockey Association (WCHA) crowns, and three NCAA national championships. Coach MacInnes also recorded four NCAA runners-up and two Coach of the Year awards from the American Hockey Coaches Association. He was named Coach of the Year six times by the WCHA and, in 1980, joined John Kelley as a charter member in the AHCA Pinnacle Club for outstanding achievement in hockey.

Under MacInnes's guidance, the Michigan Tech Huskies finished among the top four teams in the WCHA 17 times, more than any other team. Collegiate hockey's winningest coach, MacInnes died on March 6, 1983, in Houghton, Michigan. He was 57.

## Number Three

**Murray Armstrong.** With a coaching career that spanned 21 years with the University of Denver, Coach Armstrong claimed 11 NCAA championship play-offs, which eventuated in five national titles. He won his first national crown in 1958, followed with back-to-back performances in 1960 an 1961, then repeated with back-to-back titles in 1968 and 1969. In the interim, his Pioneers teams earned back-to-back runner-up spots in 1964 and 1965.

Several times the Coach of the Year, Armstrong numbers among his career highlights a 4-4 tie with the Soviet national team in 1958 and a dramatic 4-3 upset victory over Ken Dryden and Cornell in the 1969 NCAA title game. Perhaps his most cherished memory, however, is the establishment of the Murray Armstrong Fund, which will benefit the Denver hockey program, and the bronze sculpture of Armstrong, created by a former player, that is placed in the University of Denver Arena Lobby.

## Number Four

**Ned Harkness.** Coach Harkness began his coaching career at Rensselaer Polytechnic Institute in 1949 and remained with them for 14 seasons. During that time, he recorded 187 wins against only 90 defeats. He also won the NCAA national title in 1954 and placed third in 1953. In 1964 he moved to Cornell University, where he remained for 7 years and earned a 163-27-2 record. Coach Harkness won two more NCAA national titles with the Big Red and earned one runner-up spot in 1969.

An outstanding lacrosse coach as well, Coach Harkness is the only coach in history to win NCAA national titles in both ice hockey and lacrosse. Coach Harkness was inducted into the Cornell Athletic Hall of Fame in 1981.

## Number Five

**Herb Brooks.** The head coach of the 1980 Olympic hockey team that pulled a stunning upset over the U.S.S.R. for the gold medal, Coach Brooks was not unaccustomed to championship trophies. As the head coach at Minnesota, he had led the Gophers to three NCAA titles (1974, 1976, and 1979). During his tenure with the Gophers, he also earned a runner-up to the national champs Michigan Tech in 1975.

A graduate of the University of Minnesota, Coach Brooks played on five U.S. National teams and two Olympic squads. As a player or a coach, he has been on more U.S. hockey squads than any other person in history. Coach Brooks has won Coach of the Year several times, while devoting his off-season duties to insurance.

## Other Qualifiers

**Amo Bessone.** With one NCAA title, one runner-up to the national champs, and close to 300 career wins, Coach Bessone led Michigan State into the national spotlight in the mid '60s. During its strongest years, Michigan State boasted some of the leading scorers in the nation. In 1966, for example, Coach Bessone had Mike Coppo and Doug Volmar as America's leading scorers; the very next year, he had two more: Sandy McAndrews and Tom Mikkola.

**Gino Gasparini.** Coach Gasparini started his career with the University of North Dakota Fighting Sioux in 1978 and took them immediately to a Western Collegiate Hockey Association title and to a second-place finish in the NCAA final four. He concluded the very next year with a 31-8-1 record and an NCAA championship. Coach Gasparini won two more NCAA titles to rank him among the top 10 coaches in hockey history for NCAA titles.

Coach Gasparini has been Coach of the Year several times and has produced 11 All-Americans. During his tenure with North Dakota, he has sent 33 players to the NHL. His success results from an uncompromising philosophy: "Hard work produces results, and everyone must get a square deal."

**Ed Jeremiah.** One of the pioneers of collegiate hockey, Coach Eddie Jeremiah led Dartmouth to a career record of 308 victories, at the time the second-highest number of wins in the nation. Coach Jeremiah was one of the most widely respected coaches in collegiate hockey during his 30-year career (1937-1967), and he brought Dartmouth to the first two NCAA title contests in 1948 and 1949, placing second both times, once to Michigan and once to Boston College. He is a member of the U.S. Hockey Hall of Fame.

**Bob Johnson.** Coach Johnson joined the University of Wisconsin as its head hockey coach in 1966 and proceeded to take them to a career mark of 367-164-22. Under his guidance, the Badgers have won three NCAA national titles and have placed in the final four three other times. Coach Johnson has developed nine All-Americans and was the head coach of the 1976 U.S. Olympic Hockey Team, which finished fourth at Innsbruck.

Coach Johnson has been named Coach of the Year several times and in 1987 was named executive director of the Amateur Hockey Association of the United States (AHAUS). He also has served on the board of governors of the American College Hockey Coaches Association and has chaired the WCHA. Coach Johnson was elected to the Wisconsin State Hall of Fame in 1987.

**Jack Kelley.** Coach Kelley is one of only three coaches to win back-to-back NCAA championships (1971 and 1972). A dominant force in college hockey in the sixties and seventies, Boston University, under Coach Kelley's guidance, also earned a runner-up spot in 1967.

**John Kelley.** Another of college hockey's pioneers, John "Snooks" Kelley led Boston College to the NCAA's second national championship in 1949 with a 4-3 victory over Eddie Jeremiah's Dartmouth squad. The head coach of the Eagles since 1932, Coach Kelley earned a career total of 501 victories, one of the highest in the nation. He received the Lester Patrick Trophy in 1972 for coaching excellence and was inducted into the United States Hockey Hall of Fame. In 1980, the American Hockey Coaches Association established him as a charter member of its exclusive Pinnacle Club for his contributions to the sport.

**George Menard.** Coach Menard is among the top 15 coaches of all time for career wins. He earned his accomplishment at New York's St. Lawrence University, a school of fewer than 2,000 students, whose team in 1961 battled a powerful Denver team on its home ice for the national championship.

**Al Winsor.** Considered the Father of Harvard Hockey, Coach Winsor led the Crimson for 15 years to a career record of 88-26. He started his career in 1905 when a season generally averaged only 10 games. Coach Winsor also was the head coach of the 1932 U.S. Olympic hockey team, winners of the silver medal. Coach Winsor is a member of the United States Hockey Hall of Fame and is credited with many rules innovations that helped form the game.

## PROFESSIONAL ICE HOCKEY

### America's Greatest Professional Ice Hockey Coach

**William Scott Bowman**

Born in 1911 in Winnipeg, Scotty Bowman began his playing career with Ottawa in 1933 but spent most of his career with Detroit. A defenseman throughout most of his playing career, Bowman is credited with 274 games before his retirement in 1940.

Bowman didn't become a head coach until 1967 but made an almost immediate impact on the NHL. The head coach at St. Louis for four years, he reached the Stanley Cup finals three times, losing all three. He moved to Montreal in 1971 and proceeded to win five Stanley Cup titles, four of which were consecutive (1976-1979). He joined Buffalo in 1979 and proceeded to earn a career record of 739-327-210 for a .661 winning percentage, the best in professional hockey.

During his tenure with Montreal, from 1971 to 1979, Coach Bowman established a record of 419-110-105 for a winning percentage of .744, again the best in professional hockey. Coach Bowman was a recipient of the Jack Adams award in 1977, dispelling the notion that the award is a jinx. After receiving the award, he proceeded to win back-to-back Stanley Cups.

## Number Two

**Hector Blake.** The winner of more Stanley Cups than any other NHL coach, "Toe" Blake spent his entire playing and coaching career with Montreal. Born in Victoria Mines, Ontario, in 1912, Blake first played with Montreal in 1932 as a left wing. When he retired from playing in 1948, he had scored 527 points in 578 games. As a player, he won the Hart Trophy in 1939, the Art Ross Trophy in 1939, and the Lady Byng Trophy in 1945.

Seven years after his retirement from playing, Blake became the head coach of Montreal and proceeded to earn a record of 500-255-159 for a winning percentage of .510 and eight Stanley Cup titles, five of which were consecutive (1956-1960). Coach Blake retired in 1968, having been inducted into the Hall of Fame in 1966.

## Number Three

**Al Arbour.** A well-traveled defenseman during a playing career that started in 1953, Al Arbour played for Detroit, Chicago, Toronto, and St. Louis for 14 years. He retired in 1971 and 2 years later was the head coach of the New York Islanders. With a current record of over 500 victories, Coach Arbour is one of hockey's winningest coaches.

He also is living proof that the Jack Adams Award is not a jinx. The recipient of the award in 1979, Coach Arbour went on to win the Stanley Cup four consecutive times and to establish himself undeniably as one of the NHL's greatest coaches. He has been involved in 182 play-off contests and has won 113 of them for a winning percentage of .621, one of the best in the NHL.

## Number Four

**Jack Adams.** Born in Ft. William, Ontario, in 1895, Coach Adams began his playing career with Toronto in 1917 and continued playing center when his coaching career started in 1922. He moved to Detroit in 1927 to concentrate exclusively on coaching and took the Red Wings to the Stanley Cup finals seven times, winning three cups. With a career record of 423-397-162, three cups, and four runner-up finishes, Coach Adams is one of the great names in hockey.

He was inducted into the Hall of Fame in 1959, received the Lester Patrick Trophy in 1966, and received hockey's greatest honor when his peers named an award in his honor. The Jack Adams Trophy was created in 1974 to commemorate his name and to honor pro hockey's Coach of the Year.

## Number Five

**Clarence Henry Day.** Coach "Hap" Day spent his entire coaching career with the Toronto Maple Leafs and earned a career record of 259-206-81. Coach Day started his playing career for Toronto in 1924. A left wing, Day scored 213 points in a total of 635 games, retiring in 1938. He began his career as a head coach two years later and continued for 10 years, winning five Stanley Cup titles. Coach Day was inducted into the Hall of Fame in 1961.

## Other Qualifiers

**Emile Francis.** With over 400 career wins with New York and St. Louis, Emile "The Cat" Francis is among the NHL's winningest coaches. A powerful player in his day at only 5 feet 6 inches and 145 pounds, Coach Francis is equally powerful as a head coach. Since his first year with the Rangers, he has taken his teams to the Stanley Cup play-offs for 93 games, has won 40 and lost 53. His teams have been in the semifinals four times and have had one runner-up to the cup champions. Coach Francis was the recipient of the Lester Patrick Trophy in 1982 for coaching excellence.

**Dick Irvin.** Born in 1892 in Limestone Ridge, Ontario, Richard Irvin began his career with a year in Chicago (1930) and ended it with a year in Chicago (1956). In between, he spent 24 years in Toronto and Montreal and won close to 700 games. He won four Stanley Cup titles with 16 appearances in the finals, and he was inducted into the Hall of Fame in 1958.

**Tommy Ivan.** Three Stanley Cup titles in five appearances in the finals highlight Coach Ivan's career, which started in 1947 with Detroit and concluded with Chicago in 1957. An accomplished player as well as a coach, Tommy Ivan was awarded the Lester Patrick Trophy in 1975.

**Lester Patrick.** One of the pioneers of NHL hockey, Coach Patrick was also a player during his early tenure with the New York Rangers. Coach Patrick began his coaching career in 1926 and, at 6 feet 1 inch and 180 pounds, was a force to be reckoned with on and off the ice. In his 13 years of coaching, he brought New York to the Stanley Cup finals five times, winning two Cups, and earned a career record of 281-216-107. Coach Patrick was inducted into the Hall of Fame in 1945. The Lester Patrick Trophy and the Patrick Division are named in honor of his contributions to the sport.

**Art Ross.** Another pioneer of the NHL, Coach Ross began his coaching career with Montreal in 1917, eventually moving to Boston in 1924 and remaining with them until his retirement in 1945. His career record of 368-300-90 includes three trips to the Stanley Cup finals and one championship. Coach Ross was awarded the Lester Patrick Trophy in 1984 and was inducted into the Hall of Fame in 1945.

**Fred Shero.** Fred "The Fog" Shero began his coaching career with Philadelphia in 1971, moved to New York in 1978, and earned a career record of 390-225-120, including two Stanley Cup titles. Awarded the Jack Adams Trophy for Coach of the Year honors in 1974, Coach Shero was one of the few coaches to receive the honor and keep his job! (Many award winners lost their jobs the very next year after winning it.) Shero, however, was not free of the Adams Award jinx. He had won back-to-back Stanley Cups before receiving the award, but did not win another Cup for the rest of his coaching career, which ended in 1981.

# Chapter 6

# SOCCER

Soccer has changed little since it was first introduced at England's Harrow in the mid-1800s. Perhaps it is the game's very simplicity that has made it the world's most popular sport. As the forerunner of rugby and the world's other forms of football, it is joined only by Gaelic football in having retained a round ball and in focusing on kicking instead of running and passing.

Whatever the reasons for its popularity, soccer continues to fascinate *billions* of fans around the world. It is estimated, for example, that in June of 1978 more than a billion people, almost one quarter of the world's population, followed the World Cup final between Holland and Argentina (Morris, 1981). That so many millions of fans listened for reports of the game is not surprising; when the World Cup is played, the Federation Internationale de Football Association, headquartered in Zurich, flies well over 140 flags—more than the United Nations flies (Morris, 1981).

Records indicate that United States soccer started in the 1820s, more a form of hazing freshmen at Harvard and Yale than of intercollegiate competition. Although the object of the game was to kick a large ball toward the opponent's goal, accounts of those early games reveal that the ball was kicked much less often than were the shins of the freshmen players. Nonetheless, by 1884, 21 years after the creation of the Football Association in London, the American Football Association was formed in Newark, New Jersey. Composed exclusively of Irish, Scottish, and English immigrants, Association Football was born in America but gained little popularity.

The 1880s also witnessed the emergence of American football, an outgrowth of soccer and rugby, as the game that eventually became not only uniquely American but *exclusively* American. Like Canadian, Gaelic, and Australian football, the American version is only marginally popular in other parts of the world. Like children of a famous parent, each national game of football enjoys local recognition but must stand in the background as the spotlight of *international* popularity seeks out its parents.

Its name a corruption of the abbreviation *Assoc.*, for the word *association*, "soccer" is the world's one genuinely *international* game and as far back as the 1500s displayed the occasional excesses that accompany such popularity. Sir Thomas Elyot described it at the time: "Foote balle was a pastime to be utterly objected by all noble men, the game giving no pleasure, but beastlie furie and violence" (LeBow, 1978).

In spite of the Football Association's decision in the 1860s to outlaw holding, tripping, and hacking (kicking another player's legs), the game has retained some "beastlie furie" well into the present times. Since 1961, for example, when two of their fans died in the stands during a fight, the Rangers and the Celtics, two teams from Glasgow, Scotland, have been unable to play a game without some kind of disturbance. Crowded stadium conditions accounted for deaths in England as recently as 1989. The *most* violent disturbance in England was in 1971 when panic erupted in the stands and thousands of fans cascaded through exits too small to accommodate the surge of bodies. By the time the stadium cleared, 66 people had died and 108 had been seriously hurt.

A similar riot in Peru, eight years earlier, accounted for the loss of 318 lives and the hospitalization of another 500. It was a disaster unlike any in the history of sport but suggests the intense, almost hostile competition that characterizes the world's most popular game. Consider the parallels described in a London newspaper the day before England met West Germany in the 1966 World Cup: "If perchance on the morrow Germany should best us at our national game, let us take consolation from the fact that twice we have beaten them at theirs."

In spite of soccer's "backseat" in American sports, its fans realize that their sport enjoys in this country a growing circle of loyal supporters. In addition, it lays claim to a heritage of coaching excellence that has continued since the late 1800s and that represents some of the finest sport accomplishments in this country.

# HIGH SCHOOL SOCCER

## America's Greatest High School Boys' Soccer Coach

**Gene Baker**

The head soccer coach at Granite City Senior High School for 15 years and a soccer coach for a total of 21, Coach Baker has established his reputation in one of the country's most competitive states. He has dominated soccer in the state of Illinois since 1973, winning seven state championships, five of which were consecutive, and establishing a record of close to 400 wins against only 67 losses. Coach Baker's winning percentage of .820 is among the finest in the nation, and his consecutive streak of five state crowns is a national record.

Coach Baker has not been without honors. He has won the Illinois Soccer Coaches Association Coach of the Year award five times, the Regional award of the National High School Athletic Coaches Association (NHSACA) twice, and the National Coaches Association National Coach of the Year Award once. He also was the recipient of the NHSACA/Wilson National Soccer Coach of the Year Award in 1988.

Coach Baker has served on the National Federation Rules Advisory Committee and the National Soccer Coaches Ethics Committee, and he served as the chairman of both the Illinois High School Soccer Coaches

Association and the National High School Athletic Coaches Association. Coach Baker was inducted into the Granite City Sports Hall of Fame in 1986 and the St. Louis Old Timers Hall of Fame in 1985.

## Number Two

**Edward "Ebbie" Dunn.** Coach Dunn completed his 29-year career at St. Louis University High in Missouri with a national high school record: the winningest coach in the country at a single high school. Coach Dunn ended his career with a record of 444-140-79 and one state championship. Coach Dunn also ranks second in the nation for most consecutive shutouts in a single season, with 14.

In addition to receiving several state and national Coach of the Year awards, including the NHSACA/Wilson National Soccer Coach of the Year in 1979, Coach Dunn has served on several state and national committees, a fact that particularly distinguishes him among high school coaches. Coach Dunn was president of the St. Louis High School Soccer League seven times, director of the state tournament four times, and a member of the state's Rules Committee for 12 years.

Coach Dunn was instrumental in establishing his state's tournament, served as an Advisory Committee member to the Missouri State High School Activities Association for 11 years, and was a director of the National Soccer Coaches Association for Region Five.

## Number Three

**Ray Buss.** The winner of over 400 games during his 32 years of coaching, Coach Buss spent most of his career at Fleetwood High School in Pennsylvania. His 49-game winning streak in 1979 and his 19 shutouts in one season both rank among high school soccer's finest records, but perhaps his most impressive record is the fact that Fleetwood, within a six-year period, established six consecutive records for scoring the highest number of goals in a single season. No other high school soccer team has scored as many.

In addition, however, Coach Buss's teams hold the high school records for most games without being shut out. They played 99 straight games between 1978 and 1981 without being shut out. Needless to say, Coach Buss holds the national record for goals in a season, with 179. The team holding the record earned an undefeated season in 1980 and won the Pennsylvania state title.

Perhaps Coach Buss's most cherished accomplishment, however, involves the talents of two brothers who played for him in the late seventies. Doug Moyer finished his career in 1978 with 68 assists, seventh on the all-time list. Two years later, his brother Jerry completed his career with 104 assists, fourth highest on the all-time list.

## Number Four

**Bob Ashe.** The winner of five consecutive state championships in Oregon, Coach Ashe started his career in Belfast, Ireland, where he won the Irish School's Club Championship in 1962 and 1966. But it was at the Catlin Gabel School in Portland, Oregon, that he won close to 300 games, losing only 54, and earned state Coach of the Year honors four times. Coach Ashe also was selected as the NHSACA/Wilson National Soccer Coach of the Year in 1982. Coach Ashe found time to devote himself to his state's soccer organizations by serving as president of the Oregon High School Soccer Coaches Association in 1975 and 1982 and as district chairman of the Oregon High School Soccer Association in 1981.

## Number Five

**George Steitz.** Coach Steitz was a high school soccer coach for over 36 years and spent most his time at Penfield High School in New York. He won over 400 games, including eight sectional titles and 14 league crowns. Coach Steitz has won numerous local, state, and national Coach of the Year awards, including the NHSACA National Soccer Coach of the Year honor in 1984. He has coached 16 high school and college All-Americans, three of whom went on to play professional soccer.

Coach Steitz's contributions to athletics are perhaps even more noteworthy than his coaching record. He is past president of the Rochester Umpires Association, past president of the Central Western Soccer Officials Association, and secretary/treasurer of the Monroe County Athletic Association; he has also been a speaker at numerous clinics throughout the country. In addition to his involvement in soccer, Coach Steitz took part in five major campaigns in Europe during World War II.

**Bob Horgan.** The winningest coach in high school soccer history, with 571 victories, Coach Horgan divided his 32 years in coaching between two Missouri schools, Affton High School and St. Louis Christian Brothers High School. It was at St. Louis Christian Brothers that Coach Horgan established himself as one of America's best. He ranks third on the all-time list for consecutive wins, with 39, and third on the all-time list for goals scored in a single season, with 148.

Coach Horgan's St. Louis Christian Brothers also holds the number one ranking for consecutive shutouts in a single season, with 15, as well as for most shutouts in a season, with 30. Most amazingly, Coach Horgan's 571 career victories are paired with only 93 career losses.

## Other Qualifiers

**Ron Broadbent.** The soccer coach at New York's Spencerport Central High School for over 20 years, Coach Broadbent has won close to 300 games and has developed several high school All-Americans. The NHSACA/Wilson National Soccer Coach of the Year in 1980, Coach Broadbent has complemented his seven sectional championships in New York with a wide range of related activities. In addition to being the head soccer coach for the Empire State Games in '78 and '79, in which his teams won a silver and a bronze medal, he has won several Coach of the Year and service awards and has served with numerous organizations, including vice chairman of the New York State Soccer Coaches Association. Coach Broadbent is the annual challenger for the Monroe County League championship.

**Dick Danielson.** One of the top ten winningest coaches for all-time victories at a single school, Coach Danielson established a career record of 307-112-36 during his 32 years of coaching. A fixture at Manchester High School in Connecticut, Coach Danielson is one of high school soccer's best.

**David Deacon.** The head coach at William H. Hall High School in West Hartford, Connecticut, for over 30 years, Coach Deacon earned a career record of close to 300 victories, including four state championships and two runners-up. Coach Deacon never failed to win a title during his career and won several Coach of the Year awards, including the NHSACA/Wilson Coach of the Year Award in 1985. In addition to his impressive record, Coach Deacon has invested himself extensively in professional organizations. He has been a panelist for the National Soccer Coaches Association of America Convention, chaired the Central Connecticut Interscholastic League, and served as the vice chairman of Region I for the National High School Athletic Coaches Association. Coach Deacon also has been a soccer official since 1950.

**John Eden.** The head man at North Babylon High School in New York for well over 20 years, Coach Eden has won well over 300 games, including the first state championship in New York. Prior to that, he had won six sectional championships and had produced seven All-Staters and three high school All-Americans. In addition to his coaching accomplishments, Eden has served as president of the Suffolk County Soccer Coaches Association and regional chairman of the National Soccer Coaches Association. Coach Eden was selected as the NHSACA/Wilson National Soccer Coach of the Year.

**Otto Haas.** One of the coaches identified by Mickey Cochrane, Coach Haas pioneered the game in high school athletics at Chatham High School in New Jersey. Now deceased, Coach Haas was the first coach in high school soccer to win more than 400 games.

**Terry Habecker.** As head coach at Ithaca High School in New York, Coach Habecker saw his 1978 team win the state title in New York with an unblemished 24-0 record. His teams also have played 50 consecutive games without a defeat, an accomplishment that ranks his school ninth on the all-time list. Coach Habecker's 1978 team also earned the distinction of playing the most overtimes in a single game (14), versus Vestal, New York.

**Donald Hartley.** The winner of the NHSACA/Wilson Coach of the Year award in 1978, Coach Hartley spent his entire career with Red Creek Central High School in New York. Within his well over 20 years with the school, Coach Hartley has won close to 400 games, including 11 sectional crowns. In addition to several state Coach of the Year awards, Hartley has served as the sports chairman for his county soccer organization and was the assistant chairman of the New York State Soccer Coaches Association of Section V.

**George Herrick.** Coach Habecker's opponent in high school soccer's highest number of overtimes in a single game, Coach Herrick devoted more than 20 years to Vestal High School in New York, where he earned a 308-59-26 record.

**Ralph King.** Coach King has been at Brien McMahon High School in Norwalk, Connecticut, for well over 20 years. He has won close to 250 games, including at least two state championships, been runner-up twice, and won the conference title eight times more. The recipient of numerous local, state, and national awards, including the NHSACA/Wilson Coach of the Year award in 1985, Coach King has spoken at numerous clinics and has been the president and a member of the board of directors of the Fairfield County Interscholastic Association for 10 years. He also has served as the regional soccer chairman of the National High School Athletic Coaches Association, in addition to being his school's athletic director for 20 years.

**John McVicar.** Winner of five state titles in Connecticut, Coach McVicar has led the Rocky Hill Terriers to close to 300 wins during his almost 30 years with the school. One of the highlights of his career occurred in 1980, when his team was ranked number one in the state for the second consecutive year and earned a 32-game win streak. In addition to receiving several state and national awards, including the NHSACA/Wilson Coach of the Year award in 1981, Coach McVicar served as both president and chairman of the soccer committee of the Charter Oak Conference.

**Charles Sharos.** Coach Sharos has won close to 250 games during his 31 years with South Windsor High School in Connecticut. He has also won one state title and has been runner-up to the state champs three times. Coach Sharos has been Coach of the Year in both soccer and basketball and has won several service and sportsmanship awards. Coach Sharos has been president of the Connecticut High School Coaches Association and has served that organization for 13 years. He was inducted into the Connecticut High School Coaches Association Hall of Fame in 1984.

# COLLEGE SOCCER

## America's Greatest College Men's Soccer Coach

### Bill Jeffrey

Known throughout the land as "Mr. Soccer" during and after his 25 years with Penn State, Coach Jeffrey began his career in 1927 and was instrumental in establishing soccer competition on the college level. Although soccer had been played in America for almost a century, the game was, and still is, overshadowed by other college sports that originated at approximately the same time.

Bill Jeffrey was the sport's most positive influence of his time, maybe to the present day. Recognized as the sport's foremost proponent at home and abroad, Coach Jeffrey took his Nittany Lions overseas on goodwill missions for the State Department. He even traveled to Italy and Germany to teach the sport to U.S. servicemen. In 1950, Coach Jeffrey was selected to coach the American team in the World Cup Games. He accomplished a stunning 1-0 upset victory over England, shocking one member of Parliament into recommending the immediate development of a Ministry of Sports in England.

At home, Coach Jeffrey was leading Penn State to a career record of 154 wins against only 24 losses for a .865 winning percentage. His record included a win streak of 65 games, still the longest in NCAA history. Coach Jeffrey led the Nittany Lions to 13 undefeated seasons, nine of which were consecutive.

Born in Edinburgh, Scotland, Coach Jeffrey came to the United States in 1912 and passed away on January 7, 1966. College soccer's highest coaching honor, the Bill Jeffrey Award, bears his name, and Coach Jeffrey has been inducted into the United States Soccer Federation Hall of Fame.

## Number Two

**Bob Guelker.** An institution in the world of collegiate soccer, Coach Guelker, 20 years after his retirement, still ranks number five on the all-time win list with 312 career victories. Coach Guelker started his career with Southern Illinois/Edwardsville and established a record of over 200 wins and one national championship before transferring to St. Louis University where he recorded what is still the best winning percentage in collegiate soccer. At St. Louis, Guelker won 95, lost only 10, and tied 5, for a percentage of .886. In his 8 years at St. Louis, he took the Billikens into the NCAA tournament each year, winning the national championship five times and coming in once as runner-up. One of the most accomplished of all American soccer coaches, Bob Guelker retired in 1966.

## Number Three

**Jerry Yeagley.** The only soccer coach in history to have played on a high school state championship team and an NCAA national championship team and coached an NCAA titlist, Coach Yeagley has been with Indiana University since 1962, originally as a club coach and since 1973 as the varsity coach. Combining his club and varsity experience, he has compiled a career record of 333-70-25, for a winning percentage of .807. Yeagley is the only two-time winner of the National Coaches Association Division I Coach of the Year award; he also received the prestigious Bill Jeffrey Award.

In 1973, when soccer became a varsity sport at Indiana, Yeagley began a string of 10 consecutive NCAA appearances, more than any other school. The Hoosiers appeared in the championship match six of the last 12 seasons, winning back-to-back titles in 1982 and 1983. Yeagley-coached teams have ruled the Big Ten for 15 seasons, establishing a record of 52-0-1 against conference competition.

Yeagley also has chaired several prominent soccer organizations, including the NCAA Rules Committee. Most important to Coach Yeagley, he has coached 17 All-Americans, two Olympians, and 23 eventual professionals—more than any other college coach. Just as importantly, he has sent 19 former players or assistants into the coaching ranks.

## Number Four

**Joe Morrone.** During his 19 seasons at the helm at the University of Connecticut, Coach Morrone has seen 93% of his athletes earn degrees as a result of his continuing emphasis on academics. Coach Morrone spent the first 11 of his 30 years at Middlebury College and earned a 64-22-11 record. Combined with his distinguished career at Connecticut, he has recorded 325 victories against only 132 losses, making him the fourth-winningest coach in collegiate soccer history.

Morrone has taken the Huskies to the NCAA tournament 14 times, placing in the final four three times and winning the national championship once (1981). He has been involved in a wide range of committee activities, including being past president of the National Soccer Coaches Association of America (NSCAA), founder and past president of the Connecticut Junior Soccer Association and the Mansfield Junior Soccer Association, and past president of the Connecticut State Soccer Association.

Coach Morrone has received numerous New England Coach of the Year awards; he was the recipient of the Big East Conference's first Coach of the Year award. Coach Morrone was inducted into the National Intercollegiate Soccer Officials Association (NISOA) Hall of Fame in 1977.

## Number Five

**Steve Negoesco.** Head soccer coach at the University of San Francisco since 1962, Coach Negoesco is the winningest coach in the history of college soccer. His record of 411-66-43 is the best in the nation, and his winning percentage of .833 is one of the best. During Negoesco's 26-year tenure with the Dons, he has won 14 conference championships and four national titles. Earlier as a student, Negoesco played for San Francisco under the watchful eye of Gus Donoghue and earned the distinction of being the Don's first All-American soccer player. Coach Negoesco has had two undefeated seasons at San Francisco and, on September 6, 1987, when USF beat the University of Wisconsin/Green Bay 5-3, became the first collegiate coach to win 400 games.

## Other Qualifiers

**Don Batie.** With a total career record of 260-92-36, Coach Batie, particularly during his 20-year tenure with the Cal State Wildcats at Chico, has earned one of college soccer's best reputations. He has produced three All-Americans, appeared in the NCAA final four three times, won the Far West/NCAC title 14 times, and developed 22 players who have gone onto play professional soccer. Coach Batie also has been instrumental in introducing soccer to the Chico area, a labor of love that has brought the world's most popular sport to thousands of children in Northern California.

**Joe Bean.** The head coach of the Wheaton Crusaders in Illinois for 20 years, Coach Bean has established a record of 231-90-29, including six NCAA regional titles, nine conference crowns, and one NCAA Division III national championship. Coach Bean also has served as president of NSCAA, chairman of the National Ethics Committee, and editor of *Midwest Soccer News*, and has twice been named College Division Coach of the Year.

**Dr. John C. Brock.** One of the pioneers of collegiate soccer, Coach Brock helped introduce the sport to the United States in 1906 at Springfield College in Massachusetts. He enjoyed college soccer's first two undefeated seasons and posted two national championships.

**Gus Donoghue.** The father of soccer at the University of San Francisco and its head coach for 14 years, Coach Donoghue established a 121-12-11 record and earned a winning percentage of .909, one of the highest in the nation. Coach Donoghue enjoyed eight undefeated seasons with the Dons and won 11-straight conference championships.

**Anson Dorrance.** The head coach of the North Carolina Tar Heels for 12 years, Dorrance has guided his teams to a record of 158-56-20, an accomplishment that earned him Coach of the Year honors several times.

**Harry Keough.** One of the great coaches in the storied history of soccer at St. Louis University, Coach Keough enjoyed a 16-year tenure with the Billikens and posted a record of 213-50-22 for a winning percentage of .786. During his tenure with St. Louis, Coach Keough brought his teams into the NCAA tournament 15 times, winning the title five times.

**Colin Lindores.** Coach Lindores has coordinated the soccer program at Cal State/Hayward for 13 years and has steered the program into national prominence. The Pioneers have captured their league title five times, earned a 121-76-31 record, and appeared in the NCAA play-offs three of the last six years.

**Cliff McCrath.** Known as "Nub" to his players, Coach McCrath is the third-winningest coach in the history of collegiate soccer. Before arriving at Seattle Pacific University 18 years ago, Coach McCrath had guided Wheaton College to a solid reputation in Division III competition. Seattle Pacific had won only four games in the years preceding Nub's arrival. Since he took over as head coach, the Falcons have strung together 17 consecutive winning seasons, a total of 336 career wins for Coach McCrath, 16 appearances in the NCAA tournament (a record), and back-to-back national titles. Coach McCrath numbers among his favorite honors his several Coach of the Year awards and the 24 players he has sent on to professional soccer.

**Bill Shellenberger.** The founder of soccer at Lynchburg College in 1954, Bill Shellenberger has been the Hornets' only coach. During his 35 years of coaching, Shellenberger has earned the second-highest number of wins (364) and has been named Coach of the Year 15 different times by various organizations. Coach Shellenberger's teams have won 33 different championships since 1954, including the NCAA Division III regional crowns and the league title 22 times. Shellenberger has been the president of several collegiate soccer organizations, including the Virginia Intercollegiate Athletic Association and the Mason-Dixon Conference. He has served on the NCAA Rules Committee and the NCAA Selection Committee. Shellenberger was honored in *Sports Illustrated* in 1978 and was inducted into the Bluefield College Hall of Fame in 1986.

**Alfred Smith.** Another pioneer of intercollegiate soccer, Coach Smith succeeded John Brock at Springfield College, where he won the Private and Interacademic League championships 15 times. Coach Smith founded the league and is one of the motive forces behind collegiate soccer in the United States.

**Dr. John Squires.** The Dr. John Y. Squires Award is presented annually at the University of Connecticut to the soccer team's Most Valuable Player. It commemorates the contributions of Coach John Squires, who guided the Huskies' soccer team for 32 years, from 1937 to 1968. During his tenure, Connecticut established a record of 148-140-15, including one appearance in the NCAA final four and a NSCAA national championship in 1948.

**Glenn Warner.** A soccer coaching legend at the U.S. Naval Academy at Annapolis, Coach Warner guided Navy's fortunes for a great many years before his retirement in 1965. At the time of his retirement, his 253 career wins ranked number one in the nation.

## Chapter 7

# SWIMMING

Coaches of all ages are the key elements in America's most successful swimming programs. Their "strokes of genius" have created swimming dynasties across the country. From Bob Kiphuth on the East Coast to George Haines on the West Coast, American coaches have revolutionized the sport and in the process have developed some of the world's greatest swimmers. Their strategies and training techniques have resulted in world records almost from the time the American Indians Flying Gull and Tobacco introduced the "crawl" to the Swimming Society of England in 1844 (Dawson, 1988).

Invited to exhibit their unorthodox swimming style, Flying Gull and Tobacco were described by shocked Londoners as "thrashing the water violently with their arms, like sails of a windmill, and beating downward with their feet, blowing with force and forming grotesque antics." Accustomed to using only the breast stroke with the frog kick in competitions sponsored by the Amateur Swimming Association, British swimmers decided that the windmill stroke was decidedly "un-European" and refused to use it. It wasn't until the late 1800s that J. Arthur Trudgen, during a visit to South America, noticed the increased speed generated by the Indians' overhand stroke. He brought it back to England, combined it with the frog kick, and developed swimmers that chopped the 100-yard competition from 70 seconds to near 60 seconds.

But it was Frederick Cavill, another Englishman, who moved to Australia and watched the South Seas islanders "crawl" and flutter-kick through the water. When he returned from Australia, he taught the stroke to his sons, one of whom swam the 100-yard in 58.6 seconds, a world record and sufficient incentive to convince the British and the rest of the world that the "freestyle" was for real.

By 1920, the freestyle, breast stroke, and back stroke were the primary events in swimming competition, and Johnny Weissmuller of Tarzan fame was the man to beat. He and Duke Kahanamoku of Hawaii were the world's dominant swimmers. The Duke led a cadre of Hawaiians to international recognition during the 1920 Olympics in Antwerp and maintained a Polynesian stranglehold on world competition for years to come. The only man to surpass them was Weissmuller, a world record holder in 67 events and, with the help of his coach, Bill Bachrach, America's most recognized swimmer.

Even Weissmuller's records collapsed under the press of time. Today's women swimmers are surpassing his marks. In fact, the women's record in the 1,500-meter freestyle is lower than the men's mark of only 15 years ago. The gains have been so impressive that a gentleman who preceded Bachrach by almost two centuries would have been amazed at the progress made by today's youngsters. This gentleman, maybe America's *first* swimming coach, loved the sport and was devoted to the creation of water skiing, flippers, and synchronized swimming—but he also found time to coach.

His love of teaching the sport was concerned primarily with freeing non-swimmers "from the slavish terrors many of those feel who cannot swim," and he was among the first to suggest that all Colonial schools have swimming programs. Unlike Plato, who considered nonswimmers uneducated, America's first coach loved the sport for its own sake and assumed that parents would be glad to have their children skilled in swimming, "if it might be learnt in a place chosen for its safety and under the eye of a careful person" (Dawson, 1988). This first of America's "careful persons" and the man recognized by the Swimming Hall of Fame as one of the sport's first coaches? Benjamin Franklin—who else?

A succession of coaches followed him, including Bill Bachrach, who claimed initial credit for Johnny Weissmuller; Stan Brauninger, who mentored backstroker Adolph Kiefer; James "Doc" Counsilman, who won 15 consecutive Big Ten crowns from 1961 to 1976; and Bob Kiphuth, a non-college graduate who earned a full professorship at Yale and who led the 1948 U.S. Olympic team to gold medals in *every* swimming event. They are legends who epitomize the dedication of *all* of America's greatest coaches.

# HIGH SCHOOL SWIMMING

## America's Greatest High School Boys' Swimming Coach

### Dave Robertson

The dean of swimming in Illinois when the state was the geographical center of high school swimming in the country, Coach Robertson devoted 30 years of his life to the swimming program at New Trier High School, Winnetka. An additional 10 were spent at Waubonsie Valley High School in Aurora, Illinois. During Coach Robertson's 40 years of high school coaching, he earned an unprecedented 475 victories and 14 state titles and was responsible for the development of 205 high school All-Americans.

In addition to his coaching responsibilities, Robertson managed to find time to serve as both secretary/treasurer and president of the National Interscholastic Swimming Coaches Association (NISCA), Chairman of the National Federation Rules Committee, and member of the United States Swimming (USS) board of directors. But Coach Robertson is perhaps best remembered for developing interval training and promoting the teaching of swimming in stations (1954). He also was the founder of the Illinois Swimming Coaches Association, the Illinois Officials Organization, and the Illinois Diving Clinic. A speaker at numerous clinics and a recent retiree, Coach Robertson is one of the most respected men in his profession.

## Number Two

**Dick Hannula.** Few coaches achieve the remarkable successes of Coach Hannula. He started his career at Lincoln High School in Tacoma, Washington, where his teams won seven league and two state championships. He then transferred to Wilson High School in Tacoma, where he proceeded to win 24 consecutive state titles, amassing a string of 323 consecutive dual meet victories, the longest in high school history. Coach Hannula was not without a title in 32 years of coaching.

Coach Hannula has won the Washington Coaches Association Coach of the Year award several times, the Outstanding Service Award of the National and International Swim Coaches Association, a commendation from the Washington State Senate, and the Olympic Gold Medal Award from the American Swim Coaches Association. Coach Hannula also has found time to serve as president of the American Swim Coaches Association, president of the Washington Interscholastic Swim Coaches Association, and president of the Pacific Northwest Association/AAU.

Coach Hannula was selected as the NHSACA Coach of the Year in 1980 and was inducted into the International Swimming Hall of Fame in 1988.

## Number Three

**Al Neuschaefer.** Enshrined in the International Swimming Hall of Fame in 1967, Coach Neuschaefer was literally one of a kind. Originally a football coach and a professional football player for the team that was to become the New York Giants, he coached high school swimming for 27 years and established Trenton, New Jersey, as the focus of high school swimming in the U.S. During his tenure at Trenton, Coach Neuschaefer's teams won 19 state titles and 17 Eastern Interscholastic Championships when that meet was the equivalent of the High School Nationals. In spite of such unparalleled coaching success, Coach Neuschaefer listed as perhaps his greatest accomplishment the year 1942, when former swimmers at Trenton captained the Cornell, Dartmouth, and Princeton swim teams.

In addition to administrating several high school swimming organizations, Coach Neuschaefer acted as the principal liaison with the College Coaches Association for many years, served as secretary/treasurer of NISCA for 26 years, and was a member of the board of directors of the Swimming Hall of Fame. Coach Neuschaefer also served as the commissioner and vice president of the New Jersey AAU.

## Number Four

**Bob Mowerson.** With a brief stint with the 32nd Infantry Division during World War II, Coach Mowerson spent 16 years with Battle Creek Central High School in Michigan and established one of the finest reputations in the history of high school swimming. Himself a swimmer for three NCAA team champions at Michigan under Matt Mann, Coach Mowerson enjoyed the honor for most of his high school coaching career of heading up the number one high school program in the country.

Coach Mowerson went on to coach at Minnesota and Michigan State and to be the director of the U.S. Olympic trials in 1972 and 1980 as well as the chairman of the NCAA Rules Committee. Coach Mowerson has been inducted into the Minnesota Swimming Hall of Fame, the University of Minnesota Hall of Fame, and the NISCA Hall of Fame, and he received the U.S. National and Interscholastic Swimming Trophy in 1973.

## Number Five

**Don Watson.** With a dual meet record of 164-3 and 12 consecutive state championships in Illinois, Coach Watson clearly is among the nation's best. During his 16 years at Hinsdale Central High School, he won the national high school championship and developed four world record holders, two members of the U.S. Olympic team, 58 individual state champions, and 167 high school All-Americans. Coach Watson has been Coach of the Year several times, a member of the U.S. Olympic Committee, and a member of the board of directors of the American Swimming Coaches Association. Coach Watson currently is the director of the University of Texas swim center.

## Other Qualifiers

**Steve Borowski.** Punahou High School in Honolulu, Hawaii, has established itself since the mid-fifties as one of the nation's high school powerhouses in several sports, including tennis, track, and swimming. It has established a remarkable string of state championships in both boys' and girls' tennis and boys' and girls' swimming. In fact, Punahou holds the national record for consecutive state titles, at 26, and Coach Steve Borowski has been instrumental in much of that record. He is the winningest coach in the Aloha State's history and has established a high school record that is unlikely to be repeated.

**Richard Bower.** Coach Bower began his career in 1952 at Jamestown High School in New York and, five schools later, concluded it at St. Martin's in Metairie, Louisiana. During that time, Coach Bower's teams won 209 times, including six district and three state titles. Coach Bower also has chaired numerous committees; lectured in Mexico, in South America, and at AAU swimming clinics; served as president of his state's swimming organization; and been nominated by the USOC to be the U.S. Olympic coach for 1972. Bower has written scores of articles on swimming and was selected as the 1982 NHSACA Coach of the Year.

**William Burton.** The head coach at Evanston High School in Illinois for 31 years, Coach Burton established a record of 348-36, including 18 league and five state championships. In a state noted for its outstanding swimming programs, the Evanston Wildkits also finished second 10 times and third 8 times in state swimming competition. Coach Burton was named Coach of the Year in Illinois twice and was elected the NHSACA Coach of the Year in 1978.

**Richard Draz.** The winner of the NHSACA Coach of the Year award in 1986, Coach Draz has taken William C. Crawford High School in San Diego to the sectional championship five times, winning 15 league titles along the way. During his 24 years at Crawford, he has taken his team to 287 wins, including 16 first-place finishes in invitational tournaments. Coach Draz has been elected Coach of the Year five times by different organizations and has coached three high school All-Americans. He also has served as a delegate or representative to several state and national swimming organizations.

**Maurice Ervin.** As head coach at Littleton High School in Colorado for 20 years, Coach Ervin has established an enviable record of 220 wins, including seven state championships. Selected as the NHSACA Coach of the Year in 1988, Coach Ervin also has finished third in the state once and fourth once. He has been Colorado Coach of the Year seven times and has been a speaker at many state and professional clinics, including the NHSACA Convention in 1985.

**James Funiciello.** With almost 30 years of head coaching experience, Coach Funiciello has won over 300 career victories, including, at this writing, 11 New York State Section Three championships. His teams at Liverpool High School have been selected by the New York State Sportswriters Association as the best team in the state six times, and Coach Funiciello was selected to be the NHSACA Coach of the Year in 1979. Funiciello also has been chairman of the district AAU program, the New York State Empire Games, and the Section III Athletic Council.

**Glenn Kaye.** The NHSACA Coach of the Year in 1985, Coach Kaye has spent his entire 19-year coaching career at Nova High School in Ft.

Lauderdale, Florida, winning over 300 meets, including 16 district titles and six state championships. Coach Kaye's teams also have been runners-up to the state champs six times, winning some kind of championship every year of his coaching tenure. Kaye has been chairman of his state athletic organization, chairman of the national swimming organization, and member of the Swimming Rules Committee of the National Federation of State High School Associations. Coach Kaye was Florida Coach of the Year four times and has coached more than 70 All-Americans.

**Layne Kopischka.** The dominant force in swimming in Wyoming for the past several years, Laramie High School has recorded under Coach Kopischka's tenure well over 300 career victories, including 10 regional titles and eight state championships. Coach Kopischka has won a title every year of his 20-year career and has twice served as president of the Wyoming Swimming Coaches Association. He has also served as his state's representative to the National Interscholastic Swim Coaches Association and vice chairman of swimming for the NHSACA. Coach Kopischka was selected for NHSACA Coach of the Year honors in 1984.

**Terence Lowe.** As head coach at Greenwich High School for almost 20 years, Coach Lowe has earned close to 300 career victories, including 13 state championships. He has been Connecticut's Swim Coach of the Year twice and in 1983 was selected as the NHSACA Coach of the Year. In addition to his coaching accomplishments, Coach Lowe has served as president of his state's high school swimming organization and helped coordinate state meets and award banquets. During his tenure at Greenwich, Coach Lowe developed almost 50 high school All-Americans.

**Charles Schlegel.** As of 1981, with 25 years' coaching experience at Plainview High School in New York, Coach Schlegel had earned a career record of 345-26, with 18 regional championships and Long Island Coach of the Year honors 18 times. Coach Schlegel was president of his district's coaching association for 10 years and served on the program committee for the Hall of Fame of the American Swimming Coaches Association. He also was a member of the rules committee of the National Interscholastic Swim Coaches Association and was the chairman of the Empire State Games for 2 consecutive years. Coach Schlegel was selected NHSACA Coach of the Year in 1981.

# COLLEGE SWIMMING

## America's Greatest College Men's Swimming Coach

**Bob Kiphuth**

Although he became a full professor at Yale in 1950, after 32 years of service to the school, Coach Bob Kiphuth never graduated from college. His genius as a teacher was inborn, the result of an uncompromising drive toward individual perfection. During his 42 years at Yale, he compiled a win/loss record of 528-12, including 30 Eastern Intercollegiate titles, was five times the U.S. Olympic coach, and won 14 NAAU team championships. His record is unparalleled in the history of swimming and includes four NCAA team titles.

Coach Kiphuth was primarily responsible for adding dryland exercise and cross-country running to his conditioning regimen, and he included most of his coaching principles in his several books and many articles on the subject. Coach Kiphuth also was the first editor and publisher of *Swimming World* magazine.

Dedicated to swimming, Coach Kiphuth was the charter vice president of the International Swimming Hall of Fame and a director of the Boys Clubs of America, the National Art Museum of Sports, and the President's Fitness Council, as well as being the national swim chairman of the AAU. Along with many fellowships and coaching awards, Kiphuth was awarded the Presidential Medal of Freedom in 1963, this country's highest civilian peacetime honor.

Coach Bob Kiphuth was inducted into the International Swimming Hall of Fame in 1965 and died at the age of 76 in 1967.

## Number Two

**Mike Peppe.** Coach Peppe was Ohio State's first swimming coach and led the Buckeyes to 33 major titles in 33 years. With 11 NCAA team titles, he is the winningest coach in swimming history. His dual meet record was 173-37, with 12 Big Ten titles and 10 NAAU championships. Equally renowned as a diving coach, Peppe's charges at one time won 96 of a possible 125 national titles, including nine Olympic medals in four consecutive Olympics. In 1947 and again in 1956, Coach Peppe's divers finished 1-2-3-4 in the NCAA finals.

Peppe's greatness is most evident in the fact that during much of his tenure at Ohio State, 19 of the 92 members of four different Olympic teams were from Ohio State. On the '52 team alone 9 of the 25 members were Buckeyes. Coach Mike Peppe was inducted into the International Swimming Hall of Fame in 1966.

## Number Three

**James "Doc" Counsilman.** Three years after being inducted into the International Swimming Hall of Fame in 1976, "Doc" Counsilman, at the age of 58, became the oldest man to swim the English Channel. The former captain and NCAA champion at Ohio State, Coach Counsilman instilled in his swimmers his own relentless drive for personal excellence. The result was 20 consecutive Big Ten championships at the University of Indiana and six NCAA team titles, all consecutive.

Counsilman also won five AAU team titles and led the U.S. team to gold medals in the 1964 and 1976 Olympics. His coaching personally accounted for 21 Olympic gold medals and 52 world records. He numbers among his greatest swimmers Mike Troy, Charlie Hickcox, Chet Jastremski, Gary Hall, Frank McKinney, Mike Stamm, Jim Montgomery, John Kinsella, and Mark Spitz, the winner of seven gold medals in the 1972 Olympics.

Counsilman was president of the American Swimming Coaches Association and founding president of the International Swimming Hall of Fame. He also is the author of *The Science of Swimming*, the definitive work on competitive swimming.

## Number Four

**Matt Mann.** The International Hall of Fame, which inducted him in 1965, credits Coach Mann with 13 NCAA team titles. Bob Kiphuth's predecessor at Yale, Coach Mann went on to become Michigan's first swimming coach and remained there for 30 years, compiling one of swimming's greatest records and retiring from the Wolverine helm at the age of 70. In addition to his 13 NCAA titles, 8 of which were consecutive, Coach Mann led the 1952 U.S. team to an Olympic gold medal.

After he retired from Michigan, Coach Mann assumed the head job at Oklahoma, where he never lost a Big Eight swimming meet. He died at the age of 77, after a full day beside the swimming pool, a devout believer that "a coach is a coach, no matter what the sport." After his death, Fritz Crisler, famed Michigan athletic director, said, "Mann is the greatest coach who ever lived."

## Number Five

**Peter Daland.** Coach Daland was an assistant to Bob Kiphuth at Yale before assuming the reins of the USC Trojans in 1956, and he returned to Yale two years later for a meet in which he would win the NAAU team title with five USC freshmen. During his 20 years with the Trojans, Daland's teams won nine NCAA team titles in addition to the 14 NAAU titles he won as the coach of the Los Angeles Athletic Club.

Under Daland, USC won more than 160 dual meets, with 183 individual national champions. Daland was elected into the International Swimming Hall of Fame in 1977, having received two years earlier the 1975 AAU Swimming Award followed by the 1976 National Collegiate and Scholastic Swimming Trophy.

## Other Qualifiers

**Dave Armbruster.** The driving force behind the butterfly stroke's inclusion in national and international swimming competition, Coach Armbruster is the author of *Swimming and Diving*, one of history's most authoritative textbooks on competitive swimming. Armbruster coached the Hawkeyes for 30 years and in 1938 was president of the College Coaches Association when Ft. Lauderdale became the site of interest for the Swimming Hall of Fame.

In addition to his enviable coaching career, Armbruster is recognized by authorities in the sport as the critical link between coaching and teaching. He encouraged extensive research in the sport and taught such future greats as Doc Counsilman, Don Watson, and Mexican Olympic coach Ron Johnson. Coach Armbruster is a pioneer of American swimming.

**Fred Cady.** A former circus strongman and gymnast, Coach Cady was widely renowned for his waxed mustache and his production of national and Olympic champions. As swimming coach at the University of Southern California for 33 years, Coach Cady produced such Olympic champions as Dutch Smith, Mickey Riley, Paul Wolff, and Buster Crabbe. Equally renowned as a diving coach, Cady's charges at one time held every U.S. and world diving championship. Cady was inducted into the International Swimming Hall of Fame in 1969.

**Don Gambril.** The mentor of such current coaching greats as Skip Kenney at Stanford, Dick Jochums at Arizona, and Ron Ballatore at UCLA, Coach Gambril has had an influence on swimming that extends far beyond national championships. Gambril coached at Pasadena City College, Long Beach State University, Harvard, and the University of Alabama. During that time, his swimmers produced 20 world records, 10 Olympic gold medals, four NAAU team championships, one NCAA college division title, and a record of 178-22 in dual meet competition. In addition, Coach Gambril developed 114 All-Americans.

Widely respected for his ability to work with other coaches and athletes, Coach Gambril was the assistant U.S. Olympic coach in '68, '72, '76, and '80. He was head coach of the U.S. Olympic team in 1984 and still found time to serve as a member of the USOC, the AAU swim committees, the USS Board of Directors, and the NCAA Rules Committee. Coach Gambril was inducted into the International Swimming Hall of Fame in 1983.

**Skip Kenney.** "We are continuing our drive to make Stanford the most consistent swimming program in the country," said Coach Kenney when he assumed the reins as head coach at Stanford. He proceeded to transform the 15th place team into a contender for the national championship, which he won three straight years, 1985-1987. His Stanford Cardinals have won seven straight PAC-10 titles and have finished in the top four in the nation every year since 1982. In addition, Coach Kenney has produced four consecutive unbeaten dual meet seasons and 31 NCAA champions.

NCAA Coach of the Year twice and the PAC-10 Coach of the Year four times, Coach Kenney has been the assistant Olympic coach twice and the head coach of the Pan Am Games once, leading the latter team to 27 of a possible 32 gold medals in the summer of 1987. The head coach at Stanford for only 10 years, Coach Kenney is one of the finest young coaches in U.S. swimming.

**Ernie Maglischo.** Coach Maglischo has been a swimming coach at seven different schools during his 28-year career and currently is with Cal State Bakersfield with a total college record of 125-45. His teams have won seven NCAA Division II or Division III national championships and 14 conference championships at three different schools; he is the only coach in NCAA history with this record. For his accomplishments, Coach Maglischo has been named Coach of the Year eight different times and recently was presented with the Honor Award from the Aquatics Council of the AAHPERD.

Coach Maglischo has authored three textbooks and several articles for professional journals and has lectured on competitive swimming on 46 different occasions in 17 states and 12 countries. In addition, he has served on the Sports Medical Council of U.S. Swimming, on the U.S. Olympic Committee, and on the NCAA Swimming Rules Committee.

**Phil Moriarity.** Succeeding the legendary Bob Kiphuth at Yale in 1959, Coach Moriarity had worked with Kiphuth for 22 years before taking the reins at Yale. As head coach, he developed such swimming stars as Steve Clark, John Nelson, and Don Schollander. Moriarity's record was 195-25, including nine Eastern Seaboard Conference championships and 10 Eastern Intercollegiate titles, and he was named NCAA Division I Coach of the Year. Moriarity also was presented the Fred A. Cady Award and the 1978 Collegiate and Scholastic Award.

In addition to authoring two books on diving and swimming, Coach Moriarity chaired the NCAA Rules Committee and the NAAU Records Committee and designed the backstroke starting block that bears his name.

**Tom Robinson.** As head swimming coach at Northwestern University for 35 years, Coach Robinson preferred the title "teacher" to "coach" because of his reputation for having taught more than 50,000 people in the Evanston, Illinois, area how to swim. Robinson also deserves the honor of being among the top two or three first great collegiate coaches. He started at Northwestern in 1909 and led the Wildcats to 10 Big Ten championships and six NCAA championships.

Coach Robinson invented water basketball, led his team to three Big Ten championships in that sport before it was discontinued in favor of water polo. He then led his team to seven water polo titles. Coach Robinson also pioneered the development of the crawl stroke in the early 1900s. He was inducted into the International Swimming Hall of Fame in 1974.

**Gus Stager.** Having won the mythical national championship once and the state title three times at Dearborn High School in Michigan, Coach

Stager accepted the head job at the University of Michigan, where he had been a three-time NCAA finalist under the legendary Matt Mann. Although he had been advised against following in the footsteps of a legend, Coach Stager proceeded to place first or second in the Big Ten 23 times and to win four NCAA team titles.

Coach Stager also paced the 1960 U.S. Olympic team to a gold medal, the 1967 Pan Am team to a gold, and the 1973 U.S. team to the World Championships. Inducted into the International Hall of Fame in 1982, Stager also is credited with effecting the rule change involving the no-touch turn.

**Jim Steen.** Jim Steen of Kenyon College is the coach with the greatest number of NCAA team titles in history, and he won them in the shortest amount of time—16 men's and women's titles in 10 years, including four consecutive *dual* titles, an unparalleled accomplishment in coaching. During his 14 years at Kenyon, Coach Steen has produced 74 male swimmers who account for 545 All-American honors. He has also coached 50 women who have earned 385 All-American awards. For his accomplishments, Coach Steen was selected as the NCAA Division III Coach of the Year eight times and twice received the American Swimming Coach's Association Award of Excellence.

Although he has won 10 NCAA team titles in 10 years, Coach Steen is equally proud of the fact that his swimmers rank among the best in the country for winning academic and postgraduate scholarship awards.

**Nort Thornton.** One of the sport world's finest examples of a coach "making a difference," Coach Thornton became the head swimming coach at the University of California in 1974 and immediately transformed an unknown team into the fourteenth-place finisher in the NCAAs that year. Since 1977, Coach Thornton's teams have recorded 11 consecutive top-10 finishes, winning the NCAA team title in 1979 and 1980.

Coach Thornton has been named Coach of the Year three times and lists among his swimmers Graham Smith, Peter Szmidt, and 1988 Olympic sensation Matt Biondi. He is the former president of the American Swimming Coaches Association and a member of the NCAA Rules Committee.

**Randy Reese.** One of only three coaches in history to win NCAA team titles in both men's and women's swimming, Coach Reese won NCAA men's titles in 1983 and 1984 at the University of Florida. One of the swimming world's most creative coaches, Reese has had his swimmers work upstream in a nearby river, do pool workouts fully clothed, and crawl up the football field entrance ramps on their hands with wheels attached to their heels. Although Coach Reese's conditioning techniques at first were unusual, they have been copied by coaches across the country. They work.

Coach Reese's teams have also won seven SEC titles and 200 All-America honors, and they have twice earned Reese recognition as Coach of the Year. Reese's swimmers include Mike Heath, David Larson, and Olympic star Tracy Caulkins. Reese is the author of several professional articles and two books, his most recent being *Building a Championship Season with Randy Reese*.

## CLUB SWIMMING

Because many of these coaches duplicated the efforts of the top college coaches and because their records are so similar, they are presented only in alphabetical order.

**Bill Bachrach.** Bill Bachrach coached the winner of every swimming and diving event in the men's NAAU championships in 1914, so it was not for his weight being well over 300 pounds that he was considered the "heavyweight" of club coaches. As coach of the Illinois Athletic Club, Bachrach enjoys the distinction of having developed perhaps the world's greatest swimmer, Johnny Weissmuller. He also worked with Stubby Kruger, Norm Ross, Sybil Bauer, and Ethel Lackie, among others. In fact, "Bach's" swimmers accounted for 120 NAAU individual championships and two winning efforts in the Olympics.

**Paul Bergen.** The coach of the Cincinnati Pepsi Marlins for three years and once the U.S. Olympic team coach, Bergen has worked with such accomplished swimmers as Nick Nevid, Bill Schulte, Tracy Caulkins, and Kim Linehan. His swimmers have held 10 world records and won seven World Championship titles and four Olympic gold medals.

**Stan Brauninger.** The head man of the Chicago Lake Shore Athletic Club and the Medinah Towers Club in the '20s, '30s, and '40s, Coach Brauninger developed such swimming standouts as Wally Laufer, Jack Glancy, Wally Colbath (the first Jack Armstrong on radio), and Adolph "Sonny" Kiefer, the man who at one time held every backstroke record in the book. His teams won the NAAU championship six times and were runners-up on at least nine other occasions.

**Sherm Chavoor.** As owner of the Arden Hills Swimming and Tennis Club in California, Coach Chavoor developed swimmers who claimed 83 world records and 131 American records and, in 1968 an 1972, garnered 21 Olympic medals, including 16 gold. The ASCA Coach of the Year in 1968, Chavoor worked with such standouts as Mike Burton, Mark Spitz, and Debbie Meyer. Spitz and Meyer were both winners of the Sullivan Award, America's highest award for an amateur athlete.

**Ray Daughters.** The great coach of the Washington Athletic Club, Daughters helped develop Hall of Famers Helene Madison and Jack Medica and Olympic champions Marylou Petty, Olive McKean, and Nancy Ramey. During the '30s, and '40s, his swimmers accounted for 30 world records, 301 American records, and 64 national championships. Coach Daughters also served as chairman of the Men's AAU Swimming Committee and the United States Men's Olympic Swimming Committee.

**George Haines.** As coach of the Santa Clara Swim Club for 25 years, Coach Haines won 35 NAAU team championships—26 women's and 9 men's—and produced hundreds of national champions, including Steve Clark, Claudia Kolb, Don Schollander, and Donna deVarona. Coach of the Year more than any other person, Haines also coached both the men's and women's Olympic teams and was the recipient of the National Collegiate and Scholastic Swimming Trophy as well as the 1965 AAU Swimming Award. Haines was inducted into the International Swimming Hall of Fame in 1977.

**Soichi Sakamoto.** The man behind the modern swimming success in Hawaii, Coach Sakamoto developed such swimming greats as Tenabe, Woolsey, Konno, and Nakama, many of whom went on to swim for Ohio State and Indiana universities. Starting his swimmers in a nearby irrigation ditch, Sakamoto developed scores of world champions and emphasized his philosophy in these simple words: "The light of success comes only when everything seems hopeless and wasted." Coach Sakamoto was inducted into the International Swimming Hall of Fame in 1966.

**Walt Schlueter.** Coaching at the Chicago Town Club in 1950 and the Multnomah Athletic Club in 1961, Coach Schlueter produced swimmers on every Olympic team from 1948 through 1972. He was most noted for developing the perfect strokes of Don Schollander and Marilyn Ramenofsky, coaching coaches, and originating dozens of stroke drills.

**Mark Schubert.** Coach Schubert's Mission Viejo Nadadores Swim Club of the '70s and '80s was the largest competitive swimming team of its kind in the United States. It accounted for 44 national team titles, 124 individual national champions, more than 125 All-Americans, and 17 Olympic medals, 10 of them gold. Schubert was the coach of the 1984 Olympic team and the national team coach several times. He was voted Coach of the Year three times by the American Swimming Coaches

Association and has helped develop major swimming talents like Brian Goodell, Tiffany Cohen, Shirley Babashoff, Jesse Vassallo, and Mary T. Meagher. He has spoken at scores of clinics, was on the board of directors of the American Swimming Coaches Association, and was senior chairman of Southern California Swimming.

# Chapter 8

# TENNIS

Sometimes obscured by the imposing shadow of America's "Big Three," tennis is itself among the world's oldest and most popular sports and enjoys favor in America for its participant as well as its spectator appeal. Maybe its appeal has something to do with our fascination for "centre" court at Wimbledon; maybe it relates to the fashionable cleanliness of modern tennis outfits. Or more likely, maybe it has much to do with a one-to-one challenge that requires fine-tuned conditioning and both finesse and power. Whatever the reasons, tennis in the United States has become a stage for some of the sports world's most stunning athletic and coaching performances.

Like most other sports in this book, tennis existed as a recreational sport long before coaches introduced refined technique and strategy. In fact, there is some evidence that a form of the sport existed around 500 B.C. Generally, however, tennis as we know it was most popular in the "courts" of French and English monarchs during the 15th and 16th centuries. In fact, commoners were forbidden to play it.

Not so in America. Citizens of this country as early as 1659 flocked to the courts with such enthusiasm that Governor Peter Stuyvesant of New Netherland issued a proclamation on September 30 of that year forbidding play during church services (Carruth and Ehrlich, 1988). A concern of American clerics to this day, Sunday tennis remains the passion of millions of people, particularly in spring when the Wimbledon finals find many of us sharing with English spectators the traditional breakfast of strawberries and champagne.

Interestingly, America's first tournament, which was more a social event than a competition, occurred in 1876, 1 year before the first Wimbledon tournament. It was hosted by F.R. Sears on his home court in Nahant, Massachusetts. Five years later, *Richard* Sears, while a student at Harvard, won history's first U.S. Lawn Tennis Association (USLTA) singles championship. He went on to win the next six consecutive titles and to earn a charter membership in the Collegiate Tennis Hall of Fame, now housed at the University of Georgia.

Sears was the first of many American tennis greats who helped elevate the sport to its current level of popularity. Starting with Dwight Davis, of Davis Cup fame and the NCAA singles and doubles champ in 1899, through early champions like Ellsworth Vines and Bill Tilden, to consensus greats such as Don Budge, Jack Kramer, Pancho Gonzales, Bill Johnston, Bobby Riggs, Stan Smith, Tony Trabert, and Arthur Ashe, to modern greats like Jimmy Connors and Andre Agassi, tennis players gradually have established their positions in the sometimes brutal pecking order of American sports.

At the turn of the century, tennis was regarded as the pastime of women and unathletic men and received the censure of several prominent sportswriters. That effete king of France Louis X purportedly died of a chill after an especially challenging contest didn't do much for the game's reputation, particularly among the redneck sport fans of industrial America. The game persisted, however, thanks to the stubborn dedication of men like Dr. James Dwight, the first president of the USLTA and one of the men credited with introducing the game to America.

During Dr. Dwight's presidency of the USLTA, the first women's singles championship was held at the Philadelphia Cricket Club. The year was 1887 and the title was won by Ellen Hansell. Eight years later, May G. Sutton won the singles title at Wimbledon, the first American to win a singles championship in England. Soon official tennis rules evolved into essentially the rules that hold today and that continue to attract both men and women participants. Starting with Dan Penick at the University of Texas at the turn of the century, tennis also has attracted some of the sport world's greatest coaches.

# HIGH SCHOOL TENNIS

## America's Greatest High School Boys' Tennis Coach

### Jay Kramer

In a state dominated by superior high school tennis, Hinsdale Central leads the way in Illinois, and Coach Jay Kramer is a big reason. During his 28-year tenure at the school, he has been instrumental in 11 of the school's 15 state championships. In 1959, he succeeded Coach Clare Riessen, who had won four state championships and had coached his son, Marty, to four consecutive state singles championships, 1 of only 10 high school players with such an accomplishment.

During his first year at the helm, Kramer was runner-up to the state champs. In four of the next 5 years, his Hinsdale Central teams finished no lower than third in the state. In 1966, he won his first state title and followed up with another 2 years later. In between his two state titles, he finished second in the state. He finished second again in 1971 and then, for the next nine years, put together a string of consecutive state titles. Since then, Hinsdale has been either sectional champ or one of the top five teams in the state.

Coach Kramer has been Coach of the Year at least half a dozen times and in 1985 received the Hall of Fame Award from the Illinois High School

Tennis Coaches Association. He has been responsible for several national rankings for his players and has invested himself in the future of his sport. Coach Kramer was founder of the Illinois High School Tennis Coaches Association, secretary of the AAHPER National Tennis Committee, tennis chairman of the NHSACA, and a speaker at numerous clinics and conferences across the country.

## Number Two

**Robert Wood.** With the number one ranking in the National Federation's *Record Book* for all-time high school wins, University Liggett School in Grosse Pointe, Michigan, stands atop the high school tennis world for most state championships. At last count, they had recorded 25, 13 of those consecutive titles—a national record—under Coach Bob Wood. Coach Wood's teams have won over 400 dual matches, for which he has received Coach of the Year honors several times and the President's Award for outstanding service to Michigan high school tennis.

In addition to his significant coaching accomplishments, Coach Wood was responsible for founding the Michigan High School Tennis Coaches Association, was a founder of the Metro Conference, co-founded the Metro Suburban Soccer League, served as commissioner of the Michigan Independent Athletic Conference, was the tennis chairman for the NHSACA, and has been the featured speaker at several local and national clinics and conferences.

## Number Three

**James Reed.** Winfield High School and Coach James Reed have become legends in the state of Kansas. In addition to at least 14 state titles, Coach Reed has led his teams to well over 400 career victories and the number two ranking for all-time wins in the National Federation of State High School Associations' *Record Book*. Coach Reed has received Coach of the Year honors several times and has served as president of the Winfield Tennis Association and chairman of the Kansas Coaches Association.

An active representative of the sport of tennis, Coach Reed has been ranked number one in the Kansas District Junior Veterans Doubles and third in the Missouri Valley Junior Veterans Doubles. In 1977, he and his son won the championship of the Missouri Valley Father and Son Doubles. Coach Reed's obvious knowledge of the sport is reflected in his published articles as well as in the fact that more than 50 of his former players have received scholarships to play in college.

## Other Qualifiers

**Charles Buckley.** Coach Buckley in his 26 years of coaching won league championships at two different schools, Jennings County and North Central in Indianapolis, and won over 400 matches, including at least seven state championships. For his accomplishments, he has been named Coach of the Year by several different organizations and has enjoyed a winning streak of 116 consecutive matches. *USA Today*, in 1984, ranked North Central the top high school tennis team in the country. Coach Buckley's success is not surprising. With his level of energy he also has found time to serve as a director for the Indiana Tennis Hall of Fame and the All-America Prep Tennis Tournament and as president of the Indiana High School Tennis Coaches Association.

**Tom Campbell.** Nineteen years of coaching at Capital High School in Boise, Idaho, have resulted in more than 500 wins and eight state championships for Coach Campbell. He has been selected Coach of the Year four times, twice by the National High School Athletic Coaches Association, which also identified him as the Wilson Coach of the Year in 1988. Like so many other great coaches, Campbell has found the time to invest himself in his sport beyond the courts. He has twice been president of his state tennis association and twice the president of his state's tennis coaches organization.

**Chuck Morrison.** Coach Morrison is one of only two coaches in the history of high school tennis to have coached his son to four consecutive state singles championships. He has divided his time between two schools, but it was at Deerfield High School in Illinois that he earned most of his 234 career victories—against only 71 defeats. Morrison won 12 titles during his 18 years with the Warriors, including one state championship, three runners-up, and three third-place finishes. With a conference record of 103-17, Morrison's teams are perennial favorites to win the Central Suburban title and to earn additional Coach of the Year honors for Chuck.

**Harley Pierce.** The best information available on Coach Pierce reveals that he has won more than 400 matches and at least seven state championships at Sturgis High School in Michigan. He has won the regional championship a dozen other times and has been selected Michigan High School Coach of the Year. Coach Pierce also coaches football and has been the regional director and vice president of Michigan's football and tennis coaches associations.

**Tom Pitchford.** Coach Pitchford was the backbone of the tennis program at Arlington High School in Illinois for 24 of his 30 years in coaching, and he was dedicated to his sport. Although his teams never won a state championship, he finished almost consistently in the state's top five, even winning 113 conference matches in a row, for which he was recognized by *Sports Illustrated*. Pitchford served as chairman of the Illinois Tennis Advisory Committee and director of the IHSA state meet. He also served on the Originator Committee of the Illinois Tennis Coaches Association. Pitchford was named Coach of the Year many times by the Mid-Suburban League and the Illinois Coaches Association.

---

*Author's note:* During my search for information, I talked to Coach Pitchford several times on the phone to seek his help. A charming, elegant man, Tom had been suffering from cancer for several months, but, although weakened by his condition, was planning to coach again in the spring. While setting his strategy for the coming season, Coach Pitchford died—to the end a man absolutely committed to the values of coaching. His players and the sport of tennis will miss him.

**Martin Shaw.** As head coach at Scarsdale High School in New York for 29 years, Coach Shaw has won well over 300 matches while winning 19 league championships. Although New York has no state championship in tennis, Scarsdale was voted the state's number one team at least four times by the New York Sportswriters Association. Coach Shaw was given Coach of the Year honors five times, once by the NHSACA/Wilson selection committee in 1986. In addition to his coaching responsibilities, Shaw has found time to chair the New York State High School Association and to serve on the board of directors of the United States Tennis Association–Eastern Division.

# COLLEGE TENNIS

## America's Greatest College Men's Tennis Coach

### George Toley

Coach Toley's list of former players reads like a "Who's Who" of tennis champions. Rafael Osuna, Raul Ramirez, Alex Olmedo, Dennis Ralston, Bob Lutz, Stan Smith, and John Newcombe are just a few. Toley is called the "Father of Tennis" in Mexico because of his powerful influence on its development in that country. He had an equally powerful impact on tennis at the University of Southern California, where he coached for 26 years, accumulating a win/loss record of 425-90-4 for a winning percentage of .827, the third highest in NCAA history.

During Toley's 42 years of NCAA tournament competition, his Trojans won the team championship 10 times, more than any other coach. His players have dominated college and professional tennis. They have been selected as tennis All-Americans 70 times and have won a total of 274 national championships, including 27 of the Big Four: Wimbledon, U.S., French, and Australian. They have earned a final berth at Wimbledon 16 times, winning the title six times. They have made the finals of the U.S. championships 26 times, winning 14. They have played 237 Davis

Cup matches, earning a record of 163-74. And they have earned 469 national rankings in the United States.

Mexican Davis Cup captain Pancho Contreras once said, "George Toley is the greatest asset Mexican tennis ever had. He's the greatest tennis coach in the world." Our panel of experts agrees.

---

## Number Two

**Dick Gould.** The mentor of such tennis greats as Sandy Mayer, Tim Mayotte, Roscoe Tanner, and John McEnroe, Coach Dick Gould has devoted 16 years to tennis at Stanford University and has finished either first or second in the NCAA final standings 11 times. Gould-coached teams have won the NCAA team title eight times and have earned a record of 373-94.

Gould graduated from Stanford in 1960 and taught for two years at Mountain View High School. In 1962, he went to Foothill College as head tennis coach, where he won two state championships. He returned to Stanford in 1967 and has experienced nothing but success since then. In 1974, he received the Wilson Coach of the Year award and in 1983 was presented the Educational Merit Award by the United States Tennis Association. He has served in several organizational capacities and has conducted clinics across the country and in Mexico, Japan, China, and Central America.

## Number Three

**Glenn Bassett.** The successor to J.D. Morgan at UCLA and a coach who in 21 years has never had a losing season, Coach Bassett boasts a career record of 450-62-2 for a winning percentage of .877. Under Bassett's leadership, the Bruins have won 11 PAC-10 titles, averaging a 21-3 record per season. In 1950, as a UCLA co-captain, Bassett was a key factor in winning UCLA's first NCAA championship.

Following graduation, he assisted Coach Morgan for several years and assumed the reins in 1967. Since that time, the Bruins have had two undefeated seasons and seven NCAA team championships. Bassett teams also have been runners-up to the national champs five different times and have had UCLA's best season record (19-0 in 1975), longest winning streak (35 in 1975-1976), and most wins in a season (31 in 1985).

Coach Bassett is the author of two books, *Tennis Today* and *Tennis: The Bassett System*.

## Number Four

**J.D. Morgan.** Perhaps America's most successful athletic director, J.D. Morgan devoted 17 years to that job at UCLA, guiding the Bruins to 30 NCAA team titles: 10 in basketball, 7 in volleyball, 6 in tennis, 4 in track and field, and 3 in water polo. It is said of Morgan that "he is as warm, generous, and compassionate as he is relentless in pursuit of his professional goals."

Before assuming the role of AD in 1963, Morgan was relentless in his pursuit of NCAA titles, winning six from 1952 through 1961. Only his impact on intercollegiate athletics as UCLA's athletic director and as a member of the NCAA Executive Committee can overshadow J.D. Morgan's significant success as one of the finest tennis coaches in the nation.

## Number Five

**Jim Verdieck.** The top small-college coach in the country, Coach Verdieck devoted 38 years to the University of Redlands in Southern California. During his tenure there, Coach Verdieck's teams won 15 national championships: 11 NAIA titles, one small-college NCAA championship, and three NCAA Division III crowns. His teams won 34 conference championships and earned a conference win/loss record of 379-15 for a .960 winning percentage.

Coach Verdieck also coached the Redlands football team, including one undefeated team in 1956. Coach Verdieck's career win/loss record of 921-281 makes him the winningest small-college coach and one of the most successful tennis coaches of all time.

## Other Qualifiers

**Jack Barnaby.** The power behind the tennis program at Harvard for 37 years, Coach John M. "Jack" Barnaby guided his teams to a dual match record of 371-158-3 and eight Eastern Intercollegiate Tennis Association titles. His teams also claimed numerous national champions and 14 New England titles. Coach Barnaby served as president of the U.S. Professional Tennis Association.

**Paul Bennett.** Coach Bennett played football for Amos Alonzo Stagg at the University of Chicago before returning home to Canada to win the Canadian singles tennis championship. He returned to the U.S.

to serve as head coach at Northwestern University from 1930 to 1958, coaching the Wildcats to 10 Big Ten titles. Coach Bennett chaired the NCAA Tennis Committee and played a prominent role in developing the NCAA championships, which he hosted several times.

**Clarence Chaffee.** As coach at Williams College for 33 years, Coach Chaffee compiled a record of 175-99-3 and won 40 Little Three Conference titles. He complemented his coaching duties by serving as a member of the NCAA Tennis Committee and as secretary of the New England Lawn Tennis Association for 22 years.

**John Conroy.** Dr. John Conroy led Princeton's tennis fortunes for 27 years, compiling a dual match record of 270-38 and winning or sharing 15 Eastern Conference championships. From 1960-65, his teams enjoyed a string of 52 consecutive dual match victories, within that time ending Miami's 137-match streak. Coach Conroy also found time to serve for 6 years on the NCAA Tennis Committee, to host the NCAAs three times, and to author the series *Tennis Workbooks*.

**Tom Fallon.** Proving that the University of Notre Dame Fighting Irish can win on the courts as well as the gridiron, Coach Tom Fallon, during his 31-year tenure with them, earned a career record of 517-200, including an NCAA title in 1959. His tennis record is particularly noteworthy in light of his additional responsibility at Notre Dame as head wrestling coach for 15 years.

**Allen Fox.** Fox was a member of UCLA's NCAA championship teams in 1960 and 1961, winning the NCAA singles title in 1961; in 1978 he became the head coach at Pepperdine University in Malibu, California. Since that time, the Waves have never finished lower than seventh place nationally, earning runner-up honors to Stanford in 1986. A Ph.D. in psychology, Coach Fox not only has led Pepperdine to a record of 245-68 but has earned a national reputation in sport psychology.

**Harry James.** Harry James coached the University of Utah Utes for 26 years, compiling a career record of 367-188 and winning the WAC team title 11 times. In addition to his coaching responsibilities, James hosted the NCAA championships in Utah in 1970, served as president of the Intercollegiate Tennis Coaches Association (ITCA), and presided over the Intermountain and Utah Tennis Associations. He was inducted into the Collegiate Tennis Hall of Fame in 1987.

**John Kenfield.** Coach Kenfield coached at the University of North Carolina for 27 years, earning the remarkable dual match record of 424-29 and dominating the new Atlantic Coast Conference for his last two years.

Nine of Coach Kenfield's teams were undefeated, led by such tennis standouts as Wilmer Hines and Vic Seixas. Coach Kenfield was inducted into the Collegiate Tennis Hall of Fame in 1986.

**Dick Leach.** Coach Leach has been with the Southern Cal Trojans for 8 years and has never finished lower than third in the PAC-10. He won the conference championship three times, most recently in 1987 when he lost the NCAA semifinals to the eventual champion, Georgia, ending the year at 32-1. His overall coaching record at Southern Cal is 232-41 for a winning percentage of .850, one of the best in the country.

**James Leighton.** Coach Leighton coached at Presbyterian College for 12 years, leading them to national recognition and, in 1957, an upset victory over Miami that snapped the 'Canes winning streak at 72. Coach Leighton later moved to Wake Forest. His career record was 422-226-2.

**Dale Lewis.** While at the University of Indiana from 1949 to 1957, Coach Lewis earned a dual match record of 133-17, including three Big Ten titles. He moved to the University of Miami in 1958 and for the next 22 years compiled a record of 364-35, including a winning streak of 137 straight dual match victories and 19 finishes in the NCAA top-10 in 22 years, finishing second in 1965 and 1975. Coach Lewis also found time to preside over the ITCA and to chair the NCAA Tennis Committee. Coach Lewis was inducted into the Collegiate Tennis Hall of Fame in 1985.

**William Lufler.** A head coach for only 13 years, Coach Lufler began his career with Presbyterian College in 1937 and moved to the University of Miami in 1949. At Miami he compiled a dual match record of 148-2-1, with winning streaks of 57 and 72 consecutive matches. Lufler was instrumental in the establishment of tennis in Sweden and was inducted into the Collegiate Tennis Hall of Fame in 1985.

**Clarence Mabry.** Coach Mabry initiated Trinity University's tennis program in 1956 and during his 19-year tenure there led them to a dual match record of 310-36, including two runners-up to the NCAA champs in 1970 and 1971. The following year, with such stars as Dick Stockton, Brian Gottfried, Paul Gerken, and Bobby McKinley, Coach Mabry led Trinity to the NCAA team title. Coach Mabry was a chair of the NCAA Tennis Committee and was inducted into the Collegiate Hall of Fame in 1986.

**Dan McGill.** Recently retired as coach of the University of Georgia, Coach McGill took the Bulldogs to two NCAA championships, breaking what had been a California stranglehold since 1972. Coach McGill also hosted the NCAA finals for the last 11 years and serves as the director

**William Murphy.** While with the University of Michigan, Coach Murphy compiled a dual match record of 198-45 and in a 20-year period won 11 Big Ten team titles. The Wolverines also set a Big Ten record of 47 consecutive dual match victories under Coach Murphy. In 1957, Coach Murphy's Michigan team won the NCAA team title, led by singles champ Barry McKay. In 1973, Coach Murphy moved to the University of Arizona, where he compiled a record of 99-44 and three WAC team titles. Coach Murphy also chaired the NCAA Tennis Committee and served as president of the Intercollegiate Tennis Coaches Association.

**Emmett Pare.** As tennis coach at Tulane for 40 years, Coach Pare won 20 Southeastern conference team titles and tied Notre Dame for the national championship in 1959. He coached at least six All-Americans, including such Hall of Famers as Ernie Sutter and Jose Aguero. Coach Pare has been voted into the Sugar Bowl Hall of Fame and in 1983 was inducted into the Collegiate Tennis Hall of Fame.

**Daniel Penick.** With the philosophy that "you will never control a tennis ball until you learn to control yourself," Coach Penick guided the tennis fortunes at the University of Texas for almost half a century. By conservative estimates, Dr. Penick touched the lives of almost 10,000 students during his tenure with Texas, where his tennis teams won all 10 Southwest Conference championships played during his tenure. His players also won 27 of the 41 singles crowns and 31 of the 41 doubles titles. "Mr. Tennis" initiated the tennis program at Texas in 1908. He died in 1964, having lived his philosophy: "If I have been able to help anyone to be a better man, that is the best reward."

**William Potter.** During Coach Potter's 25 years at the University of Florida, his teams compiled a win/loss record of 388-107-1. They won the Southeast Conference team title four times, and Coach Potter earned Coach of the Year honors five times. He was inducted into the Collegiate Tennis Hall of Fame in 1987.

**Dennis Ralston.** Since the 1981 season at Southern Methodist University, when they finished second in the SWC and 11th in the NCAA, Coach Ralston's Mustangs have won the conference title five times and have finished no lower than sixth in the NCAA, being runners-up to Stanford in 1983. His success is not surprising. As a player, Ralston won 27 national championships, including the NCAA singles and doubles twice and the U.S. Open doubles three times. Coach Ralston was named Coach of the Year in 1983 by the NCAA and in 1987 was inducted into the International Tennis Hall of Fame.

# Chapter 9

# TRACK AND FIELD

If soccer is the world's most popular sport, track and field is the oldest, and *among* the most popular—at least every 4 years when the Olympic finals of the 100- and 200-meter dashes capture the world's attention. At the time of the first ancient Olympic games—by tradition 776 B.C. when Coroebus of Elis won the great foot race—the dashes, or "stades" as the Greeks called them, were the central events in track competition. They still take center stage but now must share the spotlight with distance and field events, which have been revolutionized by medical science and coaching technique.

From the time of America's first track meet in Saratoga, New York, on July 20, 1876, coaching has been increasingly significant in athletes' performance. Consider that first track meet. J.W. Pryor of Columbia University won the high jump with a height of 5 feet 4 inches, an effort representative of most athletes of the time. One hundred years later, with increased knowledge of the mechanics of the event and improved coaching techniques, Franklin Jacobs from Fairleigh Dickinson won the high jump with an effort of 7 feet 7-1/4 inches. Jacobs was only 5 feet 8 inches tall.

Similar athletic milestones have been reached since that July afternoon in 1876. On October 11, 1890, John Owens, in an AAU meet in Washington DC, became the first person to win the 100-yard dash in under 10 seconds. He ran it in 9.8. Almost 50 years later, on May 25, 1935, at a track meet at the University of Michigan, *Jesse* Owens (no relation to John) established or tied four world records in one day, winning the 100-yard dash, 220-yard dash, long jump, and the low hurdles.

A natural athlete (Owens ran the 100-yard dash in 10 seconds flat while still in junior high school), Jesse received superior coaching at Ohio State University and benefited from a gradual evolution of technique and knowledge that had started in the '30s and '40s. Before that time, coaches conditioned and "practiced" their athletes without the applied knowledge of anatomy, physiology, and kinesiology—which were later to evolve into the "biomechanics of sport."

Since then coaching strategies in all sports, but especially in track, include exercise physiologists who measure the anaerobic thresholds of distance runners and schedule workouts that maximize cardiovascular efficiency. Coaches today recognize that medical science is an essential complement to coaching strategy, and they seek to incorporate physiological and psychological principles into their coaching practices.

Such knowledge is not the exclusive contribution of American coaches. It is an accumulation of techniques and principles that flourish all over the world and owe much of their emphasis to the Eastern European countries, as well as to the earlier influence of American pioneers like Harry Gill of Illinois and Ken Doherty and Mike Murphy of Pennsylvania. In fact, the sport of track and field owes much to Europe for its origin and growth. It is likely to have originated in Greece and Rome and to have achieved much of its later growth in England and Scotland well before coming to America.

From the late 1800s, however, when the world's first relay race—America's unique contribution to the sport—was run in Philadelphia, to the present day, America has been a dominant force in world track and field and continues to develop some of the world's finest athletes. Most of their success is the result of collegiate coaching. More schools at every level of NCAA competition have track teams than have football teams, and only baseball and football outnumber track in *total* college-level participants each year.

Baseball, basketball, and football may receive more publicity, but track and field has a level of international popularity that has established it as a "major" sporting attraction in every part of the world. It annually showcases the athletic talents of genuinely amazing women and men who reaffirm each year the genius of innovative training and coaching techniques by establishing new Olympic and world records. These coaches are among the best in the world.

# HIGH SCHOOL TRACK AND FIELD

## America's Greatest High School Boys' Track and Field Coach

**Alan Rowan**

Punahou High School in Honolulu boasts one of the winningest programs in the United States; Coach Rowan is one of the reasons. As head track coach at Punahou for 32 of his 35 years in coaching, Rowan's teams have been either the state champs or the runners-up for all but two years of his entire career. Punahou has won at least 18 state championships during Coach Rowan's career, with close to 400 dual meet victories. His teams have lost only one dual meet since 1957.

Coach Rowan has received at least 20 different Coach of the Year awards, including the NHSACA/Wilson National Track Coach of the Year award in 1986. In addition, he has received the Outstanding Service Award from the Hawaii Athletic Directors Association. Coach Rowan also has found time to serve as a consultant for the Hawaii High School Athletic Association, and he has been a member of the Hawaii High School Athletic Association for 28 years. For the last five or six years, Coach Rowan has been a member of the National Federation of Interscholastic Coaches Association.

## Number Two

**Earl F. Quigley.** From 1926 to 1945, Coach Quigley guided Little Rock High School (now Central High School) to 18 consecutive state championships in track, a record second only to Pickford High School in Mississippi. During his 20 years of coaching, his teams lost only 2 of 100 track meets. In addition, Coach Quigley's football teams won eight state titles, and his basketball teams captured four state crowns. He even won nine state championships in baseball, a total coaching record of 760 victories and 30 state championships, an amazing accomplishment, even among the remarkable records of so many of his colleagues in this book.

## Number Three

**Richard Collins.** In his 30 or so years of coaching high school track, Coach Collins has recorded over 300 total wins and has led Andover High School in Massachusetts to 12 state crowns, eight of which were consecutive. Coach Collins has won numerous Coach of the Year honors, including the NHSACA/Wilson Coach of the Year award in 1980. He also has received the Master Coach award and has been a prominent speaker at several high school and university clinics.

A man completely committed to the sport, Coach Collins has served as president of the Rhode Island Track Coaches Association, president of the North Shore Track League, and director of the Merrimack Valley Indoor Track League.

## Number Four

**Harry "Swede" Dahlberg.** Another multisport coach who coached football, basketball, and track for more than 40 years, Coach Dahlberg guided the Butte (Montana) Bulldogs to 12 state championships between 1922 and 1966. His 12th state track title came in his last year of coaching, and Dahlberg died five years later. His school holds the annual Swede Dahlberg Invitational Track Meet, and the school district decided to name the school's football field in his honor. Dahlberg also won nine state championships in football.

Coach Dahlberg has been inducted into the Montana Coaches Hall of Fame and in 1986 was inducted into the National High School Hall of Fame.

## Number Five

**C.H. Blanchard.** "Okie" Blanchard has won 31 state championships in Wyoming and 57 district titles in a period of 35 years. Nine of his state titles were in track, the first of which was won in 1932 at Rock Springs High School. He next won three consecutive state championships at Casper High School, then moved to Cheyenne High School where he won five more. Literally a coaching phenomenon, Coach Blanchard won 13 state championships in basketball and 9 in football, in addition to his 9 in track.

Blanchard had earned three varsity letters as a fullback at the University of Wyoming and returned there to coach for a brief time before deciding that high school coaching was his first love. The Cheyenne schools have named their joint, all-purpose athletic facility in honor of Coach Blanchard, who was inducted into the National High School Hall of Fame in 1984.

## Other Qualifiers

**John Arcaro.** Coach Arcaro started his coaching career in 1956 at Baldwinsville High School in New York. He entered the army after one year and later returned to Baldwinsville in 1959. During his almost 30 years of coaching, Arcaro has won close to 300 dual matches and has dominated his league, winning virtually every title during his tenure with the school. He has received Coach of the Year honors 13 times as well as his league's Outstanding Service Award, but Coach Arcaro indicates that his greatest honor in coaching was to help develop Don Paige at Baldwinsville, the young man who went on to establish the world record in the 800 meters.

**Vince Bradford.** A man who dedicated 42 years of his life to track at two different schools, Coach Bradford spent 34 years at E.C. Glass High School in Virginia and won 34 district, 15 regional, and seven state championships. Coach Bradford has received several Coach of the Year awards and in 1970 received the Distinguished Service Award from the Virginia High School Coaches Association. Coach Bradford served with the Virginia High School Coaches Association for 20 years, a member of its Executive Committee for 7 and its president for 2. A founder and charter member of the Virginia High School Coaches Association, Coach Bradford also founded and presided over the Lynchburg Area Track and Field Club for several years.

**William Donald.** In more than 30 years of coaching, Donald has won close to 400 dual meet victories and at least six state championships. He started his career with Horn Lake High School in Mississippi and moved to Wooddale High School in Memphis, Tennessee, for the rest of his career. During his first 10 years of coaching, Donald won the county and conference championships every season, and from 1970 to 1976 his track teams were undefeated in regular season meets. Coach Donald has received Coach of the Year honors several times and has served as the director of the State Rules Committee as well as his district and league governing organizations.

**George Eastment.** Born September 4, 1904, in New York City, Coach Eastment generally is considered the father of track in the New York metropolitan area. He began his career at Bishop Loughlin High School in Brooklyn and produced 11 consecutive Catholic League titles in a state that still has no state play-off competition. Coach Eastment also led Bishop Loughlin to several national indoor titles before going on to coach at Manhattan College and ultimately to serve as the president of both the NCAA and Intercollegiate Association of Amateur Athletes of America (IC4A) Track Coaches Association and to chair the NAAU Track and Field Committee in 1964. Eastment has been nominated for induction into the National Track and Field Hall of Fame.

**Ralph Halverson.** The track coach at Cascade High School, then Great Falls High School, in Montana for 32 of his 37 years, Coach Halverson has won over 200 dual meets and recorded six state championships. His teams have been runners-up to the state champs three times, and he has received Coach of the Year honors several times, along with an Outstanding Service Award from the Montana Coaches Association. Halverson has been the president of the Class C Coaches Association, executive secretary of the Montana Coaches Association, director at large of the NHSACA, and a speaker at a wide range of high school and university clinics. He has coached 61 individual state champions who have set 14 state records. His ultimate tribute, however, involved the Class C Northern Division's decision to name their annual meet the Ralph Halverson Northern Division C Track and Field Meet.

**Art Hendricks.** Having spent most of his 36-year coaching career at Clyde High School in Ohio, Coach Hendricks has won 11 league championships, 10 district titles, and one state crown, while earning a dual meet record of 116-8. A charter member of the Ohio Association of Track Coaches, Coach Hendricks has been involved with the organization in varying capacities for 22 years, including having served as president for several years. Coach Hendricks is a member of the Ohio High School Athletic Directors Hall of Fame, the Ohio Association of Track Coaches Hall of Fame, and the National High School Hall of Fame.

**Paul Koshewa.** Coach Koshewa spent 32 of his 36-year coaching career at the Westminster School in Atlanta, Georgia, and in that time won close to 300 track meets. He has won 15 regional crowns and has been runner-up to the state champs four times. Among Coach Koshewa's most significant contributions to high school track and field, however, are his many organizational responsibilities. Coach Koshewa was the president of the Atlanta Track Coaches Association, the organizer/director of the Atlanta High School Track Club clinic, the secretary and chairman of the Georgia High School Association, the state track chairman of the Georgia Athletic Coaches Association, a member of the NHSACA and the National Coaches Association, and the host or director of several high school and university clinics.

**Bob Mosher.** A track coach for more than 30 years at Winter Park High School in Florida, Coach Mosher is among the most respected of his state's coaches. With a record of close to 300 dual meet victories, 14 district championships, and two state crowns, he has established himself among the best in his part of the country. For his accomplishments and contributions to the sport, he has received Coach of the Year honors several times, is a charter member of the Florida Athletic Coaches Association Hall of Fame, has been inducted into the Florida Track and Field Hall of Fame and the Metro Conference Hall of Fame, and has received Florida's Distinguished Service Award. Mosher has been the president and a member of the Executive Committee of the NHSACA, the president of the Florida Athletic Coaches Association, and the state track chairman.

**Russ Parsons.** An inductee into the National High School Hall of Fame in 1986, Coach Parsons established himself as one of this country's premier high school track coaches when he won his first state championship in 1944. He went on to win eight more, ranking sixth on the all-time list of consecutive state championships with a total of eight. All eight were won at Charleston's Jackson High School in West Virginia, where Parsons coached for 13 years. Coach Parsons concluded his career at Parkersburg High School, where he won the track *and* the football state crowns in 1965 and 1958 respectively.

**Henry Sanchez.** A high school legend in New Mexico where he coached at Highland High School in Albuquerque for more than 25 years, Coach Sanchez has won 250 dual meets and 10 state championships and received 11 Coach of the Year awards. Since his first year at Highland High School, Coach Sanchez has not had 1 year without a championship of some kind. He also has found time to be secretary of the Referee's Association, director of the APS Track Coaches Clinic, the Coordinator of the District Track Meet, member of the New Mexico Track Coaches Association, and representative to the State AAU and to the Special Olympics. Coach Sanchez was selected as Wilson's Track Coach of the Year in 1983.

**Paul Woodall.** With 19 of his 21 years of coaching track at Bryan Station High School in Lexington, Kentucky, Coach Woodall has taken his team to more than 250 dual meet wins, 17 Regional crowns, and seven state titles. Five of his team's seven state championships were consecutive, from 1979 through 1983. For his accomplishments, Coach Woodall has been named Kentucky Coach of the Year four times and in 1987 was selected as Wilson's National Track Coach of the Year. Coach Woodall also received the state's Distinguished Service Award and in 1970 was named a Kentucky Colonel. Coach Woodall has been the sports chairman of the NHSACA National Convention, the track chairman of the Kentucky High School Coaches Association, and a member of several other national coaching organizations.

# COLLEGE TRACK AND FIELD

## America's Greatest College Men's Track and Field Coach

**Dean Cromwell**

Known among his contemporaries as the "Maker of Champions," Coach Cromwell produced an individual champion for every Olympic Games from 1912 through 1948. In addition, his athletes accounted for 33 individual NCAA titles, 39 individual IC4A championships, and 38 individual national AAU gold medals. From 1930 to the time of his retirement in 1948, his Southern California University teams lost only three dual meets.

Coach Cromwell's most impressive coaching statistics, however, involve his national championships. During his almost 40 years with the Trojan track squad, Cromwell led the team to nine IC4A national championships and 12 NCAA national championships, nine of which were consecutive—from 1935 through 1943. One of history's "commonsense" coaches, Cromwell was in demand as an advisor to coaching organizations throughout the country and, after his retirement, as a speaker.

Shortly after his retirement, Coach Cromwell was elected to the Helms Athletic Foundation Hall of Fame (1948). In 1974, he was inducted as a charter member into the National Track and Field Hall of Fame.

## Number Two

**Michael Murphy.**   One of the early pioneers of American track and field, Coach Murphy began his career at Yale in 1887. He left Yale to coach the Detroit Athletic Club for three years, returning to Yale in 1893, leading the Eli to four consecutive intercollegiate championships. From Yale, he went to Pennsylvania, where he won eight more national intercollegiate titles, four of them consecutively.

In 1908, the first year that the Olympics enjoyed the services of a coach, Coach Murphy was given the job. He was asked to coach the 1912 Olympic team as well and would have been the coach at the 1916 Olympics had he not died in 1913. Enjoying at the turn of the century the reputation of being the world's best trainer, Coach Murphy touched the lives of his athletes with more than strategy. Said Lou Young, captain of the Penn football team in 1913: "Whenever a Pennsylvania team gets in a tight place, the words which inspire the men . . . are the words of Mike, 'The team that won't be licked can't be licked.' "

It was this philosophy that accounted for Coach Murphy's unparalleled success as a track coach and that led him to invent the crouching start for sprinters and write two books on the subject of college athletics. The University of Pennsylvania named their field house in his honor, and he was inducted into the National Track and Field Hall of Fame in 1974.

## Number Three

**Ted Banks.**   The winner of more NCAA team titles in all sports than any other coach in history, Coach Banks led the University of Texas-El Paso to a total of 17 NCAA titles from 1974 to 1981. The head coach of both track and cross-country, Banks garnered 12 men's titles and five women's in just eight years. One of the few coaches in history to win five consecutive NCAA national titles, Coach Banks won a total of six national crowns and earned the runner-up spot twice.

A gentleman who modestly credits his assistant coaches and athletes for the Miners' success over the years, Banks also has earned six NCAA national championships in cross country. Equally impressive has been his almost complete domination of the Western Athletic Conference. The UTEP Miners have won 21 of the 26 track and cross-country titles, depending upon several foreign runners in the program to lead the way. Banks has at times been criticized for his dependence on African distance runners, but he has earned the reputation of being an excellent coach and treating foreign athletes fairly, which are the primary reasons he kept winning until his retirement in 1981.

## Number Four

**Jess Mortenson.**   Coach Mortenson was a member of Dean Cromwell's USC track team and a national AAU champion in the javelin throw. He coached high school and at the University of Denver and West Point before becoming head coach at USC in 1951. During his 11 years with the Trojans, he *never lost a dual meet*, and he finished first all but once in his league. Most notably, Mortenson-coached teams won five consecutive NCAA national titles from 1951, his first year as their head coach, through 1955.

He won the national crown twice again in 1958 and 1961 and never finished lower than third in the competition. He is credited with developing such track and field standouts as Parry O'Brien, Jack Davis, Charlie Dumas, Dallas Long, and many others. Coach Mortenson died in 1962.

## Number Five

**Bill Bowerman.**   Steve Prefontaine, one of America's greatest distance runners, once said of his coach, Bill Bowerman: "I'll never forget the first time I met him. I felt like I was talking to God. I still do." In demeanor, Coach Bowerman was among America's most impressive coaches. Said Ken Doherty of him in his book, *The Track and Field Omnibook* (1976): "Bowerman is impressive: in size, in voice, in face, in past experience, both as a coach and a major in the 10th Mountain Division during World War II that fought so successfully in Italy."

Opposing coaches all acknowledge that Bowerman's personality strength and acute knowledge of the sport both account for his significant success at the University of Oregon. During his extensive tenure with the school, he accounted for four NCAA team titles (1962, 1964, 1965, and a three-way tie in 1970). He also was runner-up twice (1961 and 1967). For his several accomplishments, Coach Bowerman was inducted into the National Track and Field Hall of Fame in 1981.

**Jim Bush.**   Coach Bush was the head track coach at UCLA from 1965 through 1983, compiling a total record of 144-19 for a winning percentage of .883, including seven PAC-10 titles in 19 years. He also led the Bruins to four national NCAA titles, three of them consecutive ('71, '72, and '73). In addition, his '74 and '75 teams were runners-up to the national champs. During this period, Coach Bush helped develop such outstanding athletes as Willie Banks, Greg Foster, and Andre Phillips.

Coach Bush also accounted for 19 different Olympians and 30 NCAA outdoor individual champions. He was voted Coach of the Year several times and served as president of the U.S. Track Coaches Association in 1972 and 1973. Coach Bush also was voted into Kern County's Hall of Fame and into the National Track and Field Hall of Fame in 1987.

## Other Qualifiers

**Thomas Botts.** As head track coach at the University of Missouri from 1941 through 1972, Coach Botts led the Tigers to four Big Eight indoor titles and four outdoor titles. He won the NCAA Indoor crown in 1965 and later added two Big Eight cross-country championships to his record. Coach Botts is a member of both the Missouri Sports Hall of Fame and the National Track and Field Hall of Fame. In addition, the "Thomas W. Botts Achievement Award" is a permanent fixture in the Missouri trophy case, presented annually to a senior member of the track team for superior performance.

**Percy Beard.** An Olympic silver medalist in the high hurdles in 1932, Coach Beard headed the program at the University of Florida from 1936 to 1964. As great a coach as he was a performer, Coach Beard also is credited with developing all-weather tracks, the brush cement discus, and shotput rings.

**Ken Doherty.** The United States decathlon champ in 1928 and 1929, Coach Doherty dedicated himself to track and field as an athlete, a coach, an organizer, and a writer. As coach for more than 30 years at the high school level and at the universities of Princeton, Michigan, and Pennsylvania, Doherty was responsible for organizing the first U.S./U.S.S.R. dual track meet and has written perhaps the definitive books on track and field, *Modern Track and Field* and the *Track and Field Omnibook*. Although they were written several years ago, both are still relevant regarding motivation and coaching techniques. Coach Doherty is a member of the National Track and Field Hall of Fame.

**Bill Easton.** Runner-up to the national champs in 1956 and again in 1958, the University of Kansas, under the guidance of the legendary Bill Easton, won back-to-back national titles in 1959 and 1960. Coach Easton's NCAA championship in 1960 was especially pleasing; he led the Jayhawks past perennial favorites and track and field powerhouse Southern California to win the crown.

**Jim Elliott.** Elliott began his coaching career at the University of Villanova as an undergraduate in 1935. During his tenure with the school, he won a total of 39 indoor and outdoor team titles in IC4A competition, seven NCAA indoor team titles, and one NCAA national championship in 1957. Two of his athletes, Ron Delany and Charles Jenkins, won gold medals in the 1956 Olympics.

**Harry Gill.** Canadian-born Harry Gill became synonymous with American track and field excellence during his 30 years as head coach at the University of Illinois. He began his career in 1904 and produced 11 Big Ten outdoor and eight indoor championships. Most notably, Coach Gill was a prime mover behind the development of the NCAA championship meet in 1921, also becoming the first coach to win it. He repeated with another NCAA title in 1927. Perhaps the high point of his career, however, occurred during the 1924 Olympics, when his Illinois athletes scored more points in the Games than any other *nation*. Coach Gill is a member of the Helms Athletic Foundation Hall of Fame and the National Track and Field Hall of Fame.

**Brutus Hamilton.** Another member of the National Track and Field Hall of Fame, Coach Hamilton certainly earned the distinction. During his long association with track and field, mostly at the University of California/Berkeley, he was a national champion decathlete, the head coach of the Olympic team in 1956, an athletic director, a dean of students, and the developer of several world and Olympic champions. Most noteworthily, he was a master of psychology and a friend to his athletes. Said one of them shortly after Coach Hamilton's death in December, 1970: "Any coach can work an athlete hard, but only the great ones know when to ease off."

**Oliver Jackson.** Coach Jackson assumed the reins of Abilene Christian University in 1948 and in the next 15 years established the Wildcats as one of the premier programs in the country, guiding his athletes to 17 American records and 15 world records and developing such standout performers as 1956 Olympic triple-gold medalist Bobby Morrow, middle-distance runner Earl Young, and pole vaulter Billy Pemelton. Coach Jackson served on the NCAA Rules Committee for 4 years, serving as president of the NCAA Coaches Association as well during his final year of coaching.

**Leo Johnson.** Leo Johnson was another legendary coach at the University of Illinois. He joined the staff in 1937 as head track coach and also coached football during his tenure. A former football, track, and baseball standout at Millikin University, Coach Johnson established himself in track, where he led the Illini to 17 Big Ten crowns and three NCAA national championships. The first national title came in 1944; the next two were back-to-back titles in 1946 and 1947. Coach Johnson's teams also were runners-up to the national champs three times. His distinguished career culminated in induction into the Helms Athletic Foundation Hall of Fame in 1977.

**Clyde Littlefield.** The head coach of the University of Texas track team for 41 years, Coach Littlefield took the reins in 1921 and won 25 Southwest Conference team titles. Coach Littlefield was an assistant coach for the 1952 United States Olympic team and also coached football for seven years at Texas, leading the Longhorns to two conference crowns. He was inducted into the National Track and Field Hall of Fame in 1981.

**Jack Moackley.** The only coach that Cornell's track program knew for the first 50 years of its existence was Coach Moackley, who took over the program in 1899 and proceeded to lead Cornell to 29 IC4A titles. Nicknamed the "Miracle Man" at Cornell for the athletes he developed, Coach Moackley is responsible for several Olympians, including John Paul Jones, the 1-mile gold medalist at the 1912 Olympics.

**Dink Templeton.** Ken Doherty described Dink Templeton's coaching as "technical expertise plus fiery inspiration." "Fiery inspiration" is an understatement for the volatility that characterized his coaching and his personality. Said opposing coach Brutus Hamilton on hearing of Dink's death: "Dink was fiery, explosive, exciting, and restless, and he brought a fresh and original approach to coaching. . . . There will never be a second Templeton. . . . Never another like him."

Coach Templeton won his first NCAA championship in 1925, leading Stanford to its first national title. He would lead the Cardinals to two more, the last in 1934, an 11-point victory over his traditional rival Southern California and its coaching legend Dean Cromwell. Coach Templeton was inducted into the National Track and Field Hall of Fame in 1976.

**Leroy Walker.** As head coach of North Carolina Central University starting in 1945, Coach Walker was primarily responsible for the development of Olympians Lee Calhoun, Eddie Roberts, Norm Tate, Larry Foster, and several others. Completely dedicated to his sport, Walker served as a coach or consultant for Olympic teams in 1960, 1968, and 1972 and became the first black coach to head a U.S. Olympic contingent (1976). The author of three books on track and a Ph.D., Coach Walker chaired the men's track and field committee for the AAU from 1973 to 1976 and coordinated coaching assignments for the AAU and TAC from 1973 to 1980. Coach Walker was inducted into the National Track and Field Hall of Fame in 1983.

**Bud Winter.** Another member of the National Track and Field Hall of Fame (inducted in 1983), Coach Winter brought San Jose State to a national NCAA title in 1969 and to three runner-up positions (in '52, '59, and '64). During his 35 years of coaching, he developed 102 NCAA All-Americans and 27 Olympians, including the highly publicized trio of Lee Evans, Tommie Smith, and John Carlos. Led by these three sprinters, Winters' San Jose State athletes won more gold medals in the 1968 Olympics than the entire Soviet team. Among his accomplishments off the field, Winters is credited with organizing the first international coaches' clinic (1958).

# Chapter 10

# VOLLEYBALL

Minor sports is hardly the way to describe competitions that have been thrilling spectators for centuries. Football, baseball, and basketball burst on the scene a relatively short time ago, and although they enjoy prominent headlines in the United States, in the *world's* sports section they are buried away. But volleyball, a game that originated in the U.S. only a few years after James Naismith introduced basketball, now ranks *second* only to soccer as the world's most popular participant and spectator sport.

Its appeal in Europe is so pronounced that several countries have professional teams, many of which express annual interest in American players. Their interest is not surprising. Once the highlight of family picnics and beach parties, volleyball retains its recreational appeal but has grown in the past several years to a competition of international significance for Americans.

During the 1988 Olympics in Seoul, volleyball shared center stage with gymnastics and track and field, the traditional star players in the drama of Olympic competition. The men's second consecutive gold medal refocused the world's attention on the play and coaching strategy of the country that founded the game almost 100 years earlier.

Created by William G. Morgan, the Physical Director of the YMCA in Holyoke, Massachusetts, in 1895 and originally named "minonette," the game was designed to provide mild exercise for local businessmen at lunchtime (Sandefur, 1970). Needless to say, the game's intensity increased in proportion to its increase in competition, and as it spread internationally in the early 1900s the intensity of the competition and the sophistication of its strategy became significant.

Brazil fought the 1988 American Olympic team to the wire in a five-game nailbiter. During one of its frequent "crusades" in the early 1900s, the YMCA had introduced the game to Brazil (1917), Uruguay (1912), Puerto Rico (1909), and Cuba (1905). In 1919, the American Expeditionary

Forces brought 16,000 volleyballs to Europe for the American and Allied troops. The game spread almost immediately. It was promoted further during and after World War II when fighting and occupational forces played the game throughout Europe.

Like Americans, the Europeans enjoyed volleyball for its recreational value, but they enjoyed even more the competition it provided. By 1949, therefore, the first World Championship Tournament was hosted by Prague; by 1955 volleyball was included in the Pan Am Games, by 1964 in the Olympics. International competition contributed to the spread of the game as well as to the evolution of its rules. Filipinos, for example, limited the number of hits to three on each side; they also pioneered the "spike," a technique they called the "bomba."

In spite of the popularity of the game throughout the world, international competition has been dominated by Eastern bloc countries, most notably the Soviet Union. The U.S.S.R. won the first World Championship in 1949 and has been a major force in the game ever since. The recent resurgence of volleyball championships by the United States and the South American countries is in part a reflection of superior coaching. Some of the finest win/loss records and consecutive championships in American sports have been achieved by volleyball coaches. Given their commitment, the game is likely to remain a major sporting attraction in this country.

# COLLEGE VOLLEYBALL

## America's Greatest College Men's Volleyball Coach

### Al Scates

Coach Al Scates says it best: "You get used to winning, and when you start winning, it perpetuates itself." Under Coach Scates, winning at UCLA is a habit; it seems that his teams know little else. In volleyball's 19-year history at UCLA, the Bruins have won 12 NCAA championships, three of his teams have been undefeated, ('79, '82, and '84), and the '84 team finished the season with a mark of 38-0, a collegiate record for victories in a single season.

Coach Scates has developed 35 first-team NCAA All-Americans, including Karch Kiraly, Dave Saunders, and Steve Salmons, who were key players in the 1984 U.S. Olympic team's gold medal victory. Kiraly went on to earn the reputation of being the world's best volleyball player and to lead the U.S. team to another gold medal during the 1988 Olympics.

Coach Scates' career record of 701-101 and winning percentage of .875 set the standard for all volleyball coaches, and his four consecutive NCAA titles are unparalleled in the sport. Himself a nine-time All-American, Coach Scates is the author of three books, one of which, *Winning Volleyball*, is in its third revision.

Outside the gym, Coach Scates remains a key figure in the development of volleyball as a popular American sport. He has served as the chairman of the NCAA Volleyball Tournament Committee, is a member of the Reebok Amateur Sports Advisory Board and the National Volleyball Team Review Committee, and recently was reelected as the chairman of the American Volleyball Coaches Association's Men's Committee.

## Number Two

**Don Shondell.** Coach Shondell has led the Ball State Cardinals to 13 Midwest Intercollegiate Volleyball Association championships during his 23 years as head coach. He has earned one of the nation's finest career records with a mark of 588-177-6, making him one of only a few coaches in volleyball history to approximate the 600-win mark. He has never finished lower than second in the Midwest Intercollegiate Volleyball Association (MIVA) tournament and eight times led his team to the NCAA final four, finishing third four times and fourth four times.

The Cardinals, under Coach Shondell, are one of only two teams in volleyball history to make it to the final four five consecutive times (1970-1974). Dr. Shondell has been a professor at Ball State since 1958 and, during his tenure as volleyball coach, has served as chairman of the NCAA Volleyball Committee, president of the United States Volleyball Association, and USVBA representative to the United States Olympic Committee.

## Number Three

**Marv Dunphy.** The coach of the highly successful, world's number one, 1988 U.S. Olympic volleyball team, Marv Dunphy led the team to an Olympic gold. The gold medal was the United States team's second consecutive Olympic championship and represented a significant shift in world power in volleyball competition. Formerly the exclusive province of Eastern bloc countries, volleyball championships have been won most recently by U.S. teams, thanks to the coaching skills of men like Marv Dunphy.

A proven coach well before the 1988 Olympics, Coach Dunphy already had led Pepperdine to two NCAA titles (in 1978 and 1985) and a record of 117-32 versus some of the country's toughest competition. Coach Dunphy returned to Pepperdine after the Olympics to improve an already outstanding record.

## Number Four

**Tom Tait.** Coach Tom Tait introduced Penn State volleyball to varsity competition in 1976 and was its only coach until his retirement in 1988. During Tait's 11 seasons as head coach, the Nittany Lions earned a 356-88 record for a winning percentage of .800. His teams have made five appearances in the NCAA final four, finishing second once, third three times, and fourth once. Coach Tait, who will continue at Penn State as an associate professor of exercise science, was named the Eastern Intercollegiate Volleyball Association Coach of the Year six times and National Coach of the Year once (1986).

Widely recognized not only for his coaching accomplishments but for his promotion of the sport, Coach Tait was a three-time president of the Eastern Collegiate Volleyball League (ECVL) and was the coach of two National Sports Festivals. He also has conducted numerous camps and clinics, served as a member of the United States Volleyball Association's board of directors, and is the chairman of the NCAA Volleyball Committee.

## Number Five

**Wayne Stalick.** Coach Stalick originally founded volleyball as a club sport at George Mason University in Virginia, but in just one year helped establish an intercollegiate program and has since led the Patriots to a 414-150 record and, within the past four years, three appearances in the NCAA's final four. A Ph.D. in organic chemistry, Coach Stalick balances a full-time professorship in chemistry with coaching responsibilities that have resulted in a record three consecutive selections as the Eastern Intercollegiate Volleyball Association's Coach of the Year.

During his 14 seasons with the Patriots, Coach Stalick never finished below .500, finishing first in the East Coast Volleyball League Tournament twice and never out of the top five. The only volleyball coach in Green and Gold history, Coach Stalick has established George Mason among the volleyball powerhouses in the country.

# Chapter 11

# WRESTLING

Sparked by an inherent spectator appeal that only one-to-one competition can generate, wrestling has been fascinating sports fans for centuries. The appeal is found not so much in the sport's strategy, which hasn't changed that much over the years, as in the participants' skills and their determination to overcome fatigue as well as a worthy opponent. Temples along the Nile contain centuries-old paintings of wrestlers executing a series of holds still common today. Greek paintings, vases, and cups contain similar drawings.

Such artifacts may illustrate wrestling strategies, but they fail to capture the brutality of ancient wrestling. Leontiscus of Messina, for example, tried early in every match to break his opponents's fingers to claim quick victory. Participants in the "Pankration"—a combination of wrestling and boxing—punched, kicked, bit, and gouged each other until one of them surrendered by tapping his opponent on the back. Often the tap came too late. Arrachion of Phigalia, for example, died of strangulation trying to escape from a leg scissors hold by breaking his opponent's toes.

Fortunately, contemporary wrestling is less brutal. At the high school, collegiate, and international levels, however, it remains one of the sport world's most strenuous and physically demanding activities. Unlike many contemporary sports, it owes little to the influence of its professional counterpart, a spectacle that is more a test of showmanship than of sportsmanship. While the pros are providing aberrant answers to "Where's the beef?" amateur wrestlers are concerned only with "Which of us is the better wrestler?" Their answers have established some of the greatest accomplishments in the world of sport.

The Midwestern edition of collegiate wrestling, particularly in Iowa and Oklahoma, has produced *scores* of the world's greatest wrestlers and many of its best coaches. That domination, which started decades ago with coaches Ed Gallagher and Myron Roderick of Oklahoma State, continues into more recent times with Dan Gable at the University of Iowa. A wrestler with the unparalleled amateur record of 293 wins in 299 matches, Gable went on to coach University of Iowa wrestling to new heights in the collegiate ranks, even leading American wrestlers to seven gold and two silver medals in the 1984 Olympics.

The wrestling programs developed by such outstanding coaches create real-life matches that rival Homer's description of the bout between Ajax and Ulysses. And the freestyle technique, which is most popular in the United States, seems to be the legitimate descendant of classical Greek wrestling. Although the Greco-Roman style enjoys some popularity, freestyle wrestling is the exclusive emphasis in high schools and colleges in the United States. It has given this country some of the world's most accomplished wrestlers and many of its greatest coaches.

# HIGH SCHOOL WRESTLING

## America's Greatest High School Wrestling Coach

### William Patrick Martin

The founder of organized wrestling in the state of Virginia, Coach Billy Martin led Granby High School in Norfolk to a 259-9 record in dual meet competition in 23 years, winning the state title 21 times and finishing second once. His winning percentage of .960 is among the two or three best in history; his development of 109 individual state champions *is* the best in history.

Six of Coach Martin's protégés went on to win 10 national titles, and two competed in the Olympics. In one NCAA tournament, 10 of Coach Martin's former wrestlers competed, representing several schools. His coaching strategies were so refined that one of his innovations, the Granby Roll, is still used today.

For establishing wrestling as a major sport in the state of Virginia and for devoting so much of his time to wrestling clinics and camps, Coach Martin was elected to the Virginia Sports Hall of Fame in 1981. He already had been named to the Helms Foundation Hall of Fame in 1967 and chosen the scholastic coach of the year in 1970. Coach Martin also is a member of the National High School Hall of Fame and the National Wrestling Hall of Fame. Born in 1918 in South Creek, North Carolina, Coach Martin graduated from the University of Michigan in 1940 and retired in 1971.

## Number Two

**Michael Milkovich.** Few men enjoy as much impact on their sports as Coach Mike Milkovich. A successful high school and college wrestler, Coach Milkovich began his career at Maple Heights in Ohio in 1950, the originator of the sport in his school. After 27 years of coaching, Coach Milkovich retired with a record of 265-25 for a winning percentage of .913. Milkovich's teams won 10 state titles, eight second-place finishes, 21 conference championships, and 16 undefeated seasons.

The undefeated seasons resulted in winning streaks of 102 and 59 consecutive victories. They also produced two sons who followed in their father's footsteps. Pat won two NCAA titles, and Tom won four Big Ten and one national collegiate title. Both decided on coaching as careers.

Like all great coaches, Milkovich's influence on wrestling extended beyond the gym. He is the author of several books, the developer of a video tape that has been used nationwide, and the primary speaker at scores of clinics across the country. For his several contributions to the sport, Coach Mike Milkovich was selected in 1976 as the National High School Coach of the Year and, later, as a Distinguished Member of the National Wrestling Hall of Fame.

## Number Three

**Frank "Sprig" Gardner.** Coach Sprig Gardner is another legend of the sport who had no competitive experience in college. He introduced wrestling to Mepham High School on Long Island in 1937, and in two decades of intense competition, he led his teams to a dual meet record of 254-5-1 for an incredible .976 winning percentage. An unparalleled success story, Coach Sprig Gardner's career at Mepham included a victory streak of 100 consecutive wins. The loss that snapped that string gave way to a 130-win string of consecutive dual meet victories. In 17 years, Mepham lost but one dual meet and won 37 consecutive South Shore and sectional tournaments.

Coach Gardner's tournament teams won 40 championships, tied for one more, and placed second three times. Gardner's accomplishments became the focus of a five-page article in *Life* magazine, and two of his wrestlers won national AAU titles while still in high school. Several books and articles by Coach Gardner publicized his coaching techniques and helped revolutionize the sport. For his many contributions to wrestling, Frank "Sprig" Gardner is honored as a Distinguished Member of the National Wrestling Hall of Fame.

## Number Four

**Charles Farina.** Coach Farina was widely acknowledged as one of the nation's top high school wrestling coaches long before his induction into the National High School Hall of Fame in 1987. The head wrestling coach at Leyden High School in Illinois since 1955, Farina is the second-winningest high school coach in history, with a record of 524-79-7. During his 33 years with Leyden, he has had 31 consecutive winning seasons, two state titles, three runners-up to the title, and three third-place finishes.

Coach Farina's teams have won 27 district titles and 18 sectional championships. In 1978, his state championship team set a state record for most points scored by the state titlist (129-1/2 points). For these accomplishments, Coach Farina was named the Illinois wrestling Coach of the Year three times and the national wrestling Coach of the Year once. In addition to his enviable win/loss record, Coach Farina numbers among his finest career accomplishments the fact that 35 of his former wrestlers have gone on to coach wrestling in high school.

Farina is respected nationwide as a coach and respected locally as a fine human being. He was honored in 1986 when the Franklin Park community named the Leyden field house after him.

## Number Five

**Neil Buckley.** A first lieutenant in the second world war, Coach Neil Buckley acquired a special brand of dedication that has seen him through 40 years of coaching the wrestling program—one he created—at the Haverford School in Pennsylvania. With no collegiate experience as a wrestler, Buckley realized the advantages of such a program and introduced the sport to his school in 1946. He has been its only coach ever since and has become one of the nation's best, earning a record of 504-92-8, one of the best in high school wrestling.

During his years at Haverford, Coach Buckley developed a national prep championship team in 1973 and eight national championship wrestlers. On a local basis, he has won 30 Philadelphia Inter-Academic League Wrestling titles and was cited by the Pennsylvania Senate in 1983 as one of the state's outstanding citizens. He also has received letters of recognition from Presidents Carter and Reagan, primarily for his reputation of being a "gentleman coach" and for his total commitment to his athletes as well as to his sport.

Coach Buckley's contributions to the sport were recently recognized by his colleagues when he was inducted into the Pennsylvania Hall of Fame.

## Number Six

**Robert Saunders Siddens.** Remembered best as "Dan Gable's Coach," Coach Bob Siddens established himself as one of the sport's best well before his association with Gable. During his 27-year tenure at Eagle Grove High School in Waterloo, Iowa, Siddens established a record of 327-26 for a winning percentage of .926. During that time, he won 11 state championships and placed second or third 10 other times. In 14 undefeated seasons, Siddens' teams established a dual meet record of 88 consecutive victories.

A master of motivation, Coach Siddens enabled his wrestlers to carry his commitment to personal excellence onto the college level, where they won 19 Big Eight titles and nine NCAA championships. He was the coach of an Olympic gold medal-winning team. During the collegiate national championships in 1968, two of his former wrestlers, Gable of Iowa and Dale Anderson of Michigan State, won back-to-back NCAA titles.

Well-versed in all phases of his sport, Siddens has been an official at at least two dozen NCAA championships, more than any other official. He has written extensively about his sport and has conducted scores of clinics. For his contributions, Coach Bob Siddens has been selected as a Distinguished Member of the National Wrestling Hall of Fame. Coach Siddens retired in 1977.

## Other Qualifiers

**Stan Lampe.** With a 275-25-14 record and a winning percentage of .916 in his 28 years of coaching at Fort Morgan High School in Colorado, Coach Stan Lampe has established himself as one of the nation's premier high school wrestling coaches. Selected by the National High School Athletic Coaches Association as their 1987 Coach of the Year, Lampe has won 14 district championships and seven state titles. Beyond his outstanding coaching accomplishments, Coach Lampe has been a member of the Colorado Wrestling Officials Association for 21 years, for two years as the vice president. He also has been a member of several rules and organizational committees.

**Russell Riegel.** Championships also have come quite easily to Coach Riegel. As head coach of Hunterdon Central High School in New Jersey for 30 years, Coach Riegel earned a career record of 446-71-7.

According to the National Federation of State High School Associations, Coach Riegel's record is the third highest in the history of high school wrestling.

**Carl Ramunno.** In 31 years of coaching at Steamboat Springs High School in Colorado, Carl Ramunno has earned the enviable career record of 365 victories. He also has won his state title six times and has been runner-up six times. Beyond his coaching duties, Carl has been a member of the Colorado Coaches Association for 25 years and has been named the Coach of the Year and received the Coach's Merit Award. In addition, Coach Ramunno was named the National High School Athletic Coaches Association/Wilson Coach of the Year in 1988.

**William "Red" Schmitt.** According to the National Federation of State High School Associations, Coach Red Schmitt was the winningest coach in the history of high school wrestling. He headed the wrestling programs at Alton Western and Granite City South high schools in Illinois for 40 years, with a remarkable 602-84-5 record for a winning percentage of .871. Coach Schmitt retired in 1985.

**William Weick.** A coach for 21 years in three schools, Coach Weick started his career in Iowa at Maquoketa High School, then moved to Chicago where he coached at Tilden Tech. Many of Coach Weick's greatest successes came, however, at Chicago's Mt. Carmel High School, where Coach Weick led the Caravan to several championships and extended his career record to 383-23-4.

## COLLEGE WRESTLING

### America's Greatest College Wrestling Coach

**Danny Mack Gable**

Undefeated as a prep and collegiate wrestler in 181 matches before suffering his first defeat in the NCAA finals in 1970, Dan Gable is widely acknowledged as this country's finest amateur wrestler. He culminated his wrestling career when he won a gold medal during the 1972 Summer Olympics in Munich, not having lost one point to his opponents. The winner of three state crowns in high school, two NCAA championships in college, and an unprecedented six Midlands titles, Dan Gable was wrestling's most decorated athlete.

He has achieved nothing less as a coach. Since assuming the reins at the University of Iowa in 1977, Dan Gable has earned a Big Ten record of 72-0 and a career record of 191-9-2 for a winning percentage of .950. He was named the NCAA Rookie Coach of the Year in 1977 and the NCAA Wrestling Coach of the Year in 1978 and 1983. Only one record outshines his team's accomplishments in Big Ten competition—nine consecutive NCAA team titles.

In Gable's 11 years of coaching, only twice have his teams failed to win the NCAA crown, finishing third in 1977 and second in 1987. His successes extend beyond the Hawkeye gym. As head U.S. wrestling coach in the 1984 Olympics, Gable led the team to seven gold and two silver medals. Shortly afterward, he was elected into the United States Olympic Hall of Fame, already having been named to the United States Wrestling Hall of Fame in 1980.

Born in 1948, Gable searched relentlessly for personal and team excellence, which continues at Iowa where already he has coached 72 Big Ten champions, 82 All-Americans, and 24 national champions. His name is synonymous with the sport of wrestling and is already legendary in the record books. Dan Gable remains a model of dedication and hard work, and his *total* impact on the sport is yet to be determined.

## Number Two

**Edward C. Gallagher.** A pioneer in collegiate wrestling, Coach Ed Gallagher, after receiving a degree in electrical engineering from Oklahoma State University (then Oklahoma A & M), decided to go into coaching for his life's work. He began his career at Oklahoma State, then went to Baker University in Kansas. He returned, however, to Oklahoma State in 1916 and proceeded to establish wrestling history. During his 23-year career, Coach Gallagher produced 19 undefeated teams, all the result of his innovations in diet and training methods.

When the NCAA wrestling tournament was introduced in 1928, Coach Gallagher already had completed half his career, but the Oklahoma State Cowboys would win the first NCAA tournament and, of the 13 remaining tournaments in which they would compete, they would win 9 more and share a 10th. En route to such a remarkable record, Coach Gallagher's teams collected 37 individual titles, 32 national amateur champions, three Olympic gold medals, and a 138-5-4 record for a winning percentage of .938. Within that time, Coach Gallagher enjoyed a string of 68 consecutive victories.

Coach Gallagher died in 1940, destined to become a charter member of the National Wrestling Hall of Fame.

## Number Three

**Harold Nichols.** In 1939 the national collegiate champion at 145 pounds at the University of Michigan, Harold Nichols started his coaching career after the war, at Arkansas State University. But it was at Iowa State in 1953 that he initiated the first of his remarkable coaching accomplishments. The architect of Iowa State's wrestling domination in the 1950s, Coach Nichols guided the Cyclones to almost 400 victories and six national team titles, including four in a five-year period starting in 1969.

Iowa State also enjoyed seven runners-up to national team titles, 31 individual champions, and seven Olympians, accounting for a silver, a bronze, and two gold medals. For such accomplishments, Coach Nichols was named national Coach of the Year four times and, in 1966, honored as the Wrestling Man of the Year. Coach Nichols' selection as the third-greatest wrestling coach in history results as much from his contributions to the sport *off* the mat. He served on the NCAA rules committees, AAU and Olympic committees, and scores of clinics and summer camps. He, too, is a member of the National Wrestling Hall of Fame.

## Number Four

**Myron Roderick.** As a wrestler at Oklahoma State University in the mid '50s, Myron Roderick won 42 of 44 matches and three NCAA titles. No sooner had he won his third national championship than he was selected as the team's head coach. In just one year, at the age of 23, Coach Myron Roderick led the Cowboys to an NCAA crown, the youngest coach in history to earn such an accomplishment. He remained at Oklahoma State for another 11 years and produced six more NCAA team championships. During Coach Roderick's 13-year tenure with the Cowboys, his teams won 140 dual meets and lost only 10, in that time amassing 84 consecutive victories.

In his constant quest for the best wrestlers in the country, Coach Roderick was largely responsible for the introduction of large-scale recruiting in wrestling. Combined with his significant coaching talent, his search accounted for 20 individual NCAA champions at Oklahoma State and four gold medalists in the Olympics. When his coaching career ended, Myron Roderick became the first executive director of the United States Wrestling Federation and soon after was inducted into the National Wrestling Hall of Fame.

## Number Five

**Dale Thomas.** Coach Dale Thomas was captain of the Cornell College team in 1947 when they won the NCAA and AAU national titles and is the winningest coach in the history of college wrestling. During his 24 years at Oregon State University, he led the Beavers to a remarkable 432 victories against only 76 defeats for a winning percentage of .850. He also coached 10 NCAA champions, 21 national champs in freestyle and Greco-Roman, and 54 All-Americans. Although Oregon State never won a team NCAA championship under Coach Thomas, they were a runner-up in 1973 and placed third or fourth five times. *Dr.* Thomas also is one of the great teachers of the sport, sharing his knowledge from Canada to New Zealand. Rounding out his talents as well as his commitment to the sport, Coach Thomas was an official for the 1960 and 1964 Olympics. He also originated children's wrestling in Oregon and an international cultural exchange program for wrestlers in Oregon high schools.

The depth and breadth of his contributions to the world of wrestling resulted in Coach Dale Thomas's induction as a Distinguished Member into the National Wrestling Hall of Fame.

## Other Qualifiers

**Tommy Evans.** An accomplished wrestler before he took the reins as head coach at the University of Oklahoma in 1960, Tommy Evans was twice winner of the NCAA tournament, each time named Outstanding Wrestler. A silver medalist in the 1952 Olympics in Helsinki and a gold medalist in the 1955 Pan Am Games, Evans succeeded Port Robertson as head coach of the Sooners and led them immediately to an NCAA crown in 1960. Only one coach before him, Art Griffith at Oklahoma State, had managed such an accomplishment. Coach Evans missed the 1962 season because of active duty as a pilot but returned in 1963 to lead Oklahoma to a career record of 140-39 and two more NCAA titles. For his accomplishments, Coach Tommy Evans is a Distinguished Member of the National Wrestling Hall of Fame.

**Art Griffith.** Art Griffith just as easily could have been included in the high school section of the book. During his 15 years at Central High School in Tulsa, Oklahoma, his teams won 94 of 100 matches and 10 state titles. But it was at Oklahoma State that he achieved national recognition. Assuming the reins from Ed Gallagher in 1941, Coach Griffith took the Cowboys to a 13-year record of 78-7-4, including 10 undefeated seasons and eight NCAA championships. Perhaps Coach Griffith's most notable accomplishment, however, was the 1941 NCAA championships, when all but two of the 16 finalists had been coached by Griffith in either college or high school. Art Griffith is an inductee into the National Wrestling Hall of Fame.

**Rex Peery.** A product of Oklahoma wrestling under Coach Ed Gallagher, Rex Peery was a three-time national collegiate champion. Later, as a coach at the University of Pittsburgh, Peery established an unparalleled record. During his 16 years with the Panthers, Coach Peery earned a record of 233 wins against only 58 losses and was runner-up twice in the NCAA championships. More remarkably, within that time, he coached his eldest son Hugh to three NCAA championships and, one year later, his younger son Ed to three more. Father and sons, by 1957, had entered the NCAA championships nine times—and won all nine, one of the sports world's really remarkable achievements. A member of the National Wrestling Hall of Fame, Coach Peery served on its board of governors in addition to serving several other wrestling organizations.

**Port Robertson.** A Distinguished Member of the National Wrestling Hall of Fame, Coach Robertson is another in a long line of successful coaches at the University of Oklahoma. During his 15-year tenure with the Sooners, Coach Robertson led his teams to three NCAA titles, three national runners-up, 15 individual NCAA titles, and five Outstanding Wrestler awards. In 1960, he coached the U.S. Olympic team to three gold medals, as many as any wrestling team had achieved in 40 years of Olympic competition.

A winner of the Bronze Star and a Purple Heart in the invasion of Normandy, Coach Robertson represents the essence of amateur athletics. His own words best describe his philosophy: "First of all, a boy has to want to come here to get an education. If he thinks wrestling is more important than that, he's not going to do well in either. Then, he has to realize what it takes to be a good wrestler. He has to learn to know himself. Once he gets self-discipline in wrestling, he'll have it all his life."

**Paul Scott.** The first team in Iowa history to win an NCAA championship was not the University of Iowa, nor was it Iowa State. It wasn't even Iowa State Teachers College in 1950. The *first* Iowa school to claim an NCAA title in wrestling was little Cornell College in 1947, coached by Paul Scott, a master of the sport whom history seems to have forgotten. A wrestler and football player at Cornell in the 1920s, Coach Scott accomplished in 1947 with his school of 600 what most major universities in the country only dreamed of. He broke the Oklahoma stranglehold on NCAA titles, and he became the first wrestling coach in history to win the NCAA and the AAU team titles in the same year. The 1947 NCAA Tournament saw Cornell College run up 32 points to Oklahoma State's 15—Oklahoma State, the team that had won the tournament 11 of the past 12 years. For 3 of the next 4 years, Cornell College finished third in the tournament or in the top 10, marking Paul Scott as one of wrestling's great coaches.

**Charles M. Speidel.** Another of history's great wrestling coaches, "Doc" Speidel is almost solely responsible for bringing wrestling to the Eastern states. He coached for 38 years at Penn State, compiling a dual meet record of 191-53, including eight Eastern Intercollegiate team titles and 56 individual champions. The author of several books on wrestling and of articles for the *Encyclopedia Brittanica*, Coach Speidel was widely in demand as a speaker. He founded the National Wrestling Coaches Association, serving as its president for 2 years. But the primary reasons for his being honored as a Distinguished Member of the National Wrestling Hall of Fame are his commitment to furthering the cause of wrestling throughout the country and the fact that the Nittany Lions under Doc Speidel were the only team from the East to win the NCAA team championship.

# PART II
# WOMEN'S SPORTS

James Naismith's "basket ball" game was off the drawing board in Springfield, Massachusetts, only four years when Stanford University and the University of California hosted the first women's intercollegiate contest. One year later, the men played their first game, Yale versus Penn. That the game spread more quickly among women than men surprised no one. Basketball remained more popular with women than men until the 20th century. In fact, the participation of women in all sports increased sharply during the 1880s and 1890s, particularly in tennis, swimming, and skating.

Documentation from the period indicates that a few stalwarts even squared off in the boxing ring. The site was the Hill's Theater; the date was March 16, 1876. Nell Saunders just beat Rose Harland to claim her "purse" (an unseemly silver butter dish) and the more appropriate distinction of winning history's first women's boxing match. *Both* women, however, won the respect of an amazed audience; padded gloves weren't introduced for at least another 10 years. Fortunately, most women of the time chose less violent, if equally competitive, sports to display their physical talents.

During the summer of 1887, for example, young Charlotte "Lottie" Dod of England won the singles championship at Wimbledon. She was 15 years old and would win the title 4 of the next six years. And while Lottie was winning at Wimbledon, several of her American counterparts were organizing this country's first women's professional baseball team, a short-lived series of exhibitions that capitalized more on short pants and cut-off shirts than on long hits and extra innings.

In spite of the increasing numbers of women who were enjoying the thrill of competition, no women were allowed to compete in the first

Modern Olympics in 1896—the elitist philosophy of Baron Pierre de Coubertin would not permit it. Said the founder of the Modern Olympics: "Women have but one task—that of crowning the winner with garlands, as was their role in ancient Greece."

Decades later, a similar philosophy would be expressed by Avery Brundage, "King of the Olympics" and a social elitist of the first order. No sooner had he assumed the presidency of the International Olympic Committee in 1952 than he recommended that women be banned from the Olympics. Applauding Brundage's position, New York *Times* columnist Arthur Daley wrote: "It's probably boorish to say it, but any self-respecting schoolboy can achieve superior performances to a woman *champion!*"

While Susan B. Anthony was battling a similar mentality in the political arena of 1900, May Sutton Bundy was preparing to be the first American woman to win the singles championship on the Wimbledon Centre Court of 1904. Four years earlier, women had been permitted to compete in golf and tennis in the Olympics. Margaret Abbott was America's first woman Olympian to earn a gold medal. She won a nine-hole golf competition.

Decades later, Arthur Daley of the *Times* heralded the opinion that had prevailed since the start of the Olympics and that would continue for decades more to obstruct the progress of women athletes: "Don't get me wrong, please. Women are wonderful. But when those delightful creatures begin to toss the discus or put the shot—well, it does something to a guy. And it ain't love, Buster!" He summed up the dominant male opinion of the day: "There's just nothing feminine or enchanting about a girl with beads of perspiration on her alabaster brow."

Figure skating and swimming somehow must have enhanced the "glow of femininity" because each included women competitors early in the 20th century: figure skating in 1908, swimming in 1912. Track and field would not be open to women until 1928, gymnastics until 1960, and volleyball until 1964. That women coaches did not emerge immediately from the ranks when high schools and colleges offered programs is not surprising. They have established themselves now, but present and future generations must look back to the singular accomplishments of women athletes who made the most of the limited opportunities available to them.

In many instances, their accomplishments must be resurrected from archives long grown dusty. Consider the effort of Eleanor Churchill, who threw a baseball almost the length of a football field to win the competition in America's first AAU-sponsored track meet for women in 1923. And what about 17-year-old Jackie Mitchell? Hired for one day by manager Joe Engel of the Chattanooga Lookouts, a minor league team in the Southern Association, Jackie pitched against the 1931 edition of the New York Yankees. All she did that day was face baseball's most intimidating line-up, appropriately dubbed "Murderer's Row," and strike out Tony Lazzeri, Lou Gehrig, and Babe Ruth!

Progress was still slow. Although women competed in track and field in the 1928 Olympics, the number of events was limited to shorter distances. The 400-meter race was not sanctioned for women until 1964, the 1500 meters until 1972, and the marathon until 1984. Taking advantage of what was available to her, Babe Didrikson, the 18-year-old phenomenon from Beaumont, Texas, entered the '32 Olympics in Los Angeles and won two gold medals and one silver in the three events she was allowed to enter. Unaware that a destitute Jim Thorpe was watching her performance, Babe eventually would share with him their greatest honor. In 1950, they would be named the greatest male and the greatest female athletes of the half-century.

Even the accomplishments of the Netherlands' Fanny Blankers-Koen in the 1948 Olympics failed to relax the rigid mindset of male sports officials. The first woman to win four gold medals in a Summer Olympics, Fanny earned worldwide recognition, in spite of the attention received by 17-year-old decathlete Bob Mathias and Czech legend Emil Zatopek. Perhaps her greatest contribution to women's sports, however, involved the destruction of a couple of myths. Fanny Blankers-Koen was 30 years old and the mother of two.

In the mid-fifties, had there been a women's spotlight it would have sought out Stella Walsh, the only woman to win the U.S. pentathlon five consecutive times (1950-1954). Competing well into her 50s, Stella won more than 1,100 track and field competitions. Unfortunately for Stella, the women's pentathlon was not introduced to Olympic competition until 1964. Fortunately for the rest of us, however, a young black woman from Clarksville, Tennessee, was introduced to sports competition.

Nicknamed "La Gazelle" by the French press, Wilma Glodean Rudolph became the first woman from the United States to win three gold medals in the Summer Olympics. She won the 200- and 100-meter dashes—setting an Olympic and a world record—and anchored the 4 × 100 relay team, which set another record in the preliminaries. Bedridden for 4 years as a child, her ability ever to walk again uncertain, "Skeeter," the nickname she received from her coach Ed Temple, made an indelible mark for women and for blacks by being the first black woman to win the prestigious Sullivan Award as the nation's outstanding amateur athlete of the year.

Katherine Switzer kept the women's cause alive in 1967 when she violated the rules of the Boston Marathon prohibiting women participants and completed the course, beating several men to the finish line. Katherine shared some of the credit with her shot-putter boyfriend, who bumped race promoter Jock Semple out of the way when he tried to remove her from the race. A year later, swimmer Debbie Meyer won three gold medals in the Olympics, advancing even further the cause of women's sports, earning the Sullivan Award, and bringing recognition to Coach Sherm Chavoor's Arden Hill's Swim Club (see pages 146-147).

It was not until the mid- to late '70s, however, that real progress in women's athletics was made. In 1970, virtually no women were jogging. In just 12 years, one third of the nation's 17 million joggers were women. In the same year, one woman entered the New York Marathon and failed to finish. Ten years later, 2,465 women entered; and by 1988, 4,736 women entered the marathon, most of whom completed the course. In 1971, another significant decision of the decade resulted in the rules of women's basketball being changed to conform to the men's game.

The most significant decision of the decade, however, perhaps of all time for U.S. women's sports, involved Title IX of the Higher Education Act of 1972, which stated, "No person in the United States shall, on the basis of sex, be excluded from participation in any program or activity receiving federal financial assistance." A few months earlier, the Association for Intercollegiate Athletics for Women (AIAW) was created, in spite of opposition from the NCAA and other regulatory organizations.

Title IX not only expanded but brightened horizons for millions of women athletes; occasionally, however, it failed to provide a sense of direction. The "equality" it guaranteed was welcomed but poorly defined. Should girls and women be encouraged to play football? To wrestle? Should women receive athletic scholarships? As many as men? Should their athletic budgets be equivalent? As the implications of Title IX unfolded in successive court decisions, it became obvious that the answer to many of the questions was *Yes*.

But equality is a precious coin. It may have great worth, but it still has two sides. As girls went out for football, boys went out for field hockey, volleyball, and softball. Most were serious, seeking experiences in girls' sports that had not been available in high school but that *were* available to men in college. As a result, high schools and colleges had to reassess their respective positions and to define "equality" in terms of its maximum benefit to existing men's programs as well as to emerging women's programs.

Title IX's success, however, was remarkable. The '70s witnessed the emergence of women coaches like Margaret Wade of Delta State, who established a record of 109-6 and won three consecutive AIAW basketball championships. It saw Linda Sharp of USC win two NCAA basketball championships—and Pat Summitt, Sonja Hogg, Fern Gardner, and Sue Gunter win over 300 games in NCAA competition. It saw Jody Conradt of Texas win over 400 basketball games and Linda Dollar, head volleyball coach at Southwest Missouri State, win over 600.

The decade watched ladies' golf earnings climb from $435,000 in 21 tournaments to over $5 million. It saw tennis purses grow from just $200,000 to more than $9 million. Ironically, one of the people most responsible for this increase in earnings was a self-professed male chauvinist who lost the battle of the sexes to a woman who led women's sports out of the shadow of traditional male dominance. Bobby Riggs lost the winner-take-all prize money of $100,000 to Billie Jean King in a tennis match that attracted over 30,000 spectators and provided the added incentive for the nation's women to get in on the action.

During the first 10 years of Title IX's existence, girls on high school cross-country teams increased from 1,719 to 59,000, and the number of girls in track and field mushroomed from 62,000 to almost half a million. In the early 1970s, 215 colleges and universities had women's sports programs; by 1980, the number had increased to 900. In addition, the women's athletic budgets increased from just 1% to over 16% of the men's budget. A welcomed result of this emphasis is that 63% of all new participants in sports are women.

Another welcomed result has been the number of athletic scholarships available to women. From May 21, 1973, when swimmer Lynn Genesko received the nation's first women's athletic scholarship from the University of Miami, to the present time, thousands of young women have enjoyed the financial benefits as well as the excitement and recognition that accompany sports competition in college. And spectators have enjoyed watching them. As early as February 22, 1975, twelve thousand people bought tickets to watch a women's basketball doubleheader at Madison Square Garden.

Nine years later, thousands more flocked to Norfolk, Virginia, to watch Coach Sonja Hogg's Louisiana Tech Lady Techsters score 114 points in a preliminary game en route to the first NCAA Women's Basketball Championship. The tournament, in essence, spelled the demise of the AIAW at a time when the sport participation of women had increased from 7% in 1972 to 35% in 1982. The directors of women's programs and others who share in the enthusiasm for women's sports are still fearful that the loss of an exclusively women's regulatory organization may cloud the future of athletics for women.

To compound their fears—while Coach Linda Sharp's USC basketball team was beating Tennessee for the 1984 NCAA championship, the Supreme Court was deciding that the provisions of Title IX do not apply to athletics. Women's athletic budgets already have felt the pinch; more is expected. In the meantime, the NCAA continues to sponsor women's tournaments in a variety of sports, and the women athletes continue to amaze spectators.

# Chapter 12

# BASKETBALL

Early women's basketball was played on a surface that was divided into three sections. Players were restricted to their respective courts, with two guards, two forwards, and two centers comprising a team. This early three-court concept may have been a mistake (Bell, 1973). Clara Baer of Newcomb College, one of the game's founders, apparently misinterpreted an early diagram of the playing area. Lines that divided it into three sections were intended to illustrate the positioning of players; Baer apparently interpreted them as restraining lines.

Thus the game was born, and it was widely accepted. The dimensions of the court were consistent with the popular notion of the time that women did not have the stamina to play by the men's rules. Said one female writer of the period: "Should girls play so? The game is violent, the interest intense, the nervous strain severe, and the chance of accident large, if it is played according to the men's rules" (Foster, 1897).

Modifications were made, and the evolution of the game continued. The absence of a national organizing body in the game's early development led to variations in regional rules of play, which impeded its growth. Like so many other American sports, however, basketball for women was nurtured in college and owes much of its development to the college coaches of the time.

The first intercollegiate contest was waged between Stanford and Cal Berkeley on April 4, 1896, at Armory Hall in San Francisco. Resplendent in bloomers and sweaters bearing their schools' colors, the athletes joined 500 spectators to stage one of history's most exciting basketball games. It was also one of the closest—and probably the lowest scoring. The final score was 2-1, Stanford victorious. The *Daily Palo Alto* attributed the Cardinal success to "the superiority of the Stanford players in accuracy in throwing the ball, and finally by their teamwork."

By the end of 1938 the two-court game had become official, six players still required, each restricted to her half of the court. Coaching strategies still emphasized passing and shot accuracy; the three-bounce dribble would not become legal until 1961, the continuous dribble until 1966. The relative immobility of players made defense comparatively easy, although the use of the legs, arms, and body in guarding were not legalized until 1948.

Iowa still plays the two-court, six-player game and regularly matches the boys' games in attendance and excitement. Wrote Doug Bauer in *Sports Illustrated* on March 6, 1978: "In Iowa the girls' state championships draw better than the boys' tournament, invariably filling the 15,000 seats in Veterans' Memorial Auditorium, Des Moines, for five days in March." The passing and the uncanny accuracy of the girls' shooting continues to attract cheering fans from the smallest farm town, all on fire with a community-minded fever that makes heroines of hometown girls.

Even the increased pace of today's women's game has failed to attract Iowans. The men's rules were adopted in 1971—except in Oklahoma and Iowa. Tradition prevails; so does the "bounce-bounce-pass" and "bounce-pass-shoot" tempo of their game. As long as the media maintains support of Iowa girls' basketball and Iowans put their pride on the line each time their team takes the court, the two-court, six-player game will flourish.

Elsewhere in the country jump shots, hook shots, and fast breaks are attracting thousands of people to watch women display skills identical to their male counterparts. The almost simultaneous acceptance of Title IX and the emergence of fast-paced basketball for women led inevitably to women's AIAW championship games that watched Immaculata College and Delta State dominate the sport. Finally in 1982, the AIAW gave way to the NCAA championships, and women's basketball entered a new era.

Influenced by the same thinking that acknowledges women's rights everywhere, the new era in women's basketball echoes the position of Cathy Rush, former coach of Immaculata: "Women don't want favors, just fairness." Some collegiate programs may be suffering financially, but, by and large, women's basketball is here to stay. The brilliance of player performance and coaching strategy and the determination of athletes and coaches alike are guaranteeing a continuing bright future.

# HIGH SCHOOL BASKETBALL

## America's Greatest High School Girls' Basketball Coach

### Bertha Teague

Coach Teague is number one in many ways. She is the winningest coach in the nation with 1,152 career victories against only 115 defeats. She is among the top two or three coaches with the most state titles (8); she has one of the nation's longest win streaks (98); and she is the only high school basketball coach to be elected into the Basketball Hall of Fame in Springfield, Massachusetts.

Born in 1906 in Carthage, Missouri, Coach Teague graduated from Oklahoma State University in 1932 but already had started coaching in 1926. She devoted 42 of her 45 years of coaching to Ada Byng High School in Oklahoma, where she won 38 conference titles and 27 district championships, earned 22 state tournament berths, and won eight state crowns. Eighteen of Coach Teague's teams won 30 games or more, and five were undefeated.

One of the founders and, in 1962, the first president of the Oklahoma High Schools Girls Coaches Association, Coach Teague was reelected to the position six times while also serving on the National Rules Committee for Girls' Sport. Coach Teague was elected to the Oklahoma Hall of Fame in 1971. Two years earlier, the governor of Oklahoma had declared Bertha Teague Day.

## Number Two

**James Smiddy.** The second-winningest coach in the history of high school basketball for girls with a total of 1,072 victories against only 171 defeats, Coach Smiddy is a legend at Cleveland's Bradley Central High School in Tennessee. The winner of five state crowns and one runner-up award, Coach Smiddy has been connected with basketball for 52 years as a coach and a player. He has coached for 39 years, within that time winning two national championships (1975 and 1976). In 1984, the team's picture was exhibited in the Basketball Hall of Fame in Springfield for their record over the previous 25 years.

Coach Smiddy has been selected Coach of the Year eight times, including as the NHSACA/Wilson National Coach of the Year in 1985. He is a frequent speaker at clinics throughout the country and in 1975 was honored by the Tennessee Senate and House of Representatives and, a year later, by the Mayor of Cleveland and the Chamber of Commerce. Coach Smiddy has coached his state's All-Star team twice and in 1977 was chosen as the Alumnus of the Year by his alma mater, Cumberland College.

## Number Three

**Carrice Baker.** The primary force behind Jena High School's number-five ranking on the national list for most state championships, Coach Baker has won eight state titles during his 32 years of coaching at Winnsboro High School and Jena High School, both in Louisiana. He has earned a career record of 772-146 and has been selected as Coach of the Year eight times, including in 1980 as the NHSACA/Wilson National Coach of the Year.

Coach Baker has been a member of the National Education Association, the Louisiana Association of Teachers, and the Louisiana High School Coaching Association, having been selected by this latter group as the state's All-Star Coach in 1975.

## Number Four

**John Juneau.** The man responsible for leading Lacassine High School in Louisiana to five consecutive state championships and a number-five ranking on the national all-time list for consecutive state titles,

Coach Juneau won a sixth state crown two years later. During his almost 20 years at Lacassine, he has never been without a championship and has won close to 600 games. He has been awarded Coach of the Year honors eight times, including the 1982 NHSACA/Wilson National Coach of the Year award.

Coach Juneau has been the state representative to the National High School Athletic Coaches Association and has served on the All-Star Selection Committee of the Louisiana High School Coaches Association. He also has been the camp director of the Cardinal Basketball Camp, one of the largest in Louisiana.

## Number Five

**Wayne Merryman.** A man whose self-professed interests range from riding bulls to coaching basketball, Coach Merryman identifies as his *greatest* pleasure the fact that he coached 25 All-Staters and five All-Americans. He also has amassed a total victory record of 681 wins against only 152 losses, including three state titles and three runners-up. During his 29 years of coaching at three schools in Oklahoma, Coach Merryman has never been without a championship. For his accomplishments, he was awarded Coach of the Year honors several times, including the 1984 NHSACA/Wilson National Girls Basketball Coach of the Year.

Coach Merryman has been a member of the Oklahoma Coaches Association throughout his career, serving on the board of directors half that time. He has been a member of the National Coaches Association and both the Oklahoma and National Rules Committees. Coach Merryman is a member of the Jim Thorpe Nominating Committee and the All-State Selection Committee and chairs the Oklahoma Hall of Fame Committee. He also serves on the Advisory Committee of the Oklahoma Secondary Schools Activities Association.

## Other Qualifiers

**John Bearden.** With 20-some years' experience at three high schools in Georgia, Coach Bearden has won close to 500 games and has lost fewer than 100. The winner of two state championships and several Coach of the Year awards, Bearden has dedicated himself to his sport by participating in a range of state and national organizations. Coach Bearden was named National Girls' Basketball Coach of the Year by NHSACA/Wilson in 1979.

**Merle Gorr.** One of the winningest coaches in high school girls' basketball, Coach Gorr, during his 22 years with Shreveport Trinity

Heights High School in Louisiana, won close to 700 games with an .890 winning percentage.

**Charles Heatly.** The home of several outstanding girls' basketball coaches, Oklahoma has witnessed Lindsay High School develop one of the finest records in the state, including two state championships. Led by Coach Heatly for more than 20 years, the girls at Lindsay have won close to 550 games and have earned Coach of the Year honors for Lindsay four times. The founder of the Oklahoma Girls Coaches Association, Coach Heatly alternately served as member or chairman of the board for 17 years. Heatly also has authored a widely circulated book on high school basketball and has directed the largest girls' basketball camp in the nation. Heatly was named by NHSACA/Wilson as the National Coach of the Year in 1981.

**Thadnall Hill.** One of only three or four girls' basketball coaches in the nation to win over 1,000 games, Coach Hill led Hardy Highland in Arizona to close to 1,100 victories. During his 36-year career, he lost only 122 games, for a winning percentage of .898.

**Galen Johnson.** The head coach at Maryville Porter High School in Tennessee for 28 years, Coach Johnson is one of the top five winningest coaches in girls basketball history. During his career, he led Maryville to a remarkable 735 victories.

**Harold Jones.** Another of Oklahoma's great girls' high school basketball coaches, Coach Jones has spent his entire career with Dale High School and has led them to close to 500 victories against only 77 defeats. Coach Jones is the winner of three state championships and at least three Coach of the Year awards, including the NHSACA/Wilson National Coach of the Year in 1983. Jones has served extensively on state coaching committees, several times as president, and has spoken at numerous coaching clinics.

**Don Rippetoe.** As head coach of four high schools in Oklahoma for almost 30 years, Coach Rippetoe has led his teams to almost 600 career victories and three state championships. He has been the recipient of several Coach of the Year honors, including the NHSACA/Wilson National Coach of the Year award in 1977. Coach Rippetoe also has served with the Oklahoma High School Girls Coaches Association as a district director and, most recently, president of the organization.

**Carroll Rugland.** Also the recipient of the NHSACA/Wilson Coach of the Year Award (in 1986), Coach Rugland devoted close to 30 years of his coaching career to girls' basketball in Iowa. Most of his career was divided between two schools, Montezuma Community High School, where he won two state titles, and Hampton Community High School, where he won four regional crowns and several district championships. His career record of 545-148 ranks among the best in the country. Coach Rugland has been selected as Area Coach of the Year seven times and has served for several coaching organizations, including basketball advisory committees and the Basketball Hall of Fame jury.

**Robert Winter.** With only 12 years' experience as a head coach, Bob Winter has made his mark on South Dakota girls' basketball. During his relatively brief tenure with Yankton High School, his teams have compiled a 237-25 record, for a winning percentage of .905, and five state titles. Coach Winter also has found the time to serve as president of the South Dakota Basketball Coaches Association, to chair several committees for the NHSACA, and to speak at clinics throughout the state. Coach Winter's impact on sport was so great that he already has been inducted into the South Dakota Coaches Hall of Fame.

**Charles Womack.** Already among the nation's top coaches in boys' basketball with 896 career victories, Coach Womack is among the top ten in girls' basketball with a career record of 674-110, for a winning percentage of .860. The head coach of Hawley High School in Texas for 33 years, Coach Womack retired in 1979.

# COLLEGE BASKETBALL

## America's Greatest College Women's Basketball Coach

### L. Margaret Wade

Coach Wade was born on December 30, 1912, in McCool, Mississippi, graduated from Cleveland High School, and attended Delta State University, her hometown school of fewer than 2,000 students. She starred as a player in both high school and college and began her coaching career in high school at Marietta, Mississippi, returning to Delta State in 1973 to oversee their revived basketball program. Her first team enjoyed a 16-2 record, and her next team went on to win 28 straight games to capture the AIAW national championship.

Her third team, in 1975-1976, earned a record of 33-1, enjoyed a 73-70 victory over the Chinese National Team, and posted its second consecutive AIAW national title. Coach Wade's Lady Statesmen followed the victory the next year with a 32-3 record and their third consecutive AIAW crown, an accomplishment that has never been bettered in national competition.

Coach Wade retired in 1979 with a career record of 633-117. Her pioneering efforts for women's basketball resulted in her induction into the Mississippi Sports Hall of Fame in 1975. That same year, she was enshrined in the Basketball Hall of Fame in Springfield, Massachusetts, one of only three women to receive the honor. In 1977, the Wade Trophy, awarded each year to the nation's outstanding collegiate woman player, was instituted in her honor.

## Number Two

**Pat Summitt.** A head coach at the age of 22 at the University of Tennessee, Coach Pat Summitt has accomplished what most coaches only dream of. As a player, she won an Olympic silver medal in 1976. As a coach, she led the American team to its first gold medal in the 1984 Olympics. And in 1987, she led the Lady Vols to their first NCAA national championship. She repeated again in 1989. During her 14 years with Tennessee, she has won well over 300 games, earned a winning percentage of close to .800, led her teams to ten trips to the final four in national competition, and enjoyed 12 consecutive seasons with 20 or more wins.

Most importantly, Coach Summitt has contributed widely to the game. She has served as vice president of the Amateur Basketball Association of the United States of America (ABAUSA), is a member of the board of trustees and of the executive board of directors of the Basketball Hall of Fame, is a member of the Valvoline Sports Advisory Board, and is a member of the Target board of directors. In addition, she has been a member of the Big Brothers–Big Sisters and was the honorary chair for the Tennessee Easter Seal Society in 1985 and 1987.

## Number Three

**Marianne Stanley.** A 1976 graduate of Immaculata College, a legendary program in women's basketball, Coach Stanley became the head coach of Old Dominion at the age of 23 and in two years led them to two consecutive AIAW national championships. She has won close to 300 games with the Lady Monarchs and has earned a winning percentage of .820, one of the best in the nation. She has been named National Coach of the Year twice and Virginia Coach of the Year four times.

In NCAA tournament competition, Coach Stanley has added to her two AIAW crowns with a tie for third place in 1983, a regional runner-up in 1984, and a national championship in 1985. She has enjoyed a berth in the tournament during each of its first six years and in 1985 was inducted as a charter member into the Women's Basketball Hall of Fame.

## Number Four

**Jody Conradt.** Since the advent of NCAA women's competition in 1982, the Lady Longhorns, under the direction of Coach Jody Conradt, have earned a remarkable 187-14 record, for the unparalleled winning percentage of .930, and have never lost a Southwest Conference game, stringing together 101 victories. Coach Conradt's career record of 502-116 is the best among Division I coaches, and her record in NCAA tournament competition is remarkable.

The Lady Longhorns won the national championship in 1986, tied for third in 1987, made the final eight in 1988, and achieved regional runner-up status in both 1983 and 1984. For such accomplishments, Coach Conradt has been selected National Coach of the Year three times (in '80, '84, and '86) and in 1987 headed the United States team in the Pan Am Games, where she won a gold medal. A coveted speaker, Coach Conradt devotes each day to clinics, meetings, and workshops across the country. Her travels take her to hospitals, children's homes, clinics, and NCAA committees and have established her as the motive force behind the "Lady Longhorn Family" at the University of Texas.

## Number Five

**Linda Sharp.** One of Coach Billie Moore's outstanding players at Cal State Fullerton, Linda Sharp graduated in 1973 and became the head coach of Southern California four years later. At the time one of the nation's youngest head coaches, Coach Sharp experienced in her first year her only losing season. During her next nine, she finished among the nation's top teams every year, winning back-to-back national championships in 1983 and 1984. Coach Sharp has taken the Women of Troy to the NCAA tournament every year since its inauguration in 1982 and, in addition to her two national titles, placed second in 1986 and was regional runner-up in '82.

In 11 seasons with USC, Sharp has earned close to 250 career victories, with a winning percentage of .760, one of the best in the nation. She has been selected as the head coach of the American contingent for the World University Games and in 1984 was invited to the White House to meet President Reagan in recognition of her several contributions to women's athletics.

## Number Six

**Sonja Hogg.** Coach Hogg retired from basketball after the 1985 season at Louisiana Tech University and eventually became an assistant director of women's athletics at the University of Texas. During her 11 years with the Lady Techsters, she guided them to a 307-55 career record, for one of the best winning percentages in women's basketball, and four appearances in the NCAA Tournament, winning the championship in

1982, the tournament's first year, and placing second and third in the nation during 1983 and 1984. In 1985, her last year with LTU, her team achieved regional runner-up status.

Said Coach Hogg just before her retirement, "I enjoy being a spokeswoman for women's athletics because I believe deeply that it can play a vital part in the development of young women." Her philosophy has led her to serve on several national committees within both the NCAA and the Women's Basketball Coaches Association. It continues to compel her to speak out on behalf of women's athletics and to be one of the nation's most eloquent keynote speakers.

## Other Qualifiers

**Senda Berenson Abbott.** America's "Mother of Women's Basketball," Coach Abbott visited Dr. James Naismith shortly after he had invented basketball at Springfield College in Massachusetts. The Director of Physical Education at Smith College at the time, Coach Abbott introduced the game to her students, adapted the rules for women, and directed the first women's game on March 21, 1893. Her rules influenced women's basketball for 75 years, as did her book, the first women's *Basketball Guide*, which was published in 1901. Coach Abbott, the motive force behind women's basketball and its first legitimate coach, died in 1954.

**Joan Bonvicini.** Coach Bonvicini graduated in 1975 from Southern Connecticut, a school rich in athletic traditions. Bonvicini assumed the reins of Long Beach State nine years ago and has led them to the NCAA final four for two consecutive years ('87 and '88). She has led her team to the tournament each year of its existence and has won close to 250 games against only 50 losses for a .835 winning percentage.

**Joe Ciampi.** A graduate of Mansfield State in 1968, Coach Ciampi has been at Auburn for 11 years and has taken them to the NCAA tournament every year but one. His Tigers were regional runner-up in 1987 and went to the championship game in 1988, losing to Leon Barmore's Louisiana Lady Techsters. Ciampi has won close to 250 games and has earned a winning percentage of .774 while at Auburn.

**Fern Gardner.** Coach Gardner stepped down from the coaching ranks in 1983, after having coached at Utah for 15 years and led the Lady Utes to a record of 318-95. She took them to the NCAA tournament once (1983) and retired as the winningest Division I basketball coach. While at Utah State, Gardner won seven conference championships and appeared seven times at the AIAW national championships. In 1984, Coach Gardner became the full-time assistant athletic director at Utah.

**Sue Gunter.** One of the winningest coaches in NCAA Division I women's basketball, Coach Gunter has taken Louisiana State to the NCAA tournament three times, earning regional runner-up status in 1986. Her career record reflects close to 400 victories against only 130 defeats. A graduate of Peabody in 1962, Coach Gunter has been coaching for 18 years.

**Andy Landers.** With a career record of 310-84, Coach Landers has enjoyed eight consecutive 20-game seasons, three Southeast Conference crowns, seven straight NCAA tournament appearances, and two final-four berths. His Georgia Lady Bulldogs finished third in the nation in 1983 and second in 1985. A 1974 graduate of Tennessee Tech, a school with its own winning traditions, Landers sums up his experiences at Georgia: "It seems to me we've really accomplished everything there is, with the exception of winning the national championship. And we're going to get that done."

**Marynell Meadors.** With 18 years of experience, Coach Meadors has spent most of her playing and coaching career in Tennessee. A graduate of Middle Tennessee in 1965, she has coached Tennessee Tech to two NCAA tournament appearances and close to 400 career victories, one of the best records of active Division I coaches.

**Billie Moore.** Having coached such standout players as Ann Meyers at UCLA and Pat Summitt in the Olympics, Coach Moore has helped develop some of America's finest players and coaches. A graduate of Washburn University in Kansas ('66), Coach Moore began her coaching career at Cal State Fullerton, where she led her team to a national championship during her first year. After eight years with Cal State, she moved to UCLA, where she earned another national championship during her first year. Since that time, Coach Moore has taken UCLA to the NCAA tournament twice and has earned a career record of close to 350 victories, one of the highest in the nation among active coaches.

**Rene Portland.** A member of the Immaculata team that registered its third straight AIAW championship in 1974, Coach Portland graduated in 1975 and moved almost immediately to Penn State, where she has taken the Nittany Lions to the NCAA tournament seven straight times. During her 12-year tenure at Penn State, Coach Portland has been regional runner-up once in (1983) and has earned a career victory record of close to 300 games.

**Vivian Stringer.** A graduate of Slippery Rock in 1970, Coach Stringer has divided her time between two outstanding women's basketball programs. At Cheyney, she appeared twice in the NCAA tournament, placing second in the nation in 1982, the tournament's first year. A couple of years later, at Iowa, she appeared twice more in the tournament, winning regional runner-up in 1987. Coach Stringer has earned a career win/loss record of close to 350 wins against fewer than 100 defeats, for a percentage of .806, one of the best in the nation.

**Chris Waller.** A graduate of Maryland and now its head coach, Coach Waller has been with the Terrapins for 13 years and has guided them to five NCAA tournaments, placing third in 1982 and reaching the final eight in 1988. Coach Waller has earned a career record of close to 250 victories and a winning percentage of .700.

**Kay Yow.** With 17 years' experience, Coach Yow is one of the veterans of the women's basketball ranks. This graduate of East Carolina has taken North Carolina State to the NCAA tournament six of its first seven years and has earned a career record of close to 350 games and a winning percentage of .760. Coach Yow was the head coach of the 1988 Olympic team.

# Chapter 13

# FIELD HOCKEY

Identifying the first coach of most American sports is virtually impossible. Records are often inadequate, owing to the simultaneous organization of several teams in the sport's national birthplace. There is no such problem with field hockey for women. The sport's first coach was unquestionably Constance M.K. Applebee, "Connie" to field hockey fans and "The Apple" to her friends.

Connie arrived from England in 1901 with 22 sticks and a ball and immediately established a summer camp in the Pocono Mountains of Pennsylvania. So enthusiastic was her advocacy of the game that several Eastern women's colleges, among them Smith, Radcliffe, Vassar, and Wellesley, integrated field hockey into their sports programs. Eventually, Connie helped found the United States Field Hockey Association (USFHA) while she coached during the winter months at Bryn Mawr College.

The game was met with such excitement that in one school alone 500 girls signed up to play during its inaugural year (Hill, 1903). Its development was not restricted to the private, wealthy colleges in the East. Although field hockey remains prominent on the East Coast, it has spread to most states in America and is the primary girls' fall sport in high school.

Tradition has helped sustain it. Plaid skirts and knee socks with light blouses or sweaters are the traditional uniform today, having replaced the billowing petticoats and long skirts that inhibited play at the turn of the century. Here, too, Connie influenced the game's evolution. In 1903, she wrote that plain skirts and loosely fitting shirts should be worn, that the game could not "be safely or well played in ordinary dress" (Howell, 1982).

A member of the International Federation of Women's Hockey Associations (IFWHA), the USFHA annually coordinates travel to such countries as Great Britain, Denmark, South Africa, Hong Kong, and the Fiji Islands to play field hockey. A game enjoying worldwide popularity, field hockey is played by young and old alike and, because it's played by men and women, often becomes an interest of the entire family.

Although the outstanding women's programs are still on the East Coast, a fact reflected in our selection of America's Greatest Coaches, the game is enjoyed in other areas, particularly in the Midwest, where several outstanding women's programs have been developed.

# HIGH SCHOOL FIELD HOCKEY

## America's Greatest High School Girls' Field Hockey Coach

**Nancy Cole**

The fourth-winningest field hockey coach in high school history, Coach Cole has led Centereach High School in New York to five state titles, three of them consecutive (1981 through 1983). Since her inauguration as the mentor of the Centereach program, Coach Cole has earned a record of 238-22-15 for a winning percentage of .90. Her 1983 team ranks second on the all-time list for goals scored in a season, with 152, and fifth for goals scored in a game, with 13. Her 1986 team ranks second on the all-time list for most shutouts in a season, with 19.

One of Cole's greatest professional satisfactions, however, involves the scoring proficiency of Tracey Fuchs, a 1983 graduate. Tracey ranks second on the all-time list for career goals, with 171, only 3 behind the leader; and she ranks number one on the all-time list for goals in a season, with 82, a full 25 goals ahead of the second-place finisher. Tracey also ranks number one on the all-time list for scoring average per game, with 3.28, and for scoring in the most consecutive games, with 51. One of her teammates, Cathy Lunghi, ranks number one on the all-time list for assists in a season (33) and assists in consecutive games (15).

## Number Two

**Faith Littlefield.** The head coach of Bonny Eagle High School in Buxton, Maine, since the mid-1970s, Coach Littlefield has led her teams to six state crowns, second on the all-time list. She also ranks second on the all-time list for consecutive state titles with three (1983 through 1985). Her teams from 1976 through 1978 also won three consecutive state titles, earning another second-place finish on the all-time list.

## Number Three

**Beverley Osterberg.** The head coach of the Stowe High School field hockey team since 1973, Coach Osterberg brought almost immediate success to the program. In an area famous for its field hockey, her teams have recorded eight Vermont state championships, an accomplishment that ranks her number one on the all-time list. From 1973 through 1977, Coach Osterberg guided her teams to five consecutive state titles, another record that ranks number one on the all-time of high school records.

## Other Qualifiers

**Dorotha Edwards.** One of the nation's high school pioneers in the sport, Coach Edwards began her career with Casady High School in Oklahoma City in 1956 and guided their field hockey fortunes for 30 years. Coach Edwards established the remarkable win/loss record of 315-18-16, for a winning percentage of .950 and the number one spot in the nation as the winningest high school field hockey coach.

**Betty Lacey.** Another pioneer of the sport, Coach Lacey spent most of her career with Southern Cayuga Central in New York and established within her 21 years one of the finest winning percentages in the nation. She led Central to a win/loss record of 191-6, for a winning percentage of .96.

**Pat Mihalko.** The mentor of Cooperstown Central in New York, Coach Mihalko takes the attention of the local residents off the Baseball Hall of Fame and directs it to Central's hockey field, where she has led her squads to a career win/loss record of 226-49-38, for a winning percentage of approximately .822. Her strength over the years has involved the development of goalies. Goalie Barbara Smith, a 1981 graduate of Central, ranks fifth on the all-time list for career shutouts, with 29. Her predecessor, Kit Mulligan, a 1978 graduate, ranks 10th on the all-time list for shutouts in a season, with 14.

**Janice Edwards Lees.** The head coach of Milford Delaware Valley High School since the 1970s, Coach Lees has established her program as one of the premier field hockey programs in the country. They rank fourth on the all-time list for consecutive victories, with 39, and for most goals scored in a season, with 123. Her 1976 team ranks fifth in the nation for average number of goals per game, with 5.72, and her 1978 team ranks eight in the nation for most shutouts in a season, with 17, all of which were consecutive, a mark that ranks second on the all-time list for consecutive shutouts. Two of Coach Lees's proudest accomplishments, however, involve two former players. Carleen McAllister leads the country in goals per game, with 2.1, and Anita Emery ranks second in the nation for career shutouts, with 42.

**Gail Stevenson.** The third-winningest coach on the all-time list, Coach Stevenson has coached at Mamaroneck Rye in New York since 1962 and has earned a record of 242-20-16, for an enviable winning percentage of .916. Coach Stevenson ranks fifth on the all-time list for consecutive victories, with 37, and her 1985 team ranks fifth on the all-time list for most goals scored in a season, with 118. Perhaps her most enjoyable accomplishment, however, involves former athlete Sharon Landau, who ranks first on the all-time high school list for most goals scored during a career, with 174, and third on the all-time list for goals in a season, with 53.

# COLLEGE FIELD HOCKEY

## America's Greatest College Women's Field Hockey Coach

### Vonnie Gros

One of 23 charter members to be inducted into the new United States Field Hockey Association Hall of Fame in 1988, Coach Gros has figured prominently in the growth and popularity of American field hockey for several decades. A graduate of Ursinus College in 1957, Gros was selected the following year to play for the U.S. national team. She remained with them for 12 years, traveling around the world three times and eventually taking over the head coach position at West Chester State.

Within five years, Coach Gros led West Chester to back-to-back national championships (1975 and 1976) and was subsequently chosen the head coach of the national team in 1978. Her career record at West Chester was 118-6-13, for a .942 winning percentage, the best in the nation.

Coach Gros led the national team to two Olympics (1980 and 1984), winning a bronze medal in 1984. Said Gros of her experiences: "I really enjoy coaching. It's like coaching any sport. You're coaching because you're working with people who enjoy the sport. I really like that." It's a philosophy that made her America's best.

## Number Two

**Beth Anders.** With the most impressive win/loss record of any collegiate field hockey program, Coach Anders has led Old Dominion to the "head of America's field hockey class" since she became the head coach in 1980. Her 7-year record is 136-14-3, for a winning percentage of .899. Most notably, she has never finished lower than fifth nationally, and she has won four NCAA Division I titles, three of them consecutively (1982-1984), an NCAA record.

A 1973 graduate of Ursinus College, Anders played on both the national field hockey team and the national basketball team. She has played every position for the U.S. team but goalie and was the instrumental player for the team during the 1984 Olympics when the U.S. won a bronze medal. In fact, the U.S. Olympic Committee voted Coach Anders the Amateur Athlete of the Year for Field Hockey for an unprecedented second time. She was similarly honored in 1981.

## Number Three

**Diane Wright.** With a 13-year career record of 188-49-24, Coach Wright is one of the winningest coaches in field hockey history. Two years after taking over the University of Connecticut program in 1975, she led the Huskies to a national top-10 finish and, since then, has never finished lower than ninth. Coach Wright culminated her search for a national title in 1981 when she led her team to the NCAA Division I championship. She followed with another in 1985 while claiming two runner-up spots in the interim. In fact, Coach Wright led the Huskies to five consecutive final four berths (1981 through 1985).

A 1969 graduate of West Chester, Coach Wright directs a very successful field hockey camp during the summers and is a past member of the NCAA Division I Field Hockey Committee. She also chairs the University of Connecticut Athletic Awards and Endowment Scholarship Committee and served on the University of Connecticut Athletic Director Search Committee in 1987.

## Other Qualifiers

**Cheeseman Alexander.** A player on the national team from 1973 to 1984, Cheeseman Alexander was described by her coach as "the best goalkeeper in the world." Said Alexander of her own play: "You have to be ready; because if you make an error, it is crucial. You have to be playing every ball." The coach of Temple University during her final years of participating, Coach Alexander recorded over 100 victories and reached the finals of the AIAW title game in 1981. Under her direction, the Lady Owls also placed third in the 1984 NCAA tournament.

**Adele Boyd.** The head coach of Ursinus College since 1971, Coach Boyd was one of two coaches responsible for her school's 59-year string of winning seasons. Under her direction, Ursinus has finished in the top 20 no less than 10 times in the 13-year history of the AIAW and NCAA competition.

**Robin Cash.** The successor to Vonnie Gros at West Chester University in 1977, Coach Cash inherited a string of consecutive victories that she continued into her second year of coaching. On October 26, 1978, Penn State defeated West Chester to end a string of 70 consecutive wins, the longest in the history of the sport. During that period, Coach Cash led West Chester to back-to-back AIAW national titles (1977 and 1978).

**Judith Davidson.** Coach Davidson mentored the Lady Hawkeyes of Iowa from 1978 to 1987 before assuming the position of athletic director at Central Connecticut State University. During her tenure with the Hawkeyes, Coach Davidson earned over 200 career wins and played four times in the final four, placing second in 1984 and winning a national championship in 1986. She won the Big Ten title seven times and, during her final seven years, never finished lower than fifth in the national rankings. Coach Davidson has been the recipient of several Coach of the Year awards, has been involved in a range of professional committees, and is the author of six articles.

**Jan Hutchinson.** The head coach of Bloomsburg University in Pennsylvania for 11 seasons, Coach Hutchinson has earned a win/loss record of 177-31-15 and has won her conference title 6 straight years. She led the Huskies to the NCAA Division III national title in 1987 and in 1988 finished second to Trenton in a double overtime. Also the softball coach at Bloomsburg, Coach Hutchinson has earned a combined record of 466-109-15, for a winning percentage of .803, one of the tops in the nation.

**Karen Shelton.** A player on three AIAW national championship teams at West Chester, Coach Shelton has guided the North Carolina Tar Heels since 1981. In her own words: "It's hard to learn high-level play without being involved in high-level play. What we learned about techniques, strategy, and tactics we were able to take back and teach to young players." Coach Shelton has done it well. She has won six consecutive ACC titles and has finished in the top 10 of the national rankings in every year but one, placing second in the AIAW in 1981 and in the NCAA tournament in 1987.

**Eleanor Snell.** Perhaps the earliest pioneer of collegiate field hockey, Coach Snell was the mother of the sport at Ursinus College and guided them from 1931 to 1970, never experiencing a losing season. The debt owed to Coach Snell extends well beyond her career record. Her love of the game helped develop such outstanding players as Marion Earl in the '30s, later to become a sports journalist; Bunny Vosters in the '40s; Ruth Aucott and Vonnie Gros in the '50s, both outstanding players and coaches; and Sue Lubking, Judy Wolstenhome, and Joan Moser in the '60s. Wolstenhome and Moser were great players later to become umpires, and Lubking became the assistant athletic director of West Chester and eventually president of the USWLA.

**Suzanne Tyler.** Before she resigned as head field hockey coach of the University of Maryland in 1988, Coach Suzanne Tyler had led the Terrapins to a career record of 154-84-27 and had produced several All-Americans and All-ACC players. Most notably, she led her 1987 team to the NCAA Division I title with a 2-1 victory over North Carolina. She resigned in 1988 to become the assistant athletic director.

# Chapter 14

# SOCCER

Although soccer was first played in America in the mid-1800s, it is a relatively recent arrival for women. Because most of the programs in schools started in the 1970s, the early history of the sport for women is being written today, and its pioneers are recent college graduates. Women's soccer coaches, therefore, have yet to reach the legendary status of coaches within the more established sports, but their genius for strategy and motivation already are evident in scores of successful programs. Their recent successes have been so pronounced that several of them already rank among America's Greatest.

# COLLEGE SOCCER

## America's Greatest College Women's Soccer Coach

**Anson Dorrance**

No one has dominated the formative years of a college sport like Coach Dorrance. The winningest coach in women's soccer with well over 100 victories, Coach Dorrance has led the University of North Carolina to six national championships in seven years. The one year when the Tar Heels were not national champs (1985), they were runners-up to George Mason. Coach Dorrance has played in the championship match of every NCAA Division I tournament and has won it all but once.

He is the head coach of the U.S. women's national team and has created soccer leagues in both Connecticut and North Carolina, including the North Carolina Youth Soccer Association and the North Carolina Soccer League. Coach Dorrance also has been a member of the NCAA Women's Soccer Committee since its inception in 1982.

Well-traveled in his youth, Coach Dorrance as a child lived in Kenya, Singapore, Belgium, Switzerland, Malaysia, England, and Ethiopia. It was in Ethiopia that he met his wife, the former M'Liss Gary, a professional ballerina. The Dorrances have two daughters, Michelle and Natalie, both of whom play soccer.

## Other Qualifiers

**Jim Babyak.** The only soccer coach in Smith College history, Coach Babyak has led his teams to a Northeast Intercollegiate Athletes' Conference (NIAC) championship in 1979, a Massachusetts Association title in 1983, two Eastern Colleges Athletic Conference (ECAC) crowns, and the NCAA quarterfinals in 1986. He has led Smith to well over 100 wins, making the school only one of six in the country with that many victories. A former professional baseball player for the New York Yankees, Coach Babyak also has served on various selection committees and has been the tournament director for several championships, including the NCAA Division III championship in 1986.

**Dan Blank.** The head man at St. Mary's College for eight years, Coach Blank has led the Cardinals to a 38-2 record within the past 3 years against conference foes. His overall record is 82-30-6, and his teams have won the MIAC title three times. Coach Blank has been named the Coach of the Year twice and has served as the chairman of the ISAA West Region. He also works extensively with summer soccer camps and with clinics throughout the Midwest.

**Kalakeni Banda.** During his eight years at the University of Massachusetts, Coach Banda joined the pioneers of women's soccer by being one of only six schools to earn 100 victories. He joined Massachusetts in 1980 and when he left in 1987 had earned a career mark of 118-25-9. He concluded his first year by winning the Eastern Association of Intercollegiate Athletics championship, entered the AIAW Tournament in 1981, and qualified for the NCAA tournament for the next six years, placing second in the nation in 1987. Coach Banda retired from women's soccer at Massachusetts to become the head track coach at Amherst College in 1988.

**Dominic Garguile.** Completing his eighth year with Western Washington University, Coach Garguile has earned a career record of 82-20-9. The 1987 season marked the only time that a Garguile-coached team failed to make the NAIA play-offs since women's soccer was added in 1983. Garguile's coaching career was highlighted by the 1983 season at Western Washington. His team enjoyed an undefeated season, its second conference title, and the NAIA national championship. Coach Garguile has never finished lower than fourth in his conference and has enjoyed working with five NAIA All-Americans. Garguile has been named NCSC Coach of the Year twice.

**Terry Gurnett.** Ten years at the helm of the University of Rochester Yellowjackets has earned Coach Gurnett a career victory mark of 111 wins, but most importantly it has accounted for two NCAA Division III national championships (1986 and 1987). Prior to that, Coach Gurnett has been runner-up to the national champs twice and had won the New York State AIAW tournament four times, three of them consecutively.

Coach Gurnett also is the ISAA's National Women's Soccer Membership Chairman, a member of the ECAC Selection Committee, and a member of the NCAA Division III Ranking and Tournament Committees.

**Colin Lindores.** The head coach of both the men's and the women's programs at Cal State Hayward, Coach Lindores has led the Pioneers to four straight NCAC titles and has been named NCAC Coach of the Year three times. His 7-year record at CSH is 81-27-9 and includes two appearances in the NCAA tournament.

**Hank Leung.** With a career record of 88-25-9, Coach Leung has taken little George Mason to the top in collegiate soccer for women. He took the Lady Patriots to the NCAA tournament in five of his first six years as head coach, winning the NCAA Division I national title in 1985. A man committed to his sport, Coach Leung is also the assistant coach of the national women's team and the head coach of the National Youth Team. He has been selected national Coach of the Year three times, once by *Soccer America* magazine.

**Dang Pibulvech.** A school of only 2,000 students, Colorado College has locked horns with the major soccer powers in the nation and has earned their respect. Their success is attributable to a young native of Bangkok, Thailand, who became the Tigers' head coach in 1983. Pibulvech has posted a 76-16-5 record, for a winning percentage of .809, and has twice appeared in the NCAA's final four, placing second in the nation in 1986. Coach Pibulvech has been named Coach of the Year four times, serves on the NCAA Women's Soccer Committee, and is the chairman of the NCAA Central Region.

**Bob Scalise.** Yet another of a very few coaches to achieve over 100 wins during the first 10 years of women's intercollegiate soccer competition, Coach Scalise left Harvard with a career mark of 113-38-11. His teams won Ivy League titles three times and participated in the NCAA tournament twice, winning the NCAA District I crown in 1982. Scalise was most proud of the fact that nine of his players achieved status as All-Americans. He retired from coaching to enter the Harvard Business School.

**Len Tsantiris.** After nine seasons with the University of Connecticut, Coach Tsantiris has taken the Huskies to a career record of well over 100 wins and has appeared in a national tournament every year.

He has reached the final four in the AIAW tournament once and in the NCAA three times, finishing second in the nation in 1984 with a record of 17-4-2. His 1982 and 1983 squads finished the regular season undefeated. Coach Tsantiris has received Coach of the Year honors several times and has served on a variety of soccer boards and organizations, including membership on the NCAA's Advisory Committee and Soccer Legislation Committee and chairmanship of the ISAA Women's "Senior Bowl" Selection Committee.

# Chapter 15

# SOFTBALL

F. Scott Fitzgerald once referred to baseball as a child's game played by a few dozen illiterates. Maybe that's why it never caught on with women. Others say it was because of the hard ball and the expense of the equipment (Fidley, 1982). Still others indicate that it simply became "unfashionable" when Bloomer Girls started playing the game in immodest uniforms to attract male crowds. History does reveal, however, that coeds in certain Eastern colleges risked public censure by playing the game as early as 1876.

Softball got its "official" start, however, at the Farragut Boat Club in Chicago in 1887 when inclement weather forced a few enterprising people inside to create a variation of baseball. The resultant game, modified a few times, became "Indoor Baseball" and gained considerable popularity first among men, then among women, particularly in the Midwest. Because the game involved a soft ball, it didn't require the equipment of baseball or as much playing space.

Popular in parks and school playgrounds, by 1919 the game was being played by most of the girls in the Cleveland area and was fast becoming the girls' equivalent of baseball for boys. Known popularly as playground ball in the early '20s, softball became standardized in 1934 when the Joint Rules Committee on Softball worked with organizations such as the NCAA, the YMCA, and the Amateur Softball Association to promote the game throughout the country.

By 1935, there were some 2 million players in America and more than 60,000 teams (Fidley, 1982). Most of these were men's teams, but within a few years women were beginning to make their numbers felt. By 1938, the Los Angeles area alone boasted more than a thousand women's teams (Fidley, 1982). And the game has continued to grow in popularity; now it is one of the foremost spring sports in most schools, high school as well as college. It also boasts a history of some of the finest coaches.

The site of the first six NCAA Division I softball tournaments, Omaha, Nebraska, enjoyed some of the finest performances in recent sport history. Bias for Cornhusker wizardry on the football field gradually transformed into admiration of athletic artistry on the softball diamond. Spectators learned within days what softball fans have known for years: Few sports rival softball for sustained excitement.

The play is fast-paced, the performances are striking, and the coaching is among the nation's best. Consider just pitching—and the recent superiority of Joan Joyce, the star of the Connecticut Falcons in the late 1970s. How does she compare with the legends of baseball? Jack Chesbro set a professional baseball record in 1904 with 41 wins in a single season. Joan Joyce had 42. Walter "Big Train" Johnson holds the major league record for strikeouts with 3,508. Joan Joyce has had 7,395. Sandy Koufax and Nolan Ryan hold the professional baseball record for no-hit games with four. Joan Joyce has had 131.

A recent *high school* pitcher, Michelle Granger from Placentia, California, has pitched 11 no-hitters in a single season, a national high school record. She also holds the career record for no-hitters with 27—and for strikeouts with 1,186. Softball *coaches* are no less accomplished. The win/loss records of some of the high school coaches are remarkable. Softball is well established in high school. It has gained widespread popularity in college, however, only recently—with the advent of Title IX and scholarships for women.

# HIGH SCHOOL SOFTBALL

## America's Greatest High School Girls' Softball Coach

### Dick Rasmussen

Coach Rasmussen began his coaching career at Ankeny High School in Iowa in 1965 and immediately won the state championship. He was runner-up a few years later and from 1977 through 1980 won four consecutive state titles. Two years later, his squads strung together three more crowns (1983-1985). In the interim, Coach Rasmussen won either regional or sectional titles to give Ankeny 19 championships.

Coach Rasmussen holds the state record for the most tournament appearances and is the only coach to have won three or more consecutive state titles twice. He has been selected as Coach of the Year five times, most recently as the NHSACA/Wilson National Softball Coach of the Year (1986). He has been selected by the Ankeny Chamber of Commerce as the Citizen of the Year and has been a guest speaker at state and national clinics.

Coach Rasmussen's commitment to softball extends well beyond the diamond. He has been the state director for the Iowa High School Coaches Association. He initiated the state's All-Star game, created the state's Hall of Fame for coaches and umpires, created the state's Coach of the

Year award, and suggested the recognition of All-District teams. He has served on softball advisory committees and has chaired the Iowa Athletic Coaches Association.

Coach Rasmussen is one of this book's examples of greatness in coaching extending well beyond the field of play.

## Number Two

**Bill Hennessey.** Of Coach Hennessey's 32 years in coaching, 28 were spent at Roland-Story High School in Iowa and eventuated in a career win/loss record of 963-298 and five state titles. In fact, Coach Hennessey has never been without a championship of some kind. When not winning the state title, he has won the sectional or district title. Coach Hennessey also enjoyed the distinction of coaching two of his daughters, both of whom played on his state championship teams.

In addition to coaching softball, Coach Hennessey has coached girls' basketball, girls' track, boys' and girls' golf, and boys' baseball. His cumulative career coaching record approximates 2,000 victories, the highest in the nation. He also has found the time to be a member of the board of the Iowa Girls High School Athletic Union and to be the softball chairman of the National High School Athletic Coaches Association.

Coach Hennessey has earned Coach of the Year honors several times and has been a speaker at numerous state clinics. He also has won his state's Golden Plaque Award for superior coaching and was honored when the city of Roland named the city's softball complex "Bill Hennessey Field."

## Number Three

**Rose Scott.** Coach Scott has guided Andrew Jackson High School in Louisiana for 20 years and has earned a career record of close to 300 victories and a winning percentage of .830. She has won the state championship eight times and has been runner-up twice. Coach Scott has been Coach of the Year 11 times, including National Coach of the Year in 1985.

In addition to directing several tournaments, Coach Scott has complemented her coaching duties by chairing the District 7 Softball Committee and by speaking at various clinics throughout the state. She also has published an article for *Women's Coaching Clinic* and has helped develop her state's curriculum guide for health and physical education.

## Number Four

**Bob Dickerson and Chester Brennan.** Bob Dickerson and Chester Brennan teamed up the past 30 years to establish one of the most remarkable records in high school softball history. They assisted and succeeded each other during the period of time when Pocola High School on the Oklahoma/Arkansas border established the best record for state championships at a single school. From 1958 to 1979, Pocola High School won 11 state titles, the national record. They also teamed up to win five consecutive crowns from 1966-70 for a number-two position on the all-time list.

## Number Five

**Gerald Albert.** The head coach of Vandebilt Catholic High School in Louisiana for 10 years, Coach Albert has won close to 200 games, for a winning percentage of close to .900, and three consecutive state titles (1980-1982). He has won Coach of the Year honors in basketball and girls' softball and is the record holder in the state of Louisiana for most consecutive wins, with 85, a number that places him second on the all-time consecutive-win list nationally.

In addition to his coaching involvement, Coach Albert has participated in several state organizations. He has been the chairman of District 6AA, the softball chairman of Softball District 8-Division II, and a speaker for the Louisiana High School Coaching Clinic.

## Other Qualifiers

**Richard Beeson.** The head coach at Canby High School in Oregon for 10 years, Coach Beeson has recorded 132 wins against only 49 losses. He has been league champion twice and has earned Coach of the Year honors three times, most recently as the NHSACA/Wilson National Softball Coach of the Year in 1988. His selection was based only marginally on his softball record. Coach Beeson extended himself beyond the softball diamond by organizing his state's first All-State selection process, creating Oregon's first Softball Coaches Association (he was the first president), and formulating the state's first All-Star series.

**Edwin Coughenour.** The head coach at Kingsley-Pierson High School in Iowa for 30 years, Coach Coughenour has earned a career record of 715-119, for a winning percentage of .857, one of the best in the nation.

He has never been without a championship, winning innumerable sectional and regional titles and two back-to-back state crowns in 1967 and 1968. Coach Coughenour has been named Coach of the Year several times and has been inducted into the Iowa Athletic Coaches Association Hall of Fame (1986).

**Peter Looney.** Coach Looney has been the head coach for more than 10 years at Apponequet High School in Massachusetts, establishing the enviable record of close to 200 victories with only a handful of losses. He has won regional titles five times and the state crown once and has been named Coach of the Year innumerable times, once by the NHSACA/Wilson committee (1981) as the National Softball Coach of the Year. Coach Looney also has served as both president and vice president of the Southeastern Massachusetts Physical Education Association.

**Gary Page.** The coach of Urbandale High School in Iowa for 20 years, Coach Page has earned the career record of 922-289, for a winning percentage of .761. He has won three state titles and 19 sectional and regional championships. Coach Page holds the longest winning streak in Iowa history (68 games), has been named Coach of the Year several times, and has served extensively on advisory committees and coaches associations. Coach Page also has invented and holds the patents on four softball coaching aids that he sells commercially and uses in his summer day camp program.

**Tom Powers.** The coach at Cobre High School in New Mexico since 1979, Coach Powers has led his squads to seven straight state championships, placing him second on the all-time list for state championships and first on the list for consecutive state titles.

**Sandra Rockwell.** The coach of Rio Grande High School in New Mexico for more than 20 years, Coach Rockwell has won over 100 games, been involved extensively in state play-off competition, and won several Coach of the Year awards, including the NHSACA/Wilson National Softball Coach of the Year. More notably, Coach Rockwell has dedicated herself to athletics. She has been the president of the NMAHPER, a coach at the National Volleyball Institute, the state chairman of the AAHPER National Convention, the vice chairman of District 3AA of the New Mexico Athletic Association, and a member of various subcommittees for the NMAA. She also has found the time to be her school's assistant athletic director.

**Sherry Schaibly.** The winner of the NHSACA/Wilson National Softball Coach of the Year Award in 1979, Coach Schaibly has earned close to 200 career victories and earned the honor of being the first coach in her state (Florida) to win the state championship. In fact, she won back-to-back titles before earning runner-up status in 1978. More than a coach, however, Coach Schaibly has extended herself into the organizations that influence sport. She has served as the president of the Tampa Bay Girls Athletic Conference, the district chair of the Florida Athletic Coaches Association, the state chair of the FACA, and the vice chair of the National High School Athletic Coaches Association.

# COLLEGE SOFTBALL

## America's Greatest College Women's Softball Coach

**Sharron Backus**

As head coach of the UCLA Bruins for 13 years, Coach Backus has established a career win/loss record of 437-109-3, for a winning percentage of close to .800, and has won the NCAA Division I national championship four times (1982, 1984, 1985, and 1988). She also was runner-up to the national champs in 1987. Her postseason record in play-off competition is 51-12, for a winning percentage of .810.

Coach Backus has brought home five national titles overall and two second- and third-place finishes. She has developed 30 All-Americans, six Pan Am gold medalists, and four World Champions. In 1978 and 1982, her players did not commit a single error in regular season play and played perfect defense during the 1988 College World Series.

A player on seven Amateur Softball Association (ASA) championship teams, Coach Backus earned All-America honors for her play at shortstop and in 1985 was inducted into the ASA Hall of Fame. The recipient of several Coach of the Year awards, Coach Backus also finds time to serve on the NCAA Softball Committee and to conduct one of the top softball camps in the country.

## Number Two

**Bob Brock.** A graduate of Sam Houston in 1969, Coach Brock has done all of his coaching in Texas. After two years at Baylor, he moved to Texas A&M where he has established a softball dynasty. During his eight seasons with Texas A&M, he has established a win/loss record of 361-92 (career: 404-138) and has won two NCAA Division I national championships (in 1983 and 1987). He also has won two runner-up crowns (in 1984 and 1986). He has played in the national championship game four times.

In 1985, he led the Aggies to a fifth-place finish, having been in the Collegiate World Series every year but 1985. Coach Brock also has found time to serve on the NCAA Advisory Committee and to be a member of the National Softball Coaches Association.

## Number Three

**Judi Garman.** In just 8 years with Cal State Fullerton, Coach Garman has led the Titans to 468 career victories, one NCAA Division I national championship, and no finish lower than ninth in the national standings. She has won all but one conference title and six of eight regional crowns.

Coach Garman also has coached volleyball, basketball, and tennis at various schools throughout the country before starting the softball programs at Cal State Fullerton. Coach Garman is widely published in physical education journals and was a pioneer in the women's equality movement in sports when she played Little League baseball.

## Number Four

**Margie Wright.** The head coach at Fresno State since 1986, Coach Wright began her career at Illinois State University in 1980. Her career record is 298-129-3, for a winning percentage of .696. Since going to Fresno State, Coach Wright has won three straight league titles and has qualified for the NCAA World Series competition each year. In 1988 she led the Bulldogs to the NCAA championship game against traditional favorites UCLA and lost 0-3 but walked off with a runner-up trophy.

In addition to her coaching responsibilities, Coach Wright continues to play softball, having earned additional All-America honors as a pitcher in various amateur leagues throughout the country. She also serves as vice president of the National Softball Coaches Association (NSCA) and on the All-America Selection Committee. In addition, Coach Wright has served on the NSCA's Legislative Advisory Committee and was a member of the National Governing Body at the U.S. Olympic Festival in 1987.

## Number Five

**Carol Spanks.** In 10 short years as the head softball coach of Cal Poly Pomona, Coach Spanks has won more than 400 games. In 1988 she also guided the Broncos to their seventh consecutive NCAA Division I tournament and finished third in the nation. Her total career record is 431-169-8, for a winning percentage of .718.

Coach Spanks has coached 10 All-American softball players and has served as the head coach of the U.S. softball team that won the gold medal in the 1988 Pan Am Games. In 1985, she coached the U.S.A. All-Star team that won the gold medal in a six-country tournament held in Australia. She also served as coach and assistant general manager for the professional Santa Ana Lionettes.

Coach Spanks has been Coach of the Year several times and has been inducted into the Orange County Hall of Fame (1987) and the ASA Hall of Fame (1981).

**Gary Torgeson.** The only NCAA Division II coach to be selected among the top five college coaches in the country, Gary Torgeson has been with Cal State Northridge since 1982 and has never finished lower than third place in national competition. He has an overall record of 344-100-5 and has won the NCAA Division II national championship four times, three times consecutively (1983-1985). His squads have been national runners-up twice and in 1988 finished in third place, the only time he has not played in the NCAA title game.

Says Torgeson: "My coaching philosophy is to develop a player's potential by instilling methods of self-motivation. Our best teams over the years have had a common bond. . . . Some teams strive for this, but can never overcome the self! It is also imperative that players have a strong work ethic and not be afraid to exert themselves, both on and off the field."

Coach Torgeson's players have earned All-America honors 19 times, All-Regional 35 times, and All-Conference 59 times. He has received Coach of the Year honors 10 times and also finds the time to serve as Cal State's assistant athletic director.

# Chapter 16

# SWIMMING

A Greek vase dating back to 530 B.C. shows a woman with alternating leg and arm strokes swimming in an outdoor bath. Although the ancient Greeks did not allow women to compete in the Olympics, and American women did not enter competitive swimming until the turn of this century, women have been swimming for centuries. *Godey's Lady's Magazine* in 1858 advised women to swim, informing them that it opened the skin's pores and provided a "kinesthetic awareness" that few women realized (Kenney, 1982).

In spite of *Godey's* encouragement and regardless of the hundreds of women who graced our nation's beaches, few women actually swam. The primary reason involved moral proscriptions that clothed women in "bathing suits" that satisfied Victorian tastes but made swimming impossible. In fact, in most forms of athletics, women's early involvement was restricted by dress and, to a large extent, social position.

Inadequate facilities in colleges and universities further hindered women's involvement in swimming activities. In the late 1800s schools finally began to include swimming instruction for girls. Although the classes were not as popular as other activities, they were becoming quite commonplace in most schools. With the advent of these activities and with the need for women to replace men as coaches and lifeguards during World War I, more women were swimming, even competitively.

In fact, by 1920, during the Olympic Games at Antwerp, Belgium, American women swam off with three of the five gold medals. Americans finished first, second, and third in the 100-meter freestyle, with 17-year-old Ethelda Bleibtrey winning the gold with a world-record time of 1:13.6 minutes. The American women won the 4 × 100 freestyle relay, and 13-year-old Eileen Riggin became America's youngest gold medalist in springboard diving. In fact, the American women took all three medals in springboard diving.

Much of the credit for the women's victories in Olympic swimming was given to L.B. de Handley, coach of the Women's Swimming Association (WSA) of New York, one of several "clubs" to gain popularity in the early 1900s. The WSA and Coach de Handley helped introduce competitive swimming to America and led the nation into international dominance of the sport for the next several decades. More importantly, American women realized the benefits of athletic competition and discovered that they, like the American men, could establish themselves as world-class athletes.

One woman, just a few years after the Olympics in Antwerp, swam the English Channel, breaking the male distance record by almost 2 hours. Gertrude Ederle, clad in a swimsuit that only a few years earlier would have been censured by the press, reaffirmed the athletic talents of women and was instrumental in paving the way for all women's sports. A charter member of the swimming Hall of Fame, Ederle is one of this country's greatest athletes.

With the help of coaches like Dave Ambruster, Bill Bachrach, Ernst Brandsten, Charlie Sava, and Tom Robinson, American women have dominated pools everywhere in the world. Starting with Ethelda Bleibtrey's gold medal in 1920 and ranging through such Olympic champions as Ethel Lackie, Sandra Nielson, Ann Curtis, Sybil Bauer, Debbie Meyer, and Mary T. Meagher, American women have earned their top spot in world competition.

# COLLEGE SWIMMING

## America's Greatest College Women's Swimming Coach

**Richard Quick**

Only in his 6th year as the head coach of women's swimming at the University of Texas, Coach Quick has won four consecutive NCAA Division I titles. In addition, the Lady Longhorns have won five straight Southwest Conference titles and have developed such world-class swimmers as Betsy Mitchell, Patty Sabo, Kim Rhodenbaugh, and Tiffany Cohen.

For his accomplishments, coach Quick was the unanimous choice to be the head coach for the 1988 United States Olympic team. He has earned two national Coach of the Year awards and headed the United States contingent at the 1983 and the 1985 Pan Am Games. Before that, he had served as the head coach at Auburn University, where he developed Rowdy Gaines, one of the world's best freestylers.

An All-American for the SMU Mustangs in 1965 and 1966, Quick has devoted himself to swimming, expecting excellence from his swimmers as well as from himself. A member of numerous coaching and swimming organizations, Coach Quick is a frequent speaker at clinics throughout the country.

## Number Two

**Jim Steen.** One of the winningest coaches in NCAA history, Coach Steen has led Ohio's Kenyon College to the NCAA Division III crown 16 times, more than any other coach. Six of those titles have been in women's swimming, which gives Coach Steen more women's titles than any other coach in history. Most notably, he has won these titles in only 10 years of coaching. His women's program had never competed at the varsity level when he took over in 1980. Since then, they have won nine consecutive state, conference, or national titles.

Steen's women swimmers have earned 385 All-America honors. Steen is the speaker at various clinics throughout the country and the author of several articles. An All-Conference and NCAA competitor in 1970, Steen has most distinguished himself in coaching and twice has been the recipient of the American Swimming Coaches Association Award of Excellence.

## Number Three

**Randy Reese.** Said Tracy Caulkins, three-time gold medalist in the 1984 Summer Olympics, "In Randy Reese's program, you can prepare for the Olympics." Many of Coach Reese's athletes at the University of Florida have done just that. In addition, they have won one NCAA title in 1984, one AIAW title in 1979, three NCAA runner-up spots, six SEC crowns, a dual meet record of 85-5, and over 200 All-America honors.

A native of Daytona Beach, Florida, Coach Reese also serves as the coach of the nearby Holmes Lumber Gator Swim Club, which has produced a national title as well as 35 AAU national champs. Coach Reese has served on several local and national committees and has found time to author two books, most recently *Building a Championship Season With Randy Reese*.

## Other Qualifiers

**Peter Accardy.** The winner of NCAA titles in both men's and women's swimming, Coach Accardy has won two women's NCAA Division II crowns during his 14 years at California State/Northridge. In addition to his eight men's titles, Coach Accardy ranks third on the all-time NCAA win list with 10 NCAA crowns.

**George Haines.** Coach Haines, while with Stanford University, won one NCAA Division I crown in 1983. His coaching accomplishments, however, transcend college coaching. Haines has coached four Olympic teams, twice as the head coach. He has earned Coach of the Year honors more than any other coach. While with the Santa Clara Swim Club, he won 35 national AAU team titles, 26 of which were women's. The swimmers Haines has coached include Don Schollander and Donna de Varona.

**Bill Mann.** Coach Mann took the University of South Florida to the NCAA Division II crown in 1985, shortly after he had arrived on the campus.

**Becky Rutt.** In 6 short years, Coach Rutt took little-known Clarion State University to the top of the NCAA Division II rankings. During her tenure with the Pennsylvania university, she won three NCAA crowns.

**Carl Samuelson.** Williams College in Massachusetts is one of the most selective schools in the country. It also is the home of the 1981 and 1982 NCAA Division III women's swim champions. During his 13 years with Williams, Coach Samuelson has won two NCAA titles and five New England championships. Coach "Sam" has been named Coach of the Year several times and is responsible for the development of 48 Division III All-Americans.

**Karen Moe Thornton.** Coach Thornton has nine times led the University of California to being one of the top 12 teams in the country. When she was selected in 1987 as the Division I Coach of the Year, she became the first woman in history to receive that honor. A former Olympian and world record holder, Coach Thornton has led the Bears to NOR-PAC first-place finishes 5 of the last 8 years, finishing in second the other three. She has been fourth in the NCAA for the past 4 years and has a 9-year record of 62-33-1.

# Chapter 17

# TENNIS

When Mary Outerbridge received permission from her brother to lay out a court for tennis—a game she had discovered in Bermuda at an English garrison—in a corner of the Staten Island Cricket and Baseball Club, lawn tennis was born in this country. The game caught on almost immediately because of its relaxed pace, and by 1876 pictures were available of women playing on Staten Island. Less than 20 years later, by 1894, a sizeable number of towns had their own tennis facilities (Barney, 1894).

The game caught on so quickly that 1887 saw the first United States Lawn Tennis Association (USLTA) championship for women, won by Ellen Hansell. A few years later, in 1901, when 12-year-old May Sutton won the Pacific Coast championship, tennis affirmed its national reputation as a women's sport. Three years later, May Sutton, only 15, strengthened her hold on the number one position in American women's tennis by winning the national championship. One year later, she became the first American woman to win the women's singles championship at Wimbledon—"in a dress that could almost be considered short" (Clerci, 1975).

One young woman who broke through the racial as well as social barriers in women's tennis was Althea Gibson. Discovered in New York during a paddle tennis game, Althea was encouraged to try tennis and within one year won her first tournament. When the local tennis club financed her way to the American Tennis Association (ATA, a prominent black organization) championships, where she won two consecutive girls' division titles, Gibson was well on her way to national prominence.

Eligible for the women's singles competition, Gibson lost in the championship match but was discovered by Drs. Herbert Eaton and Robert Johnson, both of whom went on to finance her tennis future. She lived with Dr. Eaton and practiced on his private courts and traveled with Dr. Johnson to compete in national and regional tournaments. Soon

Althea graduated from high school, attended Florida A & M University with a scholarship, and ultimately went on to win the Forest Hills and Wimbledon—one of this country's great athletes.

Other names warrant mention: Maureen Connolly, Helen Wills Moody, Chris Evert, Billie Jean Moffitt King, Alice Marble, Doris Hart, Martina Navratilova, and Nancy Chaffee. They are among the dominant figures in all of tennis and have contributed to this country's traditional superiority in the game. Their coaches' accomplishments are no less noteworthy and are deserving of as much recognition.

# COLLEGE TENNIS

## America's Greatest College Women's Tennis Coach

**Frank Brennan**

Head of the Stanford Cardinals since 1980, Coach Brennan has guided his teams to five NCAA titles in 7 years, three of them consecutively ('82, '84, '86, '87, and '88). He has earned a career record of 170-25, for a winning percentage of .870, and his players have garnered All-American honors 50 times, an average of 5.5 All-Americans per year. His 1987 edition had an unprecedented seven All-Americans and enjoyed a 22-4 record.

Coach Brennan is a five-time recipient of the Northern California Coach of the Year award. He has won six other Coach of the Year awards, including 1982 NCAA Coach of the Year. He also has coached such standouts as Linda Gates, Alycia Moulton, and Caryn Copeland, his current assistant coach.

Coach Brennan is an annual favorite at clinics across the country. He was one of four nationally prominent coaches at the USTA National Teachers Conference in 1982. Three years later, he was a faculty member at the National Teachers Conference in New York. Coach Brennan also gives lectures and seminars both nationally and in such places as Mexico, Puerto Rico, and the Caribbean.

An annual member of the USTA Women's Collegiate Advisory Committee, Brennan has committed himself to his sport. From his playing days for Big Ten champion Indiana in 1964, Coach Brennan has been a national advocate for collegiate tennis and has established himself as one of the game's great coaches.

## Number Two

**Dave Borelli.** Coach Borelli has won seven national championships since he became the head coach of the Southern Cal Trojans in 1974. In his 14 years of coaching, he has earned close to 300 victories and has won three AIAW titles, two USTA titles, and two NCAA crowns since 1977. He also earned two runner-up awards in the NCAA tournament and one third-place finish. His winning percentage is .875, and his players have earned All-American honors 50 times.

Himself a player at USC, Borelli learned much of his tennis from his coach, George Toley, and credits him for his success as a coach. As a senior, Borelli received USC's Outstanding Student-Athlete Award and was awarded an NCAA postgraduate scholarship, which helped him earn his law degree from USC. The philosophy that has made him one of the nation's most successful coaches and one of the top clinicians in the country:

> We remind ourselves that we deserve to do well because we've worked hard for it, but also that we've got a lot of opportunities that a lot of people just don't have and that we should be thankful for them.
>
> We look up and see blue skies and a clear sun and say, "Hey, this is only tennis." Keeping it all in perspective really helps. The pressure isn't as frightening. You can relax more and compete harder when you appreciate your opportunities.

Scores of players have taken advantage of those opportunities, among the best Barbara Hallquist, Leslie Allen, Shiela McInerney, Stacey Margolin, and Trey Lewis.

## Number Three

**Marilyn Montgomery Rindfuss.** One of Trinity University's first nationally ranked players, Marilyn Rindfuss was ranked in the top 20 in singles and the top 10 in doubles competition for all four years in college. After her graduation in 1957, she went on the pro tour and at one time was ranked seventh in the U.S. During her playing tenure at

Trinity, the team was not officially recognized, but it did provide several outstanding competitors in collegiate tournaments.

Coach Rindfuss took over as Trinity's head women's coach in 1975, seven years after the team's formal recognition. Her teams enjoyed immediate success. During Rindfuss's first two years as the Lady Tigers' coach, Trinity sported an impressive 22-0 dual match record and back-to-back national championships. In addition to her coaching success at Trinity, Coach Rindfuss is recognized as one of the pioneers of women's athletics in America.

## Other Qualifiers

**Andy Brandi.** A product of the Trinity University tennis dynasty, Coach Brandi played professionally in the United States, Europe, and South America before turning to coaching. In fewer than 10 years with the Lady Gators of the University of Florida, Coach Brandi has guided his teams to four Southeastern Conference championships, two trips to the NCAA national tournament, where he finished third in 1987, and a national title in the 1988 ITCA Women's National Indoor Team Championships. Brandi has received Coach of the Year honors three times and has developed nine All-Americans and one national champ. Brandi's coaching strategies can be found in *Tennis Magazine* and as a guest columnist for Stan Smith's syndicated column.

**Jan Brogan.** In only 10 years as the head tennis coach of the University of California Golden Bears, Coach Brogan has won seven PAC-10 titles, come in second twice, finished in the top 10 of the NCAA seven times, and earned a career win/loss record of 74-4 in conference and 203-77 overall. In addition, Coach Brogan has developed 14 All-Americans and several Academic All-Americans.

Coach Brogan has earned Coach of the Year honors six times and is a frequent lecturer for the USTA on team tennis. She also has served on the NCAA Regional Committee, the USTA Junior Development program, and has been the head coaching coordinator for the Junior Wightman Cup.

**Emilie Foster.** The only Trinity tennis player in history—men's or women's—to win four national championships, Emilie Burrer Foster became the head coach of Trinity in 1979 and finished only once out of the top 10 in the national rankings. Currently, she has a career record of 242-62 for a winning percentage of .800 and has coached 12 All-Americans. She has been runner-up to the national champions twice and was named Division I Coach of the Year in 1983 when she led the Tigers to a record of 30-3. In 1987, Coach Foster received the National Tennis Foundation Special Educational Merit Award for Women.

**Anne Gould.** Anne Gould became the head coach of the Stanford women's program in 1976, at approximately the same time as the first scholarships were being given to women athletes. In two years she led the Cardinals to their first AIAW title with a final round win over USC in Salisbury, Maryland. During the previous two years, she had been runner-up to the national champions, Trinity and Southern California, and in her final year she again was runner up to Southern Cal.

During her tenure with Stanford as head women's coach, Gould had never finished out of the final championship match. She ended her career with a 48-10 record and devoted her time to her job as a physical education instructor at Stanford. She is the wife of Dick Gould, head coach of the men's program at Stanford.

**John Newman.** A Tiger net star from 1956 to 1960, Coach Newman led Trinity to a national championship, the USTA title in 1973. Coach Newman also is credited with helping with the development of All-American and USTA doubles champion JoAnne Russell.

**Shirley Rushing.** The dynasty that has been Trinity tennis started for the women's program years before their first national championship, but it was Coach Rushing, a member of the Athletic Department staff, who receives much of the credit. The team sponsor in the program's early years, Coach Rushing is recognized as the motive force behind two national championships (1968 and 1969) and one of the people instrumental in the success of Emilie Burrer, the USTA national champion each of those years. Burrer also teamed up with Becky Vest each of those years to win the national doubles championships.

# Chapter 18

# TRACK AND FIELD

Women did not compete in the first Olympiad in 1896. In the second, they were allowed to compete only in tennis and horseback riding. In 1912, they competed in swimming—but only the 100-meter freestyle. Each new Olympic event for women represented both an athletic opportunity and a hard-fought victory.

Track and field events, for example, weren't added until the 1928 Olympiad in Amsterdam, and then only because the Federal Sportive Feminine Internationale (FSFI) had organized its own Women's Olympics in 1922. A reaction to women's exclusion from the Olympic Games, the Women's Olympics, now called the International Ladies' Games, were held again in 1926 in Gothenburg.

Because the "Ladies' Games" represented a potential if not actual conflict with the International Olympic Committee (IOC) and the International Amateur Athletic Federation (IAAF) as well as an awareness that women's track and field had gained worldwide popularity, women were permitted to compete in Olympic track and field in 1940. The events included the 100-meter dash, the 400-meter relay, the 80-meter hurdles, the high jump, the discus, and the javelin.

Still battling social mores, the FSFI continued to sponsor what were now called the Women's World Games. Finally, in 1936, following the Olympic Games in Los Angeles, the FSFI disbanded and gave control of the women's international competition to the IAAF. By 1960, women's events also included the 800-meter run, the broad jump, and the shot put. Four years later, the 400-meter run and the pentathlon were added.

Women had come a long way since Vassar College's first "field day," an event in 1895 that grew into an annual track meet for the students. From the fence vault and the baseball throw at Vassar, women are now high jumping and hurling the javelin, in both instances higher and further than their male counterparts in early Olympic competitions.

From Babe Didrikson in 1932 and Wilma Rudolph in 1960 to Jackie Joyner-Kersee and Florence Griffith-Joyner in the 1988 Olympics, women's track and field in America has been well represented by some of the world's finest athletes. And they have been trained by many of the world's greatest coaches.

# HIGH SCHOOL TRACK AND FIELD

## America's Greatest High School Girls' Track and Field Coach

**Nino Fennoy**

Coach Fennoy, the head coach of East St. Louis Lincoln in Illinois, holds the number two spot on the all-time list for most state titles, with eight. He ranks third on the all-time list of consecutive state championships, with five. His most significant accomplishments, however, involve the athletes he has developed, perhaps the most notable of whom is Jackie Joyner-Kersee.

Coach Fennoy's most recent success story involves sprinter Carmelita Williams, who ranked 10th in the nation in 1987 in the 200-meter dash with a time of 24.14 and third in the 400-meter with a time of 54.36. The relationship Coach Fennoy enjoys with such talented young athletes has resulted in their accomplishments as well as numerous awards for Coach Fennoy. He has been awarded Coach of the Year honors several times and has served on numerous organizational and regulatory committees.

Perhaps most accomplished in the development of hurdlers, Coach Fennoy has established East St. Louis Lincoln as a national powerhouse. In 1979 Gwen Brown won the state championship in the 200-meter low hurdles with the best time in the nation, 27.7, which held as a national record for 5 years. The record was broken in 1984 by Sametra King of Romeoville, Illinois, with a time of 27.3. Most recently, it was broken again by Nicolle Thompson of East St. Louis Lincoln with a national record time of 27 seconds flat.

Coach Fennoy possesses a rare knowledge of social relationships and fundamental skills that have made his teams among the nation's best.

## Number Two

**Norman Holder.** A guidance counselor during the day, Norm Holder became Exeter High School's track coach in the afternoon. The hours he devoted to the New Hampshire school's program paid dividends because from 1963 to 1979 Exeter won 11 state championships, a total that ranks number one on the all-time list of high school state titles. Seven of Coach Holder's state crowns were consecutive (1963-1969), an accomplishment that ranks second on the all-time list for consecutive state championships.

Coach Holder participated in numerous committee activities and was named Coach of the Year several times. He retired a few years ago and now spends summers in New Hampshire and winters in Florida.

## Number Three

**Clyde Ellis.** In only eight years at John Marshall High School in Oklahoma City, Coach Ellis earned seven consecutive state championships—without losing a meet. He has been selected Coach of the Year on the state or national level eight times and earned the Coach's Achievement Award from the Oklahoma Secondary School Activities Association. Coach Ellis also has found the time to serve on the advisory board for the Oklahoma Coaches Association, to be a reference coach for the University of Florida, and to be on the board of directors of the Oklahoma City Girls' Track Association.

## Number Four

**Katie Horstman.** The coach of Minster High School in Ohio for 15 years, Coach Horstman has earned a 159-8 career record and has won 11 district titles and seven state championships. She also has been runner-up to the state champs four times and has earned honors ranging from Coach of the Year on state and national levels to Citizen of the Year by the Minster Civic Association. A coach who has never lost a conference meet, Coach Horstman also served on the board of the Ohio Women Advisory Committee and on the Ohio Track and Field Hall of Fame Committee, and she has been president of the West Central Track and Field Organization. One of Coach Horstman's greatest distinctions was being the first woman to be inducted into the Ohio Track and Field Hall of Fame, in 1986.

## Number Five

**Father Patrick O'Brien.** A diocesan priest who took over the girls' program at St. Cecilia High School in Hastings, Nebraska, for several years before moving on to Newman High School in Wahoo, Nebraska, Coach O'Brien led his teams to the number two spot on the list of all-time state titles in the *National Federation Record Book*. Within a period of 10 years, he led St. Cecilia to eight state titles, seven of which were consecutive. His seven consecutive state titles also ranks second on the list.

## Other Qualifiers

**Al Carson.** Four state championships in Georgia, all of which were consecutive, highlight Coach Carson's career, which involves either a league or a regional championship on the off years. For his successes, which started in 1967, Coach Carson has been named Girls' Track Coach of the Year seven times and, in 1982 by the NHSACA/Wilson Selection Committee, the National Track Coach of the Year. In addition, Coach Carson has been the regional director of the Georgia Interscholastic Association, the Girls' Vice Chairman of the NHSACA, and a member of the board of directors of the Georgia High School Association.

**Diane Hayes.** When Coach Hayes concluded her 13th year of coaching, she already had achieved a dual meet record of 65-3 and two state championships. Additional coaching brought Crook County High School in Oregon more titles and Coach Hayes more awards. She has been Coach of the Year four times and is included in *Who's Who in Oregon High School Track and Field*. She also is a member of the Oregon Education Association, the Oregon Track Coaches Association, and the Oregon High School Coaches Association.

**James Holdren.** The head coach at Thomas Jefferson High School in Virginia for 14 years, Coach Holdren has won a championship every year, including five state titles and five runners-up. Coach Holdren has held the longest high school girls' win streak in Virginia with 93 consecutive dual meet victories.

**William Jansen.** Coach Jansen has spent most of his time with Valley City High School in North Dakota, where he has won four state crowns, seven district or regional titles, and seven conference championships. Coach Jansen has been named Coach of the Year several times, including the NHSACA/Wilson National Track Coach of the Year in 1979, and is a member of the North Dakota Track Coaches Association.

**Harold Sharp.** Coach Sharp has devoted 31 years of his career to coaching girls' track, most of which has been with Cardinal Community High School in Eldon, Iowa. Within that time, he has enjoyed four district titles and one state championship. He has been named the state's All-Star Coach and Coach of the Year several times and has been involved extensively in his sport's organizational activities. Coach Sharp has been a regional representative of the Iowa Track Coaches Association, the president of the Iowa Division Track and Field Federation, the chairman of the Iowa Girls High School Athletic Union, and a judge at the Drake Relays. Coach Sharp is a member of the Iowa Hall of Fame.

**Carol Tumey.** Coach Tumey has divided her time between two programs in Indiana for close to 20 years of coaching. She has been the head coach of Center Grove High School and has worked with the Center Grove AAU Track Club. She has enjoyed several sectional championships, had a state champion high jumper, and worked extensively with state regulatory organizations. She was the director of Indiana Coaches of Girls Sports, an executive board member of the Indiana High School Athletic Directors Association, and the chair of the State Track and Field Association.

**James White.** With 21 years of coaching girls' track, Coach White has achieved a career record of 247 regular season victories against only 23 losses. He has won 23 district titles and three state championships and has had six runners-up. Swainsboro High School in Georgia also enjoyed 10 invitational titles under Coach White's leadership. He has been named state or national Coach of the Year four times and has served extensively with the Georgia High School Association.

**Harold Wilkinson.** Twenty-four years of coaching, mostly at Kennedy High School in Cedar Rapids, Iowa, have resulted in five state titles and three runners-up. Coach Wilkinson also has won 15 district crowns and has helped referee the Drake Relays. He has been named Coach of the Year on the state or national level eight times and was inducted into the Iowa Association of Track Coaches (IATC) Hall of Fame in 1982. In addition, he has found the time to serve on the Advisory Committee of the Iowa Girls High School Athletic Association (IGHSAA), to preside over the Iowa Division of the USTFF, and to be the regional representative of the IATC.

**Jean Wright.** Coach Wright has been with Franklin County High School in Kentucky for more than 20 years and has won two state titles, 10 regional crowns, and 13 conference championships. In addition to being named Coach of the Year on the state or national level 14 times, she has been the chair of the Girls' and Women's Sports Division of the KAHPER, the chair of the Mid-State Coaches Association, a member of the State Track Committee, and the all-sports chairman of the KAHPER.

## COLLEGE TRACK AND FIELD

### America's Greatest College Women's Track and Field Coach

**Ed Temple**

Coach Edward Stanley Temple has been the head women's track coach at Tennessee State University in Nashville since 1950 and has had athletes represent the United States in nine consecutive Olympiads. He has won 34 national team titles and has had 25 gold medal winners in the Pan Am Games, 23 Olympic medalists, one Sullivan Award winner (Wilma Rudolph), and eight former athletes inducted into the National Track and Field Hall of Fame.

Coach Temple has been the head coach of the U.S. Women's Track and Field Olympic team three times and has coached U.S. teams in competition against Germany, the U.S.S.R., Romania, and China. Currently a member of the International Track and Field Committee, Coach Temple has been inducted into the Tennessee Sports Hall of Fame (1972), the Black Athletes Hall of Fame (1977), the Pennsylvania Sports Hall of Fame (1987), and the Communiplex Women's Sports Hall of Fame (1987).

An All-State athlete in track, football, and basketball at John Harris High School in Harrisburg, Pennsylvania, Coach Temple earned his college degree at Tennessee State University and did doctoral work at Penn State.

In addition to his coaching responsibilities at Tennessee State, Coach Temple is an associate professor of sociology.

His honors and awards are too numerous to mention, but perhaps his most cherished is the fact that during his coaching career 40 members of his Tigerbelle teams have represented Tennessee State in Olympic competition. Thirty-five of these represented the United States, winning thirteen gold, six silver, and four bronze medals. Most notably, 38 of these athletes have graduated from college with one or more degrees.

## Number Two

**Nell Jackson.** One of the most dedicated of all sports figures, Nell Jackson started her professional career in 1953 as an instructor at Tuskegee Institute after establishing an American record in the 220-yard dash in 1949 and being a member of the U.S. Pan Am team in 1951. She moved to the University of Iowa in 1961 to complete her Ph.D. and finally to Michigan State University in 1973 as a full professor and the head coach of the Spartans' women's track team.

Following a successful career with Michigan State, Coach Jackson joined the U.S. Olympic Committee as a member of the International Relations Committee. She also has published at least 15 articles, two books, and several film strips. Coach Jackson's professional involvement is her most notable accomplishment. She has been the head coach of the 1956 and the 1972 Women's Olympic Track and Field teams, the manager of the Women's Track and Field team at the Goodwill Games in Moscow in 1986, the chair of the AAU Women's Track and Field Committee, a member of the board of directors of the U.S. Olympic Committee, the organizer and coach of the Illini Track Club for Girls, a presenter at over 50 clinics and workshops throughout the world, and the chair of the AIAW Track and Field Sports Committee.

Coach Jackson also has served as the vice president of the Athletic Congress of the United States, the primary governing body of amateur track and field in this country; the project director of the National Youth Sports Program, and a member of the Jury of Appeals in the 1983 Pan Am Games. Coach Jackson died in 1988. A tribute to her commitment to track and field can be seen in the Black Athletes Hall of Fame.

## Number Three

**Terry Crawford.** The 1988 Olympic Track and Field Coach, Terry Crawford spent her first 9 years as a head coach at the University of Tennessee, where she finished second in the NCAA national championships twice, second in the outdoor championships twice, and made the final four in NCAA and AIAW competition four more times.

Coach Crawford moved to the University of Texas in 1985 and immediately established the Lady Longhorns as a national power. She placed second in the NCAA indoor championships in 1985 and won the national titles twice (1986 and 1988). She also won the NCAA outdoor title in 1986. She has rarely failed to win her conference championship and from 1981 through 1987 did not lose a dual meet.

Coach Crawford has been named Coach of the Year several times and has been instrumental in the development of such outstanding performers as hurdler Sharrieffa Barksdale, middle-distance runners Delisa Walton and Joetta Clark, and distance runner Brenda Webb. She also has been an assistant coach during the Pan Am Games and the gold-medal-winning coach of the South track team during the nation's first National Sports Festival in 1978.

## Number Four

**Cleveland Abbott.** A graduate of South Dakota State College in 1916 and the Director of Physical Education and Athletics at Tuskegee University by 1923, "Cleve" Abbott was coaching women athletes well before they were allowed in the Olympics. Although women had some track and field events in the 1928 Olympics, the 400-meters was not sanctioned for women until 1964, other events a few years earlier.

Coach Abbott's women's teams won the national AAU indoor and outdoor championships consistently from 1937 through 1950. Members of the Tuskegee Women's Track team represented the United States in almost every early Olympic competition. And while Coach Abbott was developing women track athletes, he also was coaching the Tuskegee football, baseball, and basketball squads to conference and national titles.

Coach Abbott was the deputy commissioner of the Southern Association of the Amateur Athletic Union, a member of the National AAU Women's Track and Field Committee, and the man responsible for the annual Tuskegee Relays and the Southern Intercollegiate Athletic Conference basketball tournament. He died in 1955 and is buried next to Booker T. Washington and George Washington Carver in the Tuskegee University cemetery.

## Number Five

**Loren Seagrave.** Coach Seagrave joined the LSU Lady Tigers in 1983 and in only 2 years guided them to the NCAA Division I tournament and a runner-up spot to the national champs, Oregon. In 1987,

Coach Seagrave led the Lady Tigers to national titles in both the indoor and the outdoor competitions, the first time one school had won both in the same year. He followed up the next year with another national crown in the NCAA outdoor championships for a record-tying three national championships in women's track and field.

From 1984 to 1988, Coach Seagrave led LSU to four of the five SEC indoor titles and three of four outdoor titles. In the process, he was instrumental in the development of 112 All-Americans. A graduate of the University of Wisconsin, Coach Seagrave started his career as a high school track coach, winning two state championships, then accepted an assistantship at Wisconsin before moving to LSU. Coach Seagrave also finds the time to be a member of The Athletic Congress (TAC) Women's Development Committee.

**Brooks Johnson.** A graduate of Tufts University in 1956, Brooks Johnson gained world recognition in 1960 when he established a new world record in the 60-yard dash. Shortly afterward, he went on to coach the U.S. national indoor team (1969) and the U.S. national women's team (1969 and 1973). He then moved to Santa Fe College, where in two years he produced 20 All-Americans and 13 national champions. During his two years with Santa Fe, he led them to second- and third-place finishes in the national indoor championships.

Shortly after serving as the 1976 U.S. Olympic sprint coach, Johnson moved to Stanford University, where he became the first black head coach in Stanford's history and where he led the women's cross-country team to a third-place finish in 1981 and second-place finishes in 1982, 1983, and 1984 at the NCAA cross-country championships. He also led them to third-place finishes in both the indoor and the outdoor national championships.

Coach Johnson has received Coach of the Year honors several times and has served as a member of the House of Delegates for the United States Olympic Committee. Coach Johnson also is the national coordinator of the U.S. Women's Development Committee. He also is responsible for the founding of the Sports International Track Club for men and women, which won five national team titles in the '70s.

## Other Qualifiers

**Scott Chisam.** UCLA is among the nation's top schools for total NCAA championships, and Coach Chisam has made his contribution. During his relatively short stay with the Bruins, he led the women's track and field team to back-to-back NCAA Division I outdoor titles, the first two in NCAA women's championship competition.

**Tom Heinenon.** In a school famous for its track and field, Coach Heinenon helped keep the tradition alive by leading Oregon to the NCAA Division I national outdoor title in 1985.

**Teri Jordan.** A magna cum laude graduate from Kansas State University in 1976, Coach Jordan established herself as one of the premier distance runners in the world in the early '70s. Since coming to Penn State in 1984, she has been named Coach of the Year twice. She has won Eastern Colleges Athletic Conference (ECAC) titles twice (1985-1986) and has served as the President of the U.S. Women's Track and Field Coaching Association and as an executive board member of the National TAC Governing Board.

**Bob Kersee.** The head coach of women's track and field at UCLA since 1983, Coach Kersee helped establish his reputation by assisting with the development of Jackie Joyner-Kersee, probably the greatest female track and field athlete in the world. He achieved runner-up status to the NCAA outdoor champs in 1988 and won the first two women's PAC-10 titles in history.

**Gary Pepin.** The Big Eight Coach of the Year in 1987, Coach Pepin guides both the men's and women's programs at the University of Nebraska. His women's team has claimed three of the first six NCAA Division I indoor championships, never finishing lower than sixth. His athletes have earned 89 NCAA indoor All-American awards and 63 outdoor. He has coached such standout performers as world-record holder Merlene Ottey-Page, four-time NCAA champion Rhonda Blanford, and two-time NCAA champ Linetta Wilson.

**Mamie Rallins.** The 14-year career of Coach Rallins at Ohio State University is highlighted by 48 Big Ten indoor and outdoor champions and 17 All-Americans. After leading the Buckeyes to a second-place finish in the Big Ten in 1987, she assumed the role of head coach of the U.S. team at the World Indoor Track and Field Championships. Rallins may be best known as a coach for developing world-class hurdler Stephanie Hightower, an Olympian and a world-record holder. A world-class hurdler in her own right, Rallins was voted the world's best hurdler in 1969. She assumed her duties at Ohio State in 1976.

**Doug Williamson.** Runners-up to the national champs during the 1986 and the 1987 NCAA outdoor championships, the University of Alabama made a bid for the top spot in the nation during Coach Williamson's first year with the school. The Crimson Tide, under Williamson's direction, also have won two SEC titles.

**Gary Winkler.** Coach Winkler established his credentials as one of the nation's best with Florida State University when he guided the Seminoles to the NCAA national outdoor championship in 1984 and followed up a year later with a runner-up to the national champs, Oregon. During that same year, 1985, he won the NCAA national indoor championship. He currently is at the University of Illinois at Urbana-Champaign.

# Chapter 19

# VOLLEYBALL

From the time the YMCA in Springfield, Massachusetts, drew up the first set of volleyball rules in 1897, to the establishment of the International Volleyball Association (IVA) in 1975 as the world's first professional volleyball league, women have figured prominently in the sport. The United States Volleyball Association (USVBA), founded in 1928, has governed men's and women's competition and conducts its own national championships, as do the AAU and the NCAA.

Men's competition for the USVBA title, particularly during the first 40 years of the organization's existence, was dominated by YMCA teams, first in the Midwest and then in California. The game has long been associated with beaches and blue skies; since 1949, the first year of the USVBA women's title, volleyball competition for women has been dominated by California clubs, the Santa Monica Mariners and the Long Beach Shamrocks being the most prominent.

The game owes much to former players and to prominent coaches who helped establish it as the world's second most popular team sport. Consider the names: Holly Brock, Carolyn Gregory Conrad, Lois Ellen Haraughty, Linda Murphy, Nancy Owen, and Jane Ward—all Hall of Famers who dedicated themselves to the game and who tried to lead U.S. volleyball into the international spotlight.

And consider contemporary names like Mary Jo Peppler, Kathy Gregory, Terrie McGahan, and Flo Hyman—who *did* establish the United States as a world power in volleyball. To them and to the coaches who coordinated their play, we offer the following recognition.

## HIGH SCHOOL VOLLEYBALL

### America's Greatest High School Girls' Volleyball Coach

**Norma Bellamy**

As head coach of Safford High School in Arizona for 20 years, Coach Bellamy has won more state championships than any other high school volleyball coach in history. Under Bellamy's leadership, Safford won 13 consecutive championships from 1968 through 1980 and walked off with the state crown 18 times. Volleyball was not recognized as an interscholastic sport in Arizona until 1968, and since that time Coach Bellamy and Safford High School have established two national high school records—for most all-time wins and most consecutive wins of a state title.

Safford has won with such consistency that they also rank fourth on the list of most consecutive state titles. Following their string of 13, Safford won five more consecutive crowns from 1982 through 1986. For her accomplishments, Coach Bellamy has been named Coach of the Year seven times, receiving the NHSACA/Wilson National Coach of the Year Award in 1980. Through 1980, Bellamy's teams were 52-0 in state play-off competition, another national record. Coach Bellamy also has found the time to serve extensively with the Arizona Interscholastic Athletic Volleyball Advisory Committee.

## Number Two

**Laurice "Low" Hunter.** With more than 20 years as the head volleyball coach of Evergreen High School in Colorado, Coach "Low" Hunter won eight state titles in a nine-year period of time. Seven of her titles were consecutive, placing her second on the all-time high school list for consecutive state championships.

A coach who is active in a variety of state and national volleyball organizations, Coach Hunter is in demand as a speaker for clinics and workshops and has devoted herself to her sport. Her efforts have paid off. In addition to her number three ranking for most state titles and her number two ranking for most consecutive state titles, Coach Hunter ranks third on the list for most consecutive match wins. From 1978 through 1984, Hunter led Evergreen High School to 176 straight victories in volleyball.

## Number Three

**Louise Crocco.** Having earned a 511-53 career record for a winning percentage of .900, Coach Crocco has taken Cardinal Gibbons High School in Ft. Lauderdale to nine state championships in 12 years, giving them the number five ranking on the all-time win list for state championships. Five of those titles were consecutive (1976 through 1980). Coach Crocco also enjoys a winning streak of 227 straight regular-season matches in her state's classification.

Coach Crocco has been named Coach of the Year five times, once by the NHSACA/Wilson National Coach of the Year Award Committee, and she enjoys the distinction of being one of the winningest coaches in the country. In addition to her coaching responsibilities, Coach Crocco has served on the executive board for the Broward Athletic Conference, has been a board member for the Miami Athletic Conference, and was a national vice chairman for the NHSACA.

## Number Four

**Joan Wells.** Coach Wells became the head coach of Lawrence High School in Kansas in 1971 and two years later took her team to the state championship game. She finished as runner-up to the state champs in 1973 and again in 1974. In 1975, Coach Wells won her first state championship, initiating a string of six consecutive titles, the third highest in the history of girls' high school volleyball. She was runner-up to the state champs again in 1981 and in the process took her teams to a total career record of over 300 victories and a winning percentage of close to .850.

Most notably, Coach Wells has served extensively on state and national coaches associations. She was the national volleyball chairman in 1981 and her state's volleyball chairman in 1977. She has served on many advisory councils and has been a speaker at state and national clinics too numerous to mention. She has been Coach of the Year many times, including having won the NHSACA/Wilson National Coach of the Year award in 1983.

**Eileen Covington.** During her career at Woodrow Wilson Senior High School in Washington, DC, Coach Covington missed the state championship game only once. She was runner-up to the titlist three times and won the crown eight times, three times consecutively. She has won approximately 150 games, for a winning percentage of .960, and has been named Coach of the Year six times, once by NHSACA/Wilson (1986).

Coach Covington has served on her state's Volleyball Coaches Association, is a member of the District of Columbia Coaches Association, and coordinates various volleyball leagues in the area.

## Number Five

**Gene Chyzowych.** Coach Chyzowych accepted the position of head coach of the Columbia High School volleyball team in 1977 and has yet to lose a match. As of the summer of 1988, his record stood at 241-0, including 11 number one rankings in the state of New Jersey. Says Chyzowych, "There is no magic to our success, just hard work and total concentration. Many fans say that if you want to see our matches, you'd better be at the gym early, because they may be over in 15 minutes."

**Sally Kus.** Coach Kus has won the area championship in New York nine consecutive times, along the way earning a total career record of 360-12, for a remarkable winning percentage of .968, and establishing a national record for consecutive victories in any sport—boys' or girls'—for her string of 274 volleyball wins from 1978 through 1985. For her accomplishments, Coach Kus has been named Coach of the Year three times and has won numerous coaching awards from state and national organizations, including the National Organization of Women (1986).

Coach Kus has chaired the Volleyball Committee for Section VI as well as the Erie County Interscholastic Conference. She has chaired the Empire State Games, has served on various state and national clinics, and was the coach of the National AAU Junior Olympics for seven years. Coach Kus received the NHSACA/Wilson Coach of the Year award in 1987.

## Other Qualifiers

**Wanda Bingham.** According to the *National High School Sports Record Book*, Coach Bingham is the second-winningest girls' volleyball coach in history, with close to 400 career victories against fewer than 100 losses. Coach Bingham spent 14 years with a single high school establishing her record, Churchill High School in San Antonio, Texas.

**Winifred Hamilton.** Coach Hamilton has spent her entire career with Westhill High School in Stamford, Connecticut. She has won well over 200 victories with a winning percentage of .900, has won the state title twice (1975 and 1980), and has been runner-up four times. She has won her state's sectional crown eight times and been named Coach of the Year three times, once as the National Coach of the Year by the NHSACA organization. Also selected as Connecticut's Coach of the Year in tennis, Coach Hamilton has devoted herself to athletics in her state by serving on several athletic and volleyball organizations both nationally and statewide.

**Mary Hines.** With two state championships in almost 20 years of coaching, Coach Hines has brought Catalina High School in Tucson, Arizona, to the forefront of her sport. She has won almost 250 games and has earned a winning percentage of .930, while winning league titles every year and earning runner-up to the state champs four times. In addition, Coach Hines has found the time to serve on the Volleyball Rules Committee for the NFSHSA and to be the director of the Arizona Volleyball Coaches Association. She also is a board member of the National Volleyball Coaches Association and has won Coach of the Year honors six times. Coach Hines was selected as the NHSACA/Wilson National Coach of the Year in 1985.

**Anita Lake.** While battling the physical and psychological effects of a double mastectomy, Coach Lake managed to accumulate one of the most enviable records in girls' volleyball history. She was undefeated in Michigan high school competition, earning a record of 66-0, and when she organized a community team of junior high and high school students, she earned a record of 280-20 for a total career record of 346-20.

Beyond her involvement in coaching, Coach Lake has been a volleyball camp director, the keynote speaker at several state and national clinics, and the vice chairman of the NHSACA District IV Volleyball Committee. She has been honored as Coach of the Year 10 times, including as 1979 NHSACA/Wilson National Coach of the Year.

**Linda Martin.** During her years with Brockport Central School in New York, Coach Martin has taken her teams to the Section V Class A title four consecutive times and has won her league title seven consecutive times. She has earned close to 200 career victories and has been honored as Coach of the Year three times, once by the NHSACA/Wilson organization (1981).

Coach Martin also was the first woman to serve on the New York State Athletic Association Executive Committee and later served as president of the Women's Council. She also has served on numerous other state and national committees.

**Catherine Neely.** According to the *National High School Sports Record Book*, Coach Neely is the winningest girls' volleyball coach in high school history. During her 23 years with East Ridge High School in Chattanooga, Tennessee, she earned 459 victories against only 170 defeats.

**Linda White.** During her tenure with Wando High School in Mt. Pleasant, South Carolina, Coach White earned more than 300 victories and three state championships, all consecutive from 1976 through 1978. During that time, her teams compiled a record of 113-2. She earned Coach of the Year honors five times, once from the NHSACA/Wilson organization (1982).

Coach White also has served as president of the South Carolina Coaches Association of Women's Sports and was the first woman to serve on the South Carolina High School League. Coach White also has served on several advisory and regulatory committees on a statewide basis.

# COLLEGE VOLLEYBALL

## America's Greatest College Women's Volleyball Coach

### Dave Shoji

In 14 years as head volleyball coach at the University of Hawaii, Coach Shoji has earned over 400 victories and an impressive winning percentage of .834. Even more impressively, he has won four national championships and during AIAW competition never finished lower than third nationally. He has been runner-up to the national champs twice (1977 and 1988). In 11 of his 14 years with Hawaii, Coach Shoji has led the Wahines to the final four of the national tournament.

An All-American at the University of California/Santa Barbara in 1969, Shoji returned to the Islands to coach club volleyball for a year and high school volleyball at Punahou for two. When he started at the University of Hawaii in 1975, he also coached the men's team for 10 years. Coach Shoji was inducted into the UC-Santa Barbara Hall of Honor in 1987.

## Number Two

**Andy Banachowski.** Coach Banachowski ranks fourth on the all-time win list, having logged 20 or more wins every year he has been with the UCLA Bruins. Banachowski began his career with UCLA in 1970, having been an All-American with Coach Al Scates's UCLA teams in the 1960s. During his 23 years with the school, he has logged four national titles, three when intercollegiate titles were first awarded in the 1970s and one NCAA crown in 1984. The Bruins also have finished second twice (1981 and 1983).

Coach Banachowski has helped develop 14 All-Americans and has won numerous Coach of the Year awards. He also has served on the NCAA's Women's Volleyball Committee, after having served in a similar capacity with the AIAW. Coach Banachowski is the author of *Power Volleyball* and is the motive force behind several clinics and camps in the area.

## Number Three

**Mick Haley.** The winner of the NCAA Division I volleyball tournament in 1988, Coach Haley recorded his second national title after winning the AIAW volleyball championship in 1981. Coach Haley has been with the University of Texas Lady Longhorns since 1981, compiling a record there of 251-65-1 for a winning percentage of .792. He also finished third in the NCAA tournament in 1986 with a record that year of 29-6.

Before moving to the University of Texas, Coach Haley spent 7 years with Kellogg Community College in Battle Creek, Michigan, where he won two national championships and never finished lower than fourth. His combined record is close to 550 wins, making him one of only five coaches nationally to achieve such a mark.

The coach of several All-American players and the recipient of many Coach of the Year honors, Coach Haley has extended his coaching to include national teams. He helped coach the U.S. national women's squad in 1973, and he headed up the 1977 U.S. women's team during the World University Games in Sofia, Bulgaria. He also served as president of the Collegiate Volleyball Coaches Association and vice president of the United States Volleyball Association (USVBA).

## Number Four

**Linda Dollar.** The only coach of women's volleyball to win over 600 games, Coach Dollar began her career with Southwest Missouri State University in 1972 after graduating from that university in 1970. The motive force behind volleyball at SMSU, Coach Dollar has taken the Lady Bears to the national tournament 12 consecutive times. During the reign of the AIAW, Dollar logged six finishes among the nation's top 10 teams.

Coach Dollar has complemented her coaching with a lengthy term on the board of directors of the American Volleyball Coaches Association.

She also is on the board of directors of the USVBA. In addition to several Coach of the Year awards, Coach Dollar was inducted into the SMSU Women's Athletic Hall of Fame in 1982.

## Number Five

**John Dunning.** A collegiate coach for only four years, Coach Dunning already has elevated himself to the ranks of America's greatest. As coach at Fremont High School in California for 10 years, Dunning earned a career record of 283-32 before founding the Bay Volleyball Club in 1980. During the club's first year, they won the Northern California (NorCal) Junior Championship and repeated two years later.

Coach Dunning became the head coach of Pacific University in 1985 and led them to an immediate 36-3 record and an NCAA Division I title over Stanford at the tournament held in Kalamazoo, Michigan. He followed up his first-year success with a 39-3 record in 1986 and another Division I title, this time over Nebraska in front of a home crowd in Stockton, California. Pacific won 30 or more matches in the next 2 years but failed to make the final four. With such success in such a short period of time, Coach Dunning is likely to achieve an even higher rank among America's greatest coaches.

**Elaine Michaelis.** Under Coach Michaelis's direction, Brigham Young University has appeared in national meets 17 times, second only to UCLA's 19. They have placed in the top five seven times, and in the top ten 14 times. They have won their conference title 14 of 19 times and have never finished lower than second. A graduate of Brigham Young, Coach Michaelis became the head coach in 1969 and within her tenure with the "Y" has earned a career record of 520-132-5, fourth highest in the nation.

Coach Michaelis is among the nation's most popular coaches at clinics, has chaired the AIAW Volleyball Sports Committee and the AIAW Rules Committee, and has been a member of the AIAW Executive Committee. Coach Michaelis has been awarded Coach of the Year honors several times and in 1987 was inducted into the Utah Summer Games Hall of Fame.

## Other Qualifiers

**Joan Boand.** One of college volleyball's pioneers, Joan Boand has been the head coach at Grand Valley State University for 20 years and has led the Michigan school to close to 450 victories. Currently, Coach Boand ranks 15th on the all-time win list for all colleges and is second for Division II schools.

**Larry Bock.** The names of Juniata College volleyball and Coach Larry Bock are synonymous. Bock has been with the Division III program since its inception in 1977 and has established an overall record of 410-82 with an unprecedented seven straight Middle Atlantic Conference championships since 1981. Under Bock's leadership, the Juniata "Tribe" has been to the NCAA Division III final four in five of the last seven seasons, finishing second once and third once. For his accomplishments, Bock has been named Coach of the Year twice, once by the NCAA Division III committee.

**Carol Dewey.** During her years at Purdue University since 1975, Coach Dewey has won close to 400 games and has established a winning percentage of over .700. She is the winningest coach in Purdue's history, men or women. She has coached Purdue to four Big Ten titles and in 1982 compiled a 33-1 record and a fifth-place finish in the NCAA tournament. Coach Dewey has been a member of the NCAA Division I Women's Volleyball Committee and has served on the Russell All-America Selection Committee. Dewey was named Big Ten Coach of the Year in 1982.

**Chuck Erbe.** The mentor of the Southern California Trojans for 12 years, starting in 1976, Coach Erbe earned a win/loss record of 310-121-3 and established the Women of Troy as an annual powerhouse in collegiate volleyball. The Trojans won national championships in 1976 and 1977 and again in 1980 and 1981, the latter one of the first NCAA titles.

Coach Erbe retired from his head coaching responsibilities in 1988 and served as the assistant women's coach at the University of Illinois.

**Carol Fritz.** The only volleyball coach in Western Maryland's history, Coach Fritz since 1968 has led the Green Terrors to a record of 523-122-3. The 1988 season concluded with a record of 45-9, a school record for most wins in a single season. Coach Fritz's teams have appeared in five consecutive Division III tournaments and have won the Maryland State tournament three times consecutively ('81, '82, and '83). The former president of the Middle Atlantic Conference, the biggest conference in Division III competition, Coach Fritz won the first five MAC tournaments. Combined with her coaching records in softball and basketball at Western Maryland, Coach Fritz has earned a combined collegiate coaching record of 673-216-4, one of the best in the country at any level.

**Peggy Martin.** In 12 short years with Central Missouri State University in Warrensburg, Coach Martin has established herself among the top 20 coaches in the country for total wins. She has led her Division II program to a career record of 410-117 for a winning percentage of .778. Her record in 1987 was an enviable 42-4, good enough for another

Missouri Intercollegiate Athletic Association (MIAA) championship and Division II Coach of the Year.

**Marilyn McReavy.** Another women's coach listed in the top 20 for total career victories, Coach McReavy has taken the Division I Florida Gators to a career record of 448-143 for a winning percentage of .758. Her '87 record in the Southeast Conference was an enviable 37-6, one of the best in the nation.

**Marlene Piper.** One of the nation's winningest coaches, with a 18-year career record of 517-186, Coach Piper has established a winning percentage of .735 while coaching Portland State to the AIAW and the NCAA Division II final four three different times. Currently at the University of California/Davis, Coach Piper is a popular clinician and has served as a coach for the U.S. Olympic Committee at the U.S. Olympic Festival.

**Geri Polvino.** Another of the nation's winningest volleyball coaches, Coach Polvino has earned a career record of 480-270 during her 21 years with Eastern Kentucky. The only certified female instructor in the International Volleyball Federation, Dr. Polvino has established an international reputation as a teacher and coach. The recipient of Coach of the Year honors seven times, Coach Polvino has served on the selection committee of the USVBA All-America Committee and is a voting member of the American Volleyball Coaches Association. She has been president of the Coaches Academy and has chaired the Volleyball Rules Committee.

**Rhesa Sumrell.** Prior to her retirement from Missouri Western in 1986, Coach Sumrell had earned a career record of 493-158 to earn her a spot in the top five for career victories. Her winning percentage of .757 was also among the best in the nation.

**Rudy Suwara.** The coach of both men's and women's volleyball during his 17-year career, Coach Suwara has earned a career record of 516-252-6. His record at San Diego State University with the women's program is 344-151, for a winning percentage of almost .700. His 300th victory came after only 11 seasons. Suwara's teams have captured three first-place finishes in the Western Collegiate Athletic Association conference and have rarely finished lower than third. His teams have been in the top 10 nationally for 6 of the last 9 years and he has produced several All-Americans, many of whom, like Sue Hegerle and Mary Holland, had little or no previous experience. A 15-time All-American and a member of the 1968 U.S. Olympic volleyball team, Coach Suwara was inducted into the Volleyball Hall of Fame in 1976.

**Sheila Wallace.** The coach of one of the finest Division III programs in the country, Coach Wallace has led Ohio Northern University to a career record of 467-173 during her 19-year career. Her winning percentage of .730 is one of the best in the nation, and her career win/loss record ranks among the nation's top 10, highlighting seasons such as 1987 when her team enjoyed a 39-6 record.

# REFERENCES

Baker, W.J. (1982). *Sports in the western world.* Totowa, NJ: Rowman & Littlefield.

Barney, E.C. (1894). American sportswoman. *Fortnightly Review,* **62**, 263-277.

Bell, M. (1973). *Women's basketball.* Dubuque, IA: William C. Brown.

Best of the bosses. (1988, May). *Sports Illustrated,* pp. 46-48.

The best twenty teams. (1985, September). *Women's Sports and Fitness,* pp. 17-20.

Brasch, R. (1970). *How did sports begin?* New York: David McKay.

Burke, P. (1976). Taking Title IX into your own hands. *Women's Sports,* p. 13.

Campbell, N. (1987). *Grass roots and schoolyards.* Lexington, MA: Greene.

Carruth, G., and Ehrlich, E. (1988). *Facts and dates of American sports.* New York: Harper & Row.

Cheatum, B., and Ebert, F. (1972). *Basketball: Five player.* Philadelphia: W.B. Saunders.

Clerci, G. (1975). *The ultimate tennis book.* Chicago: Follett Publishing Co.

Cohane, T. (1973). *Great college football coaches of the twenties and thirties.* New Rochelle, NY: Arlington House.

Cramer, J. (1986). Amateurism—Kappan special report: Winning and learning. *Phi Delta Kappan,* pp. 37-41.

Danzig, A. (1956). *The history of American football.* New York: Prentice-Hall.

Dawson, B. (1988). *An era to remember: Weissmuller to Spitz.* Fort Lauderdale, FL: International Swimming Hall of Fame.

Delano, A. (1966). *Field hockey.* Dubuque, IA: William C. Brown.

Doherty, K. (1976). *Track and field omnibook.* Swarthmore, PA: Track and Field News.

Einstein, C. (1956). *The fireside book of baseball.* New York: Simon & Schuster.

Emery, L. (1982). The first intercollegiate contest for women: Basketball, April 4, 1896. In R. Howell (Ed.), *Her story in sport* (pp. 417-423). Champaign, IL: Leisure Press.

Fidley, M. (1982). The establishment of softball for American women, 1900-1940. In R. Howell (Ed.), *Her story in sport* (pp. 527-540). Champaign, IL: Leisure Press.

Finley, M.I., and Pleket, H.W. (1976). *The Olympic Games: The first thousand years.* New York: Viking.

Fischler, S., and Fischler, W. (1983). *The hockey encyclopedia.* New York: Macmillan.

Foster, A.B. (1897). Basketball for girls. *American Physical Education Review,* **2**, 152.

Good, P. (1985). Who's going to bat for women's sports? *Women's Sports,* **7**, 16.

Guttman, A. (1978). *From ritual to record.* New York: Columbia University Press.

Harris, H.A. (1972). *Sport in Greece and Rome.* New York: Cornell University Press.

Hill, L. (1903). *Athletics and outdoor sports for women.* New York: Macmillan.

Howell, R. (1982). *Her story in sport.* Champaign, IL: Leisure Press.

Kenney, K. (1982). The realm of sports and the athletic woman, 1850-1900. In R. Howell (Ed.), *Her story in sport* (pp. 107-140). Champaign, IL: Leisure Press.

Landers, D. (1976). *Social problems in athletics.* Champaign, IL: University of Illinois Press.

LeBow, J. (1978). *All about soccer.* New York: Newsweek Books.

Mack, C. (1932). I'm not ready to quit. *The Rotarian,* 16-18, 45-47.

McCallum, J.D. (1978). *College basketball USA: Since 1892.* New York: Stein & Day.

McCallum, J.D., and Pearson, C.H. (1972). *College football USA: 1869-1972.* New York: McGraw-Hill.

McNab, T. (1980). *The complete book of track and field.* New York: Exeter Books.

Menke, F. (1963). *The encyclopedia of sports.* New York: A.S. Barnes.

Morris, D. (1981). *The soccer tribe.* London: Jonathan Cape Publishers.

Nasty Dan and his wrestling empire. (1988, April). *Sports Magazine,* p. 38.

The new American athlete. (1986, January). *Women's Sports and Fitness,* pp. 21-23.

The new breed of coaches. (1985, October). *Runner's World,* pp. 12-13.

Noonkester, B. (1982). The American sportswoman from 1900-1920. In R. Howell (Ed.), *Her story in sport* (pp. 178-222). Champaign, IL: Leisure Press.

Once and future champs. (1988, March). *Southern Living,* p. 126.

Pearce, W., and Pearce, J. (1971). *Tennis*. New York: Prentice-Hall.
Pellowski, M. (1979). *The great sports question and answer book*. New York: Playmore Publishers.
Potera, C. (1986). Are women coaches an endangered species? *Women's Sports and Fitness*, 8, 34.
Prestidge, J. (1979). *The love of gymnastics*. New York: Crescent Books.
Revealing the top coach. (1988, February). *Sport Magazine*, pp. 22-24.
Ruden, S. (1986). The chosen few. *Women's Sports and Fitness*, 8, 38-39.
Sachare, A. (Ed.) (1988, April 25). *NBA News*.
Sandefur, R. (1970). *Volleyball*. Pacific Palisades: Goodyear Publishing.
Scott, P., and Crafts, V. (1964). *Track and field for girls and women*. New York: Appleton-Century-Crofts.
Shondell, D.S., and McNamara, J.L. (1971). *Volleyball*. New York: Prentice-Hall.
Stagg, A.A. (1924). *Touchdown!* New York: Longman's Greene & Company.
Stengel, C. (1961, October). My own story. *Saturday Evening Post*, pp. 57-70.
Ten great years: A celebration of women's sports. (1985, October). *Women's Sports and Fitness*, pp. 5-6.
Then and now. (1988, January/February). *Women's Sports and Fitness*, p. 58.
3,000 years in the making. (1984, July). *Women's Sports*, pp. 12-15.
Treat, R. (1973). *The official encyclopedia of football*. New York: A.S. Barnes.
Turkin, H., and Thompson, S.C. (1968). *The official encyclopedia of baseball*. New York: A.S. Barnes.
Twombley, W. (1976). *200 years of sport in America*. Maplewood, NJ: Hammond.
Unhappy return of the native. (1966, April). *Sports Illustrated*.
Voight, D.Q. (1966). *American baseball*. Norman, OK: University of Oklahoma Press.
Wade, P. (1983). *Winning women*. New York: Times Books.
Wallace, F. (1966). *Notre Dame: From Rockne to Parseghian*. New York: David McKay.
Warner, G.S. (1927). *Football for coaches and players*. Palo Alto, CA: Stanford University Press.
Women and sports: What's the scene in '86? (1986, October). *Glamour*, p. 72.
Yost, F.H. (1905). *Football for player and spectator*. Ann Arbor, MI: University Publishing.
Young, F. (1984). *Winning basketball for girls*. New York: Facts on File Publications.

# INDEX

## A

Abbott, Cleveland, 264
Abbott, Senda Berenson, 213
Abdul-Jabbar, Kareem, 41
Accardy, Peter, 246
Adams, Paul, 64
Adkins, Pete, 64
Agassi, Andre, 150
Albert, Gerald, 237
Alexander, Cheeseman, 223-224
Allen, Forrest Clare "Phog," 35, 45-46
Allen, Francis, 94, 98
Allen, George, 85
Almquist, Oscar, 105, 106
Alston, Walter, 7, 23
Anders, Beth, 223
Anderson, George "Sparky," 26
Anson, Cap, 6
Applebee, Constance M.K., 217
Arbour, Al, 115
Arcaro, John, 165
Armbruster, Dave, 142-143
Armstrong, Murray, 110
Ashe, Bob, 123
Astorino, Louis, 107
Auerbach, Arnold "Red," 37, 50

## B

Babb, Julius W. "Pinky," 62
Babyak, Jim, 229
Bachrach, Bill, 146
Backus, Sharron, 240
Baer, Clara, 203
Baker, Carrice, 206
Baker, Eugene V., 56
Baker, Gene, 121-122
Banachowski, Andy, 275-276
Bancroft, Frank, 5
Banda, Kalakeni, 229
Banks, Ted, 170
Barnaby, Jack, 157
Barringer, Tom, 41
Barrow, Eddie, 6
Bassett, Glenn, 156
Batie, Don, 129
Bazemore, A.W., 64
Bean, Joe, 130
Beard, Percy, 172
Bearden, John, 207
Bee, Clair, 47
Beeson, Richard, 237
Bellamy, Norma, 270
Bellisle, Bill, 106
Bennett, Paul, 157-158
Bergen, Paul, 146
Berra, Yogi, 7
Bessone, Amo, 109, 111
Bingham, Wanda, 272-273
Blaik, Earl, 79
Blake, Hector, 115
Blanchard, C.H., 42, 63, 164-165

285

286  Index

Blank, Dan, 229
Blankers-Koen, Fanny, 199
Bleibtrey, Ethelda, 243
Blood, Ernest, 40
Boand, Joan, 277
Bock, Larry, 278
Bonvicini, Joan, 213
Borowski, Steve, 137
Borelli, Dave, 252
Botts, Thomas, 172
Boudreau, Lou, 27, 35
Bowen, Murl, 10
Bower, Richard, 137-138
Bowerman, Bill, 171
Boyd, Adele, 224
Boyd, Jennings, 42
Bradford, Vince, 165
Brandi, Andy, 253
Braun, Walt, 64
Brauninger, Stan, 146
Brazell, David, 15-16
Breadon, Sam, 6
Brennan, Chester, 237
Brennan, Frank, 251-252
Brickhouse, Jack, 28, 30, 31
Broadbent, Ron, 124
Brock, Bob, 241
Brock, John C., 130
Brockmeyer, Win Otto, 62-63
Brogan, Jan, 253
Brooks, Herb, 111
Brown, Paul, 80-81
Brundage, Avery, 198
Bryan, Jimmie, 42
Bryant, Paul "Bear," 68-69, 76
Buckley, Charles, 153
Buckley, Neil, 187-188
Buller, Ed, 64
Bundy, May Sutton, 198
Burton, William, 138
Bush, Jim, 171-172
Buss, Ray, 122-123
Buwick, Greg, 94, 98

C

Cady, Fred, 143
Camp, Walter, 55, 56, 57, 59, 71-72
Campbell, Nelson, 37
Campbell, Tom, 153
Carson, Al, 259
Cartwright, Alexander, 3
Case, Everett, 42
Cash, Robin, 224
Chaffee, Clarence, 158
Chamberlain, Wilt, 38
Chance, Frank, 6
Chavoor, Sherm, 146-147, 199
Cheff, Ed, 16
Chisam, Scott, 265
Churchill, Eleanor, 198
Chyzowych, Gene, 272
Ciampi, Joe, 213
Cichy, Sid, 65
Cisco, Galen, 17
Cochems, Eddie, 58
Cole, Nancy, 219
Collins, Jimmy, 6
Collins, Richard, 164
Connors, Jimmy, 150
Conradt, Jody, 211-212
Conroy, John, 158
Coughenour, Edwin, 237-238
Counsilman, James "Doc," 134, 141
Coviello, Joe, 63-64
Covington, Eileen, 272
Crabbe, Buster, 143
Craig, Roger, 27
Crawford, Terry, 263-264
Crocco, Louise, 271
Cromwell, Dean, 169
Cronin, Joe, 27-28
Crouse, Art, 107
Crum, Denny, 47
Cummins, Ralph, 65

Cunningham, Billy, 52-53
Curran, Jack, 10

**D**

Dahlberg, Harry "Swede," 164
Daland, Peter, 142
Daley, Arthur, 198
Danielson, Dick, 124
Daughters, Ray, 147
Davidson, Judith, 224
Day, Clarence Henry, 116
Deacon, David, 124
Deane, Bill, 24, 25, 28, 30, 31
Dedeaux, Raoul "Rod," 12, 18
de Handley, L.B., 244
Devaney, Bob, 72
Dewey, Carol, 278
Dickerson, Bob, 237
Diddle, Ed, 47
Didrickson, Babe, 199, 256
DiMaggio, Joe, 27
Dinneen, Bill, 6
Dod, Charlotte "Lottie," 197
Dodd, Bobby, 71
Doherty, Ken, 162, 172
Dollar, Linda, 200, 276
Donald, William, 165
Donoghue, Gus, 130
Dorais, Gus, 58, 59, 67
Dorrance, Anson, 130, 228
Doubleday, Abner, 3
Draz, Richard, 138
Dugan, Ken, 16
Dunn, Edward "Ebbie," 122
Dunning, John, 277
Dunphy, Marv, 180
Durocher, Leo, 24-25
Dwight, James, 150
Dykes, Jimmy, 28

**E**

Eastment, George, 166
Easton, Bill, 172
Eden, John, 124-125

Ederle, Gertrude, 244
Edwards, Dorotha, 220
Elliott, Jim, 172-173
Ellis, Clyde, 258
Erbe, Chuck, 278
Ervin, Maurice, 138
Etter, E.B., 65
Evans, Clint, 16
Evans, Tommy, 193
Ewbank, Wilbur "Weeb," 86
Exendine, Albert, 57

**F**

Fallon, Tom, 158
Farina, Charles, 187
Faust, Gerry, 65
Fennoy, Nino, 257-258
Ferguson, Bob, 4
Fitch, Bill, 51
Fitzgerald, Ed, 22
Fletcher, Vergil, 39
Fohl, Leo, 7
Foley, Tom, 4
Folsom, Fred, 57
Foster, Emilie, 253
Fox, Allen, 158
Francis, Emile, 116
Franklin, Benjamin, 134
Fraser, Ron, 15
Frey, Hal, 98
Frisch, Frankie, 6, 24
Fritz, Carol, 278
Funiciello, James, 138

**G**

Gable, Danny Mack, 183, 190-191
Gagliardi, John, 77
Gaines, Clarence "Bighouse," 47
Gaither, Alonzo "Jake," 76
Gallagher, Edward C., 183, 191
Gambril, Don, 143
Gambucci, Serge, 106
Gardner, Fern, 200, 213
Gardner, Frank "Sprig," 186

Garguile, Dominic, 229
Garman, Judi, 241
Gasparini, Gino, 111
Gehrig, Lou, 7, 55
Genesko, Lynn, 201
Gibson, Althea, 249-250
Gill, Harry, 173
Gillman, Sid, 79, 86-87
Goosen, Greg, 22
Gorr, Merle, 207-208
Gould, Anne, 254
Gould, Dick, 156
Graham, Otto, 35
Grange, Harold "Red," 60, 84
Granger, Michelle, 234
Grant, Bud, 87
Greene, Lofton, 42
Griffith, Art, 193
Griffith, Clark, 28
Griffith-Joyner, Florence, 256
Grimm, Charlie, 7, 28
Gros, Vonnie, 222
Grossfeld, Abie, 96, 97
Guelker, Bob, 128
Gunter, Sue, 200, 214
Gurnett, Terry, 229-230
Gustafson, Cliff, 13

**H**

Haas, Otto, 125
Habecker, Terry, 125
Haines, George, 133, 147, 246
Halas, George, 35, 60, 84-85, 87, 90
Haley, Mick, 276
Halverson, Ralph, 166
Hamilton, Brutus, 173
Hamilton, Winifred, 273
Haney, Fred, 7
Hannula, Dick, 136
Harkness, Ned, 110-111
Harris, Bucky, 28
Hartley, Donald, 125
Havenstrite, Winston, 10

Hayes, Diane, 259
Hayes, Woodrow "Woody," 72, 73
Heatly, Charles, 208
Heinenon, Tom, 266
Heinsohn, Tom, 52
Heisman, John, 57, 58
Hendricks, Art, 166
Hennessey, Bill, 236
Herrick, George, 125
Herzog, Whitey, 25
Heyliger, Vic, 109
Hicks, Joe, 16-17
Hill, Thadnall, 208
Hines, Mary, 273
Hirsch, Elroy "Crazylegs," 62
Hobson, Howard, 36
Hogg, Sonja, 200, 212-213
Holder, Norman, 258
Holdren, James, 259
Holman, Nat, 37, 42
Holmes, Oliver Wendell, 3
Holtz, Lou, 72-73
Holzman, Red, 51-52
Horgan, Bob, 123-124
Hornsby, Rogers, 6, 29
Horstman, Katie, 258-259
Houk, Ralph, 7, 26, 29
Howard, Elston, 21
Howard, Frank, 17
Hudson, Frank, 59
Huggins, Miller, 6, 29
Hulbert, Bill, 5
Hunter, Laurice "Low," 271
Hutchinson, Jan, 224

**I**

Iba, Henry, 47-48
Irvin, Dick, 116
Ivan, Tommy, 116

**J**

Jackson, Nell, 263
Jackson, Oliver, 173

Jacobs, Franklin, 161
James, Harry, 158
Jansen, William, 260
Jeffrey, Bill, 127-128
Jennings, Hugh, 6
Jeremiah, Ed, 112
Johnson, Bob, 112
Johnson, Brooks, 265
Johnson, Galen, 208
Johnson, Leo, 173-174
Jones, Harold, 208
Jones, K.C., 51, 52
Jordan, Michael, 37, 38
Jordan, Teri, 266
Joyce, Joan, 234
Joyner-Kersee, Jackie, 256
Juneau, John, 206-207

**K**

Kahanamoku, Duke, 133-134
Kaiser, Jack, 10-11
Karow, Marty, 17
Kasberger, Joseph, 10
Kaye, Glenn, 138-139
Kelley, Jack, 112
Kelley, John, 112
Kemp, Jack, 87
Kemp, Steve, 13
Kenfield, John, 158-159
Kenney, Skip, 143
Keogan, George, 48
Keough, Harry, 130
Kersee, Bob, 266
Kindall, Jerry, 14-15
King, Billie Jean, 201
King, Ralph, 125
Kingman, Dave, 13
Kiphuth, Bob, 133, 140-141
Klein, Ronald, 11
Knight, Bob, 46
Knox, Chuck, 87-88
Kopischka, Layne, 139
Koshewa, Paul, 166-167
Kramer, Jay, 151-152

Krzyzewski, Mike, 48
Kubek, Tony, 22
Kuhn, Bowie, 22
Kundla, John, 53
Kus, Sally, 272

**L**

Lacey, Betty, 220
Lake, Anita, 273
Lambeau, Earl "Curly," 88
Lambert, Piggy, 36, 45
Lampe, Stan, 188
Landers, Andy, 214
Landry, Tom, 81-82
Lapchick, Joe, 33, 53
Lasorda, Tom, 30
Lazzeri, Tony, 7
Leach, Dick, 159
Leahy, Frank, 73
Lees, Janice Edwards, 221
Leighton, James, 159
Leonard, Brother, 107
Leopold, Brother, 107
Leung, Hank, 230
Lewis, Dale, 159
Lindores, Colin, 130, 230
Littlefield, Clyde, 174
Littlefield, Faith, 220
Loken, Newt, 98-99
Lombardi, Marie, 79
Lombardi, Vince, 63, 78-80
Looney, Peter, 238
Lopez, Al, 30
Lowe, Terence, 139
Lucas, Henry, 5
Lufler, William, 159
Lynn, Freddie, 13

**M**

Mabry, Clarence, 159
MacInnes, John, 109, 110
Mack, Connie, 6, 8, 20-21, 23, 32, 60
Madden, John, 88-89
Maglischo, Ernie, 144

Mainieri, Demie, 17
Mann, Bill, 247
Mann, Matt, 142, 145
Mantle, Mickey, 21
Marquess, Mark, 17
Martin, Billy, 25, 26
Martin, Linda, 273-274
Martin, Peggy, 278-279
Martin, William Patrick, 185-186
Matthewson, Christy, 20, 60
McCarthy, Joe, 7, 22-23, 28
McCracken, Branch, 36
McCrath, Cliff, 131
McGill, Dan, 159-160
McGraw, John J., 6, 19-20, 23, 60
McGuire, Al, 48
McGuire, Frank, 48
McKechnie, William, 6, 23
McKissick, John, 65
McReavy, Marilyn, 279
Meade, Bill, 96
Meadors, Marynell, 214
Menard, George, 112
Menke, Denis, 10
Merritt, John, 77
Merryman, Wayne, 207
Meusel, Bob, 7
Meyer, Debbie, 199
Meyer, Ray, 37, 49
Meyer, Vince, 9-10
Michaelis, Elaine, 277
Mihalko, Pat, 220
Milkovich, Michael, 186
Miller, Ralph, 48
Mills, Abraham G., 3
Mitchell, Jackie, 198
Moackley, Jack, 174
Moore, Billie, 214
Morgan, J.D., 157
Morgan, William G., 177
Morrison, Chuck, 153
Morrone, Joe, 129
Mortenson, Jess, 171
Moser, Chuck, 65

Mosher, Bob, 167
Motta, Dick, 53
Mount Pleasant, Frank, 57
Mowerson, Bob, 137
Murphy, Michael, 162, 170
Murphy, William, 160
Murtaugh, Danny, 7, 30-31

## N

Nagurski, Bronco, 62
Naismith, James, 33, 38, 45, 177, 197
Neely, Catherine, 274
Negoesco, Steve, 129
Neuschaefer, Al, 136
Nevers, Ernie, 69
Newman, John, 254
Nichols, Harold, 191-192
Noll, Chuck, 89

## O

O'Brien, Father Patrick, 259
O'Malley, Walter, 30
O'Neill, James "Tip," 6
O'Neill, Steve, 31
Osborne, Tom, 73
Osterberg, Beverley, 220
Outerbridge, Mary, 249
Owen, Steve, 89-90
Owens, Jesse, 161
Owens, John, 161

## P

Page, Gary, 238
Page, Joe, 23
Panek, Pat, 65-66
Pare, Emmett, 160
Parseghian, Ara, 73
Parsons, Russ, 167
Paterno, Joe, 70-71
Patrick, Lester, 116
Peery, Rex, 193-194
Penick, Daniel, 160
Pepin, Gary, 266
Peppe, Mike, 141

Pettine, Mike, 66
Phipps, James, 11
Pibulvech, Dang, 230
Pierce, Bemus, 59
Pierce, Harley, 153
Piper, Marlene, 279
Piper, Ralph, 99
Pitchford, Tom, 153-154
Polvino, Geri, 279
Pond, Charles P., 96-97
Portland, Rene, 214
Potter, William, 160
Powers, Tom, 238
Price, Hartley, 97
Pruett, Hub, 7

Q

Quick, Richard, 245
Quigley, Earl F., 164

R

Radbourn, Charles, 5
Rallins, Mamie, 266
Ralston, Dennis, 160
Ramsay, Jack, 53
Ramunno, Carl, 189
Rasmussen, Dick, 235-236
Reade, Bob, 76-77
Reed, James, 152
Reese, Randy, 145-146, 246
Rice, Grantland, 69-70
Richardson, Bobby, 22
Rickey, Branch, 6
Riegel, Russell, 188-189
Riggin, Eileen, 243
Riggs, Bobby, 201
Riley, Pat, 37, 51
Rindfuss, Marilyn Montgomery, 252
Rippetoe, Don, 208
Robertson, Dave, 135-136
Robertson, Port, 194
Robinson, Eddie, 75-76
Robinson, Jackie, 35
Robinson, Tom, 144

Rockne, Knute, 58, 59, 60, 67-68
Rockwell, Sandra, 238
Roderick, Myron, 183, 192
Roethlisberger, Fred, 99
Roosevelt, Theodore, 58
Ross, Art, 117
Ross, Larry, 106
Rowan, Alan, 163
Roy, Spat, 107-108
Rudolph, Wilma Glodean, 199, 256
Rugland, Carroll, 208-209
Rupp, Adolph, 35, 45
Rush, Cathy, 204
Rushing, Shirley, 254
Russell, Bill, 53
Ruth, Babe, 6, 22, 24, 29, 59
Rutt, Becky, 247

S

Sakamoto, Soichi, 147
Samuelson, Carl, 247
Sanchez, Henry, 167
Saunders, Nell, 197
Scalise, Bob, 230
Scates, Al, 179-180
Schailby, Sherry, 238-239
Schembechler, Bo, 73-74, 77
Schier, Karl, 99-100
Schlegel, Charles, 139
Schlueter, Walt, 147
Schmitt, William "Red," 189
Schwartz, John, 11
Scolinos, John, 17-18
Scott, Paul, 194
Scott, Rose, 236
Seagrave, Loren, 264-265
Seltz, Dick, 11
Sharos, Charles, 126
Sharp, Harold, 260
Sharp, Linda, 200, 212
Shaw, Martin, 154
Shellenberger, Bill, 131
Shelton, Karen, 224

Shero, Fred, 117
Shoji, Dave, 275
Shondell, Don, 180
Shotton, Burt, 20
Shublom, Walt, 41
Shue, Gene, 53
Shula, Don, 82, 83-84
Shurlock, Art, 100
Siddens, Robert Saunders, 188
Smalley, Roy, 13
Smiddy, James, 206
Smith, Alfred, 131
Smith, Dean, 33, 46, 52
Smith, Mayo, 26
Smith, William Boyce, 66
Snell, Eleanor, 225
Spalding, Al, 5
Spanks, Carol, 242
Speidel, Charles M., 194
Squires, John, 131
Stafford, Gil, 18
Stager, Gus, 144-145
Stagg, Amos Alonzo, 34, 56, 70
Stalick, Wayne, 181
Stanley, Dolph, 40
Stanley, Marianne, 211
Stanton, Tom, 42
Staples, Eric, 42
Steen, Jim, 145, 246
Steinbrenner, George, 25
Steitz, George, 123
Stengel, Casey, 7, 21
Stevenson, Gail, 221
Stram, Hank, 90-91
Stringer, Vivian, 214-215
Stuhldreher, Harry, 68
Summitt, Pat, 200, 211
Sumrell, Rhesa, 279
Suwara, Rudy, 279
Sweeney, Charles, 5
Switzer, Barry, 7
Switzer, Katherine, 199
Szypula, George, 94, 100

**T**

Tait, Tom, 181
Tanner, Chuck, 31
Tarkanian, Jerry, 49
Tasker, Ralph, 37, 41
Teague, Bertha, 205-206
Temple, Ed, 262-263
Templeton, Dink, 174
Thomas, Dale, 192-193
Thompson, Cliff, 105
Thompson, John, 49
Thornton, Karen Moe, 247
Thornton, Nort, 145
Thorpe, Jim, 57, 59, 60, 69, 199
Toley, George, 155-156, 252
Torgeson, Gary, 242
Trout, Arthur, 42-43
Tsantiris, Len, 230-231
Tumey, Carol, 260
Tweed, "Boss," 4
Tyler, Suzanne, 225

**V**

Van Huss, Walter, 43
Verdieck, Jim, 157

**W**

Wade, L. Margaret, 200, 210-211
Walker, Leroy, 174
Walker, Paul, 43
Wallace, Sheila, 280
Waller, Chris, 215
Walsh, Bill, 91
Walsh, Stella, 199
Warner, Glenn, 131
Warner, Glenn Scobey "Pop," 55, 56, 59, 69-70
Watson, Don, 137
Weaver, Earl, 31-32
Weick, William, 189
Weissmuller, John, 133, 134, 146
Wells, Joan, 271-272
Wettstone, Gene, 95-96
White, Byron "Whizzer," 36

White, James, 260
White, Linda, 274
Wilkinson, Charles "Bud," 74
Wilkinson, Harold, 260-261
Williams, Dick, 32
Williams, Harry, 58
Williams, Ted, 27
Williamson, Doug, 266
Willson, Mike, 100-101
Winkler, Gary, 267
Winsor, Al, 113
Winter, Bud, 175
Winter, Robert, 209
Wolfe, Dick, 101
Womack, Charles, 209
Wood, Gordon L., 61-62
Wood, Robert, 152
Woodall, Paul, 168

Wooden, John, 37, 44-45
Woodruff, George, 55, 59, 74
Wootten, Morgan, 41
Wright, Diane, 223
Wright, Harry, 4, 32
Wright, Jean, 261
Wright, Margie, 241

**Y**

Yeagley, Jerry, 128
Yost, Fielding "Hurry Up," 57, 74
Young, Denton True "Cy," 6
Younger, Maxmillian (Max), 101
Yow, Kay, 215

**Z**

Zuppke, Bob, 35, 60, 84

# ABOUT THE AUTHOR

Dr. Michael Koehler's involvement with sport dates back many years. Being the grandson of the legendary Jim Thorpe, athletics were a natural for him. He was a high school All-American and played football at Marquette University, Milwaukee, WI, and the University of Nebraska.

Dr. Koehler has been coaching high school football since 1963 and teaching college since 1974. He has also written several articles and four books on football and athletics and lectured nationwide. He is recognized as a sport authority and is well known by dozens of big-time coaches.

Dr. Koehler is a football coach and a guidance counselor at Deerfield (IL) High School and teaches graduate-level courses at Northeastern Illinois University. In his leisure, he enjoys fishing, boating, and outings with his wife, Pat, and three lovely daughters.